The
Avowal
of
Difference

SUNY series, Genders in the Global South
Debra A. Castillo and Shelley Feldman, editors

The *Avowal* of *Difference*

Queer Latino American Narratives

Ben. Sifuentes-Jáuregui

Cover photo courtesy of Eduardo Hernández Santos, photographer; taken in 2005, El Malecón, La Habana, Cuba.

Published by State University of New York Press, Albany

© 2014 State University of New York

All rights reserved

Printed in the United States of America

No part of this book may be used or reproduced in any manner whatsoever without written permission. No part of this book may be stored in a retrieval system or transmitted in any form or by any means including electronic, electrostatic, magnetic tape, mechanical, photocopying, recording, or otherwise without the prior permission in writing of the publisher.

For information, contact State University of New York Press, Albany, NY
www.sunypress.edu

Production, Ryan Morris
Marketing, Michael Campochiaro

Library of Congress Cataloging-in-Publication Data

Library of Congress Cataloging-in-Publication Data

Sifuentes-Jáuregui, Ben.
 The avowal of difference : queer Latino American narratives / Ben. Sifuentes-Jáuregui.
     pages cm. — (Suny series, genders in the Global South)
 Includes bibliographical references and index.
 ISBN 978-1-4384-5425-2 (hc : alk. paper) 978-1-4384-5426-9 (pb : alk. paper)
 ISBN 978-1-4384-5427-6 (ebook)
 1. Spanish American fiction—20th century—History and criticism.
 2. Homosexuality in literature. 3. Gays in literature. I. Title.
 PQ7082.N7S55 2014
 860.9'353—dc23
                                                      2014003517

10 9 8 7 6 5 4 3 2 1

For Mark

Contents

Acknowledgments ix

Introduction: Written Through a Body 1

Part 1. Unwriting the Self

Chapter 1. *Modernismo*, Masochism and Queer Potential in Nervo's *El bachiller* 25

Chapter 2. Queer Losses in Barbachano Ponce's *El diario de José Toledo* 49

Chapter 3. Adonis's Silence: Textual Queerness in Zapata's *El vampiro de la colonia Roma* 69

Part 2. Interventions

Chapter 4. Epistemerotics: Puig, Queer Subjects, and Writing Desire 87

Chapter 5. La Manuela's Return: Transvestism/Identification/the Abject in Lemebel's *Loco afán* 115

Part 3. The Body Politic

Chapter 6. Homosociality, Disavowal, and Pedagogy in Vargas Llosa's *Los cachorros* 137

Chapter 7. Sadomasochism in *Paradiso*: Bound Narratives and Pleasure 157

Chapter 8. On the Homo-Baroque: Queering Sarduy's Baroque Genealogies 173

Part 4. Queer Latina/o Narratives

Chapter 9. Queer *Latinidad*: Thomas's *Down*   197
These Mean Streets and Díaz's *Drown*

Chapter 10. Traveling North, Translating Queerness: 213
Rivera-Valdés and the Trouble with Discipline

Notes   231
References   263
Index   275

Acknowledgments

This book is part of ongoing conversations and debates on Latino American sexualities and queer theories, and was written in constant dialogue with friends and colleagues whom I would like to thank. First, I want to thank Yolanda Martínez-San Miguel, who has always been a thoughtful, ideal reader, interlocutor, and friend, offering me encouragement to move my ideas in new and rich directions. I thank César Braga-Pinto, who has been a perspicacious reader and friend, helping me work though difficult theoretical questions.

At Rutgers, I am grateful to my colleagues in American Studies and Comparative Literature for their intellectual support: I especially thank Louise Barnett, Elin Diamond, Ann Fabian, Leslie Fishbein, Nicole Fleetwood, Angus K. Gillespie, Allan Isaac, Susan Martin-Márquez, and Michael Rockland for reading and commenting on my work.

Over the years I have been very fortunate to present material from the book in many professional venues. From the Latin American Studies Association meetings and the Tepoztlán Institute to lectures at different universities and other places where I shared my work, I received important critical responses to the ideas I offer here. I want to thank Jossianna Arroyo, Marisa Belausteguigoitia, Francisco Cos Montiel, Juan José Cruz, Monica Cyrino, Guillermo de los Reyes, Héctor Domínguez-Ruvalcaba, Anita Figueroa, Claudia Hinojosa, Bill Johnson-González, Lawrence LaFountain-Stokes, Sylvia Molloy, the late Carlos Monsiváis, Graciela Montaldo, Patrick O'Connor, Michael O'Rourke, Donald Pease, Joseph Pierce, José Quiroga, Israel Reyes, Rubén Ríos-Ávila, Abel Sierra Madero, and Benigno Trigo, among so many individuals who engaged with and responded to my work.

This book would not have been possible without the support of Debra Castillo; I am indebted to her for the professional and intellectual generosity she has always given me. She introduced me to my editor Beth Bouloukos at SUNY Press. I thank Beth, along with Ryan Morris, for guiding this book project forward with such care. I also owe a big thank-you to the anonymous reviewers, whose comments and recommendations made this a stronger work of criticism.

I know that, like most research projects, this book gathers much of its impetus from the classroom: my undergraduate students have always been fount of creative new ideas. I was lucky to have Danica Arahan, Jonathan Levin, and Kenya O'Neill work with me as undergraduate research assistants—I thank them for their help in finding bibliographical materials. My present and former graduate students—especially Chris Rivera, Mia Romano, and Elena Valdéz—shared with me their work, and brought to my attention recent scholarship: I am grateful to them all.

As always, I thank my family, who has been a source of support; and especially my mother Graciela, who has always taught me about courage and love. Finally, I thank Mark Trautman—he joined me every day in the writing of this book, reading and commenting on each page more than once. For fifteen years, he has been the most important emotional and intellectual presence in my life—and I dedicate this book to him with love.

* * *

An earlier version of chapter 3 on Zapata was originally published, "Espacios raros en *El vampiro de la colonia Roma* de Luis Zapata," in *Cultura Moderna* I, 1 (Spring 2005): 33–44. Chapter 5 appeared in a shorter version as "El retorno de la Manuela: travestismo/identificación/lo abyecto en *Loco afán* de Lemebel" in *Inti: Revista de literatura hispánica* 69–70 (2009):171–185. Chapter 7, "Sadomasochism in *Paradiso*: Bound Narratives and Pleasure," was first published in *Foucault in Latin America*, edited by Benigno Trigo (New York: Routledge, October 2001), 263–276. An abridged version of chapter 9 appeared under the title "Queer Ellipsis and Latino Identities," in *Textual Identities of "Identity Politics": Debates from Afar on Recent US Cultural Texts*, edited by Juan José Cruz (Tenerife: Universidad de la Laguna, 2009), 49–60.

I wish to thank Ediciones Cátedra for permission to cite from Octavio Paz's *El laberinto de la soledad* in the "Introduction" and chapter 3. Also, I thank the Heirs of Manuel Puig (c/o Guillermo Schavelzon & Asoc., Agencia Literaria) for permission to cite from *The Buenos Aires Affair* in chapter 4. I thank Eduardo Hernández Santos for permission to use his photograph as the book's cover image. This photograph appears in his book *El muro: The Wall*. I also thank his agent Roberto García, publisher Steven C. Daiber of Red Trillium Press, and Flavio Risech for helping obtain me permission to use the image. Finally, I thank Rutgers for awarding me a University Research Council Subvention grant to support in part the publication of this book.

Introduction
Written Through a Body

Para nosotros el cuerpo existe; da gravedad y límites a nuestro ser.
—Octavio Paz, "Máscaras mexicanas"[1]

Antes de ser una realidad, los Estados Unidos fueron para mí una imagen. No es extraño: desde niños los mexicanos vemos a ese país como al *otro*. Un *otro* que es inseparable de nosotros y que, al mismo tiempo, es radical y esencialmente el extraño.
—Paz, "El espejo indiscreto"

Wild speculations

Some years ago, I wrote about an exchange that I had with a Mexican friend and intellectual about the place of gay and lesbian identities. He "was fascinated by some project I was describing, but interrupted: 'Why are U.S. academics so obsessed with the question of "gay identity"?' I was baffled. On other occasions, I have been told by other Latin American intellectuals, 'I don't like being classified as a lesbian author.' Or, 'I know so-and-so would die before being labeled a gay author.'"[2] While this disclaimer of a gay or lesbian identity could be read as an act of closetedness, or taken to the extreme, as an act of queer self-hatred, I proposed another reading. I suggested that the very refusal to claim and assume a "gay" or "lesbian" identity should not be simply read as a marker of indifference toward an identity that could be said has been "imported" from the other side, but rather this refusal might be phrased more strongly as a postcolonial affront to the imposition of identities and categories that do not (cor)respond to the experiences and needs of a particular cultural context. If we follow this more assertive way of reading Latin America's reluctance to take on gay and lesbian identities as those that define a sexual minoritarian status, then it may be easier to try understanding such a disidentification.[3]

But these labels—queer, lesbian, bisexual, and so forth—are quite persistent, and they transform and travel. I remember in the late 1990s when I first talked about queer theory at the Colegio de México, how enthusiastic some of the students were by the term queer and its applicability to their own lives, precisely because of the breadth of the term. More recently however, I have become less comfortable with such ease of applicability, or shall we say by its universality.[4]

One of the most comprehensive works that traces the emergence of "queer" as a critical tool is Annamarie Jagose's *Queer Theory, An Introduction*.[5] She outlines some of the ways in which queer theory has been *historically* produced from a series of conversations that have come out of feminism, early homophile movements, poststructuralist theory, and so forth. She rightly points to the contradictory task of historicizing "queerness," which by its very nature resists that kind of emplotment; but nonetheless, she manages to situate "queerness" in a historical context, and shows how it borrows methodological force from interdisciplinarity. I would like to propose something very obvious that seems to escape Jagose and other theorists: queer theory—certainly the genealogy that has circulated in the United States and other Western countries—is also the result of a cultural context. I would like to put forth and to sketch out with broad strokes a particular genealogy of how queer theory takes shape out of a very United States experience and intellectual scene. For this, I would like to look at the practice and notion of "coming out of the closet"—and try to gauge the degree to which this specific cultural act frames the articulation of queer theory.

I am interested in this powerful "coming out" narrative, especially how this narrative lies at the core of theories of queer performativity. Already critics such as Judith Butler and Eve K. Sedgwick—among legions of other U.S.-based scholars—have explored how this narrative not only names a subject's gay, lesbian, or queer status, but also inaugurates her into a subjectivity of outness. Importantly, this narrative gets mobilized as a chant—"out of the closet, and into the streets!"—thereby interpellating the subject into a political realm. That is, if "out of the closet" signifies a subject's coming into being, then "into the streets" gives him a desired visibility and marks his entrance into the political realm.

"Out-of-the-closet-ness" as a category of identification and its potential for political coalition has become such an overwhelming imperative that for a long time it did not occur to me just how strange this idea of "coming out of the closet" might sound *outside* the United States. In fact, this practice's conceit for universality in naming a homosexual subject denotes an ideology that promotes what Dennis Altman calls the "Americanization of the homosexual," the way in which homosexual male styles and aesthetics circulate in the global sexual marketplace.[6] You see, there is something strange about speaking of "coming out of the closet" in places where *architecturally* they have not always existed. Where I grew up in Mexico, we did not have closets, we had armoires—somehow, no matter just how fabulous the idea of "coming out of the armoire" may sound . . . well, it is just not the same thing. In other words, the trope of the closet is a surplus space that does not exactly allow for a global homosexual identification, queer identification, or both.

So, what I am wildly advancing is that there seems to be much more of a cultural affinity to talk about performativity in places where "coming out" is read as a historically and culturally effective event. Now, where that experience of "coming out" is not autochthonous to a given location, might there be other genealogies that we can draw (on), thereby giving ourselves new alternatives for sexual narratives and identifications? Here I am echoing José Quiroga's proposal that "homosexual praxis is *effective* in [the Americas] in ways in which homosexual identity is not."[7] In other words, the practices of sexuality do not necessarily eventuate into the same sexual identities—in fact, they may be different. Conversely, sexual identity labels do not connote the same series of practices. Uncovering how these sexual and queer practices get narrated and silenced allows us to understand how circuits of desire produce subjects differently. It is worth stressing this point: the sexual narratives of America are not only those that are excessively visible, *but also those that are unspoken, silent.* This silence around sexuality goes by many names—from repression to oppression.

And how we read such silences involves putting forth a new scaffold or reading practices.⁸

Reading silences

I am here reminded of that fleeting moment, unfathomable, when Gustav Aschenbach reaches out to embrace Tadzio, his youthful object of desire:

> He sat quite still, quite unseen in his elevated location and looked into himself. His features were active; his brows rose; an alert, curious, witty smile crossed his lips. Then he raised his head and with both his arms, which were hanging limp over the arms of his chair, he made a slow circling and lifting movement that turned his palms forward, as if to signify an opening and extending of his embrace. It was a gesture of readiness, of welcome, and of relaxed acceptance.⁹

I consider this particular scene and gesture from Thomas Mann's *Death in Venice* a monad for the impossibility to articulate of male-male desire and to capture the significance of its expression.¹⁰ The protagonist reveals a certain acknowledgment of something within himself, as well as a slow hesitancy to name it. It is through this awkward embrace that he finally performs a "relaxed acceptance," in other words, a resignation. We might readily say that Gustav has resigned himself to accept his queer desires. This scene of resignation should be thought of as a resignification of the self, after all, the passage begins with a private moment during which Gustav looks on from "his elevated location" "into himself." This inner gaze thus leads the subject to "welcome" a transformative desire that remains silent, yet powerfully resignifies the self. Resignation is indeed a form of private resignification. It is here that I want to insist on the idea that resignation should not be read as defeat, rather as a potentiality to change one's life in tacit and silent new directions.

This scene from *Death in Venice* is emblematic of a particular expression of queer identity: self-recognition as queer, followed by the necessity of silence and privacy. So, in this private moment, what is Gustav trying to embrace? Is it the boy, an ideal? Is it the spirit of place? The object of his embrace is necessarily unknown. And so, must we always be privy to the other's pleasure? From the outside, the undecidability of the object of his desire might make for a frustrating scene of reading; however, within himself, not naming that object makes for a heightened moment of pleasure. Thus, I find in Gustav's passion a reminder of other similar moments in Latin American queer writing where the object is not—really, must not be—named.

I want to discuss Latin American texts that narrate queer sexual desires from the place of silence, not necessarily a question of unknowing and ignorance, rather from a conscious position of unspoken knowledge, an assertive refusal to name that desire—and to link it with an identity. How does desire play itself out when it remains under a mantle of self-imposed privacy? I do not want to summon the figure of the closet as epistemology. How do certain identifications happen when they are opted out from being given a voice?

Self-knowledge with the need for privacy—this particular figuration propels fascinatingly queer and other sexual moments. I would like to speculate on this queer figuration as it applies to Latin American letters to explore some of the theoretical issues it raises. More importantly, I want to consider this idea of a private, queer self-knowledge as a central trope inflected and effected by a Latin American cultural context. If knowingness is not offered as a thing or subject of analysis, where might we locate queer figurations and identities? What becomes an epistemology to render queer desires understandable?

I want to define *queerness* as the circuits of desire that disobey any imposed heteronormativity or even homonormativity; appreciating how these circuits function contributes to new subjectivities. If we consider that the "coming-out-of-the-closet" narrative figures as a master narrative or an ideological template in Anglo-American gay and lesbian subjectivities, we must then ask how to use a different conceptualization of queerness-through-silence to grasp Latino American sexual identities.

Foundational narratives

Let us begin then with a rather queer foundational text, that is, with Octavio Paz. His essay "Máscaras mexicanas" offers one of the most succinct, yet deceptive, articulations of his theorization of the

Mexican national subject: "el mexicano se me aparece como un ser que se encierra y se preserva: máscara el rostro y máscara la sonrisa."[11] ["the Mexican appears before me as a being that hides and guards himself: his face is a mask, his smile, a mask."] Throughout the essay, Paz goes on to reveal an anatomy or radiography of *lo mexicano* (Mexicanness) as a closed, hermetic identity. Paradoxically, he wants to open up a discussion to reveal Mexican identity, one that he initially has claimed only closes itself off to the world. This opening gesture is quite complicated because as he notes "abrirse es una debilidad o una traición."[12] ["to open oneself up is a weakness or a betrayal."] In other words, his essay—if successful—would be a betrayal to Mexicanness, his *own* Mexicanness. To speak openly about being Mexican would in fact make him a *rajado* who, accordingly, "es de poco fiar, un traidor o un hombre de dudosa fidelidad, que cuenta los secretos y es incapaz de afrontar los peligros como se debe."[13] ["the *rajado* is not to be trusted, he is a traitor or of doubtful loyalty, one who tells secrets and in incapable of face danger as one should."] This paradox is central to Paz's oeuvre, and it is never resolved completely.

If we go back to the first line for a moment, we notice a fascinating doubling "el mexicano se me aparece..." ["the Mexican appears before me"]; here the "I" encounters this other subject, and it becomes an object of analysis. Moreover, "el mexicano se me aparece" can be read as a discovery from within: "the Mexican appears within me." Paz is always teeter-tottering that line between being a subject who critiques and being subjected to his own critique. A third reading of "el mexicano se me aparece" is mirrored in the second part of the sentence, "máscara el rostro y máscara la sonrisa." The Mexican (the idea of a national subject) is an exterior mask (a visage of the other) that is placed over the author's own face and smile. These different formulations of *lo mexicano*—as the other, as a subjectivity within, and as a mask—are tightly tangled together, and therein we can see how Paz approaches his understanding of national identities and identifications. It is fairly safe to speculate that these three—and maybe there are more—articulations of the subject and their overlaps are paradigmatic of how the Latin American subjects are written.

Going back to that question of Paz's own inability or unwillingness to see himself implicated in his own description of a *rajado* by revealing some secrets of *lo mexicano*, I wonder if what makes him blind to this contradiction is more than just a particular social, class, gender, or cultural privilege, but rather a performance of *machista* bravado, on the one hand, as well as a desire to fashion himself as a cosmopolitan subject, on the other. Let me briefly comment that Paz disavows the possibility of being *rajado* (or castrated) himself by displacing that anxiety in a series of female figures in his oeuvre—from Malinche to Sor Juana, eventually onto Woman. I will bracket off his paradoxical stance and the powerful feminist critiques of the sexism in his theorization;[14] instead, I want to focus on the essay's most important cultural insight, that is, how national identity is written alongside gender and sexuality, specifically *through the body*. In other words, how Paz thinks about national identity through the display and deployment of the body. It is this critical practice of writing through the body that, I argue, lies at the heart of a Latin American difference on matters of gender and sexuality.

Woman beyond *la chingada*

If being a *rajado* is the thing a Mexican is *not* (supposed to be), then if we follow Paz's superficial insights, a Mexican cannot be a woman: "Las mujeres son seres inferiores porque, al entregarse, se abren. Su inferioridad es constitucional y radica en su sexo, en su 'rajada,' herida que jamás cicatriza."[15] ["Women are inferior beings because, when they give of themselves, they open up. Their inferiority is constitutional and lies in their sex, in their slit ("rajada'), a wound that never heals."] Despite his overtly sexist politics, it is important nonetheless to account for this view. On the one hand, Paz excludes women "constitutionally" from the body politic as well as the national imaginary. On the other hand, he links the production of a national identity or a national spirit with gender and sexuality; it says that the nation can be written as a gendered category. I would like to go further in the Pazian description of woman—she is also a melancholic, for hers is an open wound that never heals.[16]

Furthermore, Paz goes on to reveal that

> Como casi todos los pueblos, los mexicanos consideran a la mujer como un instrumento, ya de los deseos del hombre, ya de los fines que le asigna la ley, la sociedad o la moral. Fines, hay que decirlo, sobre los que

nunca se la ha pedido su consentimiento y en cuya realización participa sólo pasivamente, en tanto que "depositaria" de ciertos valores.[17]

[As with almost every people, Mexicans consider woman as an instrument, be it of men's desires, or of the ends that the law, society or morality assign to her. It is important to say that her consent has never been asked for to accomplish these ends, and she only participates passively in their realization, to the degree that she is a 'repository' of certain values.]

This is a stunning passage, because it reminds us of Gayle Rubin's "traffic in women."[18] Rubin, in fact, is rewriting Lévi-Strauss's 1949 *The Elementary Structures of Kinship* to show how women function explicitly and precisely as a "repository" of legal, social, and cultural desires. She is interested in demonstrating how women occupy a subordinate position within cultural structures and systems. I do find Paz's understanding of women as "instruments" of male desires, also as a "repository" of values to be quite illuminating. He concludes that "la mujer es sólo un reflejo de la voluntad y querer masculinos."[19] ["woman is only a reflection of masculine will and want"].

So far, for Paz, the Mexican woman is a melancholic and a reflection of masculine desire. However, Paz surprises us by going in another direction:

Se dirá que al transformar en virtud algo que debería ser motivo de vergüenza, sólo pretendemos descargar nuestra consciencia y encubrir con una imagen una realidad atroz. Es cierto pero también lo es que al atribuir a la mujer la misma invulnerabilidad a que aspiramos, recubrimos con una inmunidad moral su fatalidad anatómica, abierta al exterior. Gracias al sufrimiento [el mito de la "sufrida mujer mexicana"], a su capacidad de resistirlo sin protesta, la mujer trasciende su condición y adquiere los mismos atributos del hombre.[20]

[Some will argue that by transforming something that should be a cause for shame into a virtue, we are only trying to relieve our sense of guilt and to cover up with an image an atrocious reality. That may be true but it is also true that in attributing to woman the same invulnerability that we (men) aspire to, we cover her up again with a moral immunity her anatomic fatality, always open to the exterior. Thanks to suffering and her ability to endure it without protest, woman transcends her condition and acquires the exact attributes of man.]

In other words, suffering—or, more precisely, withstanding such suffering—makes a woman into a "man." This notion of bravery, of putting up with aversion, of withstanding pain or humiliation produces a shield (or another mask) of "moral immunity" that covers up the wound to make woman reach the same "invulnerability" that "we aspire to"—notice the implicit and tacit masculine "nosotros." Woman becomes a model of masculinity, because she can put up with the atrocity of her bodily condition. Importantly, those traits of "aguantarse" or containment are the classic tropes that define and shape masculinity—writ large. Moreover, masculinity is most present or persistent when most challenged; it is the continuous challenge to masculinity that will define it. Passive masculinity is an oxymoron. As I suggested earlier, Paz opens up about *lo mexicano*, because he implicitly knows that by going through the possible humiliation of opening up, he is indeed reaffirming his own masculinity.[21]

I would like to return to that "moral shield" (or other mask) that transforms woman into man because it does something very interesting to the earlier discussion of woman as "repository." The moral shield is a kind of fetishistic disavowal that gives Paz's Mexican women back a phallus in the form of a superior morality, it rewrites and values that open wound into moral discourse of rectitude, of masculinity.

I wonder how Rubin's theory might be different if she had read Paz's essays. For Woman in Paz is also the metaphor for colonialism; his fixation on her *rajada* has to do with narcissistic gaze of being an heir to *la chingada*, *un hijo de la chingada*. Her body is not exclusively an object of exchange (as Rubin argues), but her body is punctured and ripped to become the very enactment of a colonial rape, only to then be undervalued and discarded; in other words, her body is resignified. Paz's *chingada* acquires its value not on its own terms, but through a different circuit, a memory of what has been lost. The *chingada*'s body is displayed and re-membered differently as emblematic of the nation. This kind of maneuvering and refunctioning of the body is what I give more weight in the rethinking of queer identities in this project.

Following the work of Rubin and René Girard, Eve K. Sedgwick has proposed that classic triangulation and the traffic in women structures male homosocial bonds. The presence of woman in this triangle permits that the erotic desire between men is displaced, sublimated, and she seals the alliance of male-male power relations under the figure of a gift, woman's own body.[22] That is, her body hides and "normalizes" that desire between men; she makes that homoerotic desire into something unrecognizable—or at least unnameable.

I wonder how Sedgwick's theory might be different, if she had read Paz's essays? Consider, for instance, Sedgwick's idea of homosexual panic that is the overvaluation of the women's presence in the triangle to ensure heteronormativity, that is, it helps guarantee that the male-male relation be regarded as social or political, and not erotic or sexual. Now, if we change the idea of "woman"—from Sedgwick's model to Paz's—this does not mean that homosexual panic ceases to exist. On the contrary, some would argue that homosexual panic might appear more virulently in Mexican and other Latin American contexts. I would argue then that if woman, according to Paz, can morally become a "man," her presence in the triangle must take on a different form: specifically, it is my contention that she becomes more importantly heightened as a bodily presence. Paz will argue that "[n]o nos da miedo ni vergüenza nuestro cuerpo; lo afrontamos con naturalidad y lo vivimos con cierta plenitud—a la inversa de lo que ocurre con los puritanos."[23] ["we are not afraid or ashamed of our body; we face it with naturalness and we live it a certain amount of pleasure—it is the opposite of Puritanism."] It is this investment in the body that marks a central difference in how Latin American sexual identities and others are produced and conceived.

Judith Butler and her school propose that gender is produced in parallel fashion to speech acts,[24] and this performative production of gender gets installed in a body (in *Bodies that Matter*, she uses the term *process of sedimentation* to denominate the materialization and embodiment of the performative).[25] In other words, the body in Butler's work does not contribute to the initial production of gender, rather the body coheres with gender,[26] a kind of Saussurian arbitrary bonding between signifiers and signifieds. My project is about insisting on *the priority of the body in the construction of Latino American gender and sexual identities*. It is truly a rather modest project, but given that the preponderance of "gender theory," "sexuality and queer studies" in the U.S. academy has been so overwhelming, it has become necessary to reread classics such as Paz's to restate what might appear obvious (this, of course, is a question of professionalization). Let me just note that from the critical perspective that we have inherited from Butler as a canonized figure in queer theory, Paz has been criticized for essentializing gender and sexual orientation. I am sure he does some essentializing; however, he is also presenting another model, a different intervention—to use Quiroga's term—to articulate Latino American sexualities.[27] His project might be conceived as an attempt to describe gender in bodily terms—and not necessarily performative ones.[28] By focusing on Paz, we begin to dislodge Butler's and other U.S. scholars' centrality as the only way to talk about sexuality; also, we begin to see the *cultural* and *historical* underpinnings of Butler's own work, underpinnings that she herself has disavowed in the name of philosophy (her disciplinary training), with a certain conceit to universality. Moreover, by learning to recognize other critical perspectives (from the South, in this case), we also interrupt the directionality of how theory travels from North to South, to read Latin American cultures, moving away from imposition toward something that resembles more a dialogue.

Again, this does not leave Paz off the hook for his sexism or his homophobia, but it does free us to reread Paz and others in a new light. And we reveal some amazing things: for instance, how different someone like, say, José Martí sounds, when he declares "Nuestra Grecia es preferible a la Grecia que no es nuestra."[29] ["Our Greece is preferable to the Greece that is not ours."] Just *how* gay does that line always sound to me! But seriously, remember the masculine body that he sets forth as the American citizen (the citizen of the Americas), a body that does not show "el brazo de uñas pintadas y pulsera" ["the arm with painted nails and bracelets']. In "Nuestra América," Martí first gives us the abjected body, which "we" are not, then he draws out a body: "Con los pies en el rosario, la cabeza blanca y el cuello pinto de indio y criollo..."[30] [With the feet on the rosary, the white head, the neck colored of Indian and Creole...] Later on, he adds, "Éramos una vision, con el pecho de atleta, las manos de petimetre y la frente de niño."[31] (164) ["We were a vision with the chest of an athlete, the hands of a fop, and the forehead of a child.] This figuration of the citizen is followed by a litany of other bodies, the *indio*, the *negro*, the *campesino*, the *genio*, and so forth.³² I just give this brief example to underscore the importance of the body in foundational Latin American narratives. Many others would follow.³³ As an aside, though very much in the center of this discussion, I am thinking of Sylvia Molloy's beautiful figuration of body and language in *En breve carcel*: "una piel de voces" ["a skin of voices"]: "Con una voz, con su propia voz rota, habrá de unir fragmentos si quiere vivir. Agregará a la infancia que evita y a la que vuelve [. . .] esas entonaciones que, como las pieles, no tiene que olvidar."³⁴ ["With one voice, with her own fragmented voice, she will have to unite the pieces if she wants to live. She will add to the childhood that avoids and to which she returns [. . .] those intonations that, like skin, she does not have to forget."] Later, Molloy brings back together "Pieles y voces, tan parecidas, tan vulnerables y caducas."³⁵ ["Skins and voices, so similar, so vulnerable and easily shedding."] Voices and skins, a skin of voices, language, and body become inseparable, yet transitory.

I turn our attention to another masking strategy, one that Quiroga presents in his *Tropics of Desire*. In his analysis of the 1993 Gay Pride March in Buenos Aires, when masks were given to those participants who wanted to make their presence known, yet all the while protecting themselves from the real danger of being identified and potentially suffering the consequences for being "out" or simply "supportive." While he understands that the closet is part of this instance of gay and lesbian representation, it is not the only part of such a representation. He adds that "[t]he mask spoke of broader circuits that did not necessarily end with an 'outing,' or an identity as conclusion."³⁶ Quiroga concludes that the mask is a "figure [that] memorializes its own absence, insisting on its own presence as erasure. It responds to the demands of identity with the silence of No One."³⁷ In other words, and similar to my analysis of Paz's bodily deployments, the mask here functions as a prosthetic that enables gay, lesbian, and queer identities, by covering or recovering the body politic—and fashioning new codes of representation.

Finally, Carlos Monsiváis offers yet another example of queer masking in the persona of the gay Mexican poet and essayist Salvador Novo. Monsiváis identifies in Novo's wit and sharp sense of irony a critical tool for queer self-figuration—Novo "vuelto espejo de la afectación más reprochable"[38] ["becomes mirror to the most reprehensible behaviors"]. According to Monsiváis, Novo uses a series of strategies to deflect homophobia as well as affirm his queer persona: "En la mecánica del ghetto, común a todas las minorías acosadas, el vituperio de sí y de los semejantes mediatice el filo del exterminio de los epítetos machistas. 'Lo que me digan yo ya me lo dije pero con la elegancia, la ironía y la malicia que ustedes desconocen.'"[39] ["In the operations of the ghetto, familiar to all harassed minorities, the vituperation of the self and those like him mediates the sharp-edged extermination of sexist epithets. 'What you say to me, I have already said to myself but with the elegance, the irony and the malice that is unfamiliar to you.'"] In other words, Monsiváis identifies in Novo's work and self-figuration certain strategies of self-preservation that both save the homosexual, while making him thrive. He proposes first the "mechanics of the ghetto" offer a context, or a space of sameness; this might be read as a space where queer self-figuration might thrive and replenish itself after constantly being marginalized. Second, he puts forth the idea that the use of abusive language against the self might serve a means to "soften" the deadly force of external invectives. We might consider interpreting these two strategies as distinct "masks" that Novo used—the former strategy suggests the formation of a hermetic space for the self; the latter strategy anticipates the external naming, and projects an identity and offers a futurity for the queer self—an identity and futurity that has more "elegance," "irony," and "malice" than the other could ever imagine. It would appear that Novo's queer strategies look inwardly (the idea of the ghetto) and anticipate outwardly other possibilities for the self—this double movement reveal a practice of queer self-figuration that extends on Paz's articulation of the (national) subject—to recall, first as the other, second as a subjectivity within, and as a mask. I like to go further and suggest that Novo's own words— "What you say to me, I have already said to myself but with the elegance, the irony and the malice that is unfamiliar to you"—introduce yet another element to this genealogy of masks and queer Latino identities, and that is a dimension of aesthetics. Novo might in fact be constructing an elegant and nuanced narrative of the self in the process of becoming and imagining potential ways of being, announcing a new visionary defense of queer identity. Monsiváis argues that in his poetics Novo discredits "refined taste" with the intention of being a provocateur. Novo uses overt expressive misery (la "sordidez" expresiva) to neutralize those who expel him from "proper" society (las "buenas costumbres"). To summarize Monsiváis in his overall assessment of the poet and essayist, the body in Novo's queer constellation becomes erotic and playful—the body serves as a mirror that reflects and distorts homophobic society's "buenas costumbres" ["good manners" or "good intentions"].[40] The body signifies and imposes itself on others—and in so doing we are being taught an original and audacious lesson for writing queer Latino narratives anew.[41]

Limits and Forms

"Para nosotros el cuerpo existe; da gravedad y límites a nuestro ser." ["For us the body exists; it gives weight and limits to our being."] This insight seems to encapsulate Paz's understanding of the body as an anchor and containment of the self. Said differently, the body offers us a race, a gender, a colonial status—claiming the body as our own resists its naturalization as masculine and universal. Nevertheless, Paz's text is quite obsessed with other weights and limits to the self: "Quizá nuestro tradicionalismo—que es una de las constantes de nuestro ser y lo que da coherencia y antigüedad a nuestro pueblo—parte del amor que profesamos a la Forma."[42] ["Perhaps our traditionalism—that is one of the constants to our being and what gives coherence and timelessness to our people—stems from the love we profess to the Form."] This idea of the Form is based on Paz's reading of Georg Simmel; Paz argues throughout the essay that the subject is defined alongside or against those structures that he identifies as constitutive of the Self. These Forms often constrain the self, and reduce him; other times they overwhelm him, and force him to become something greater. In any case, the Forms require that the self set up a relation to them. We are reminded again of the ways in which Paz began his essay, where the Mexican (national subject) appears as the other, as a subjectivity within, and as a mask; and the author has to position himself versus each of these formal expressions. I would like to suggest that the relational nature of how the subject accommodates himself to the Form might help explain one of the most misunderstood, though most infamous, passages from the essay, that is, Paz's discussion of homosexuality.

Queer endings

Paz's introduces his view of homosexuality: "Es significativo [...] que el homosexualismo masculino sea considerado con cierta indulgencia, por lo que toca al agente activo. El pasivo, al contrario, es un ser degradado y abyecto."[43] ["It is significant (...) that male homosexualism as it pertains to the active agent is considered with a certain degree of indulgence. The passive one, on the contrary, is a degenerate and abject being."] And later on, he adds that "el homosexualismo masculino es tolerado, a condición de que se trate de una violación del agente pasivo. Como en el caso de las relaciones heterosexuales, lo importante es 'no abrirse' y, simultáneamente, rajar, herir al contrario."[44] ["male homosexualism is tolerated, on the condition that it is about the rape of the passive agent. As is the case with heterosexual relations, what is important is 'not opening up' and simultaneously, cutting, wounding the other"].

What this particular situation refers to is what has come to be known as the "penetration paradigm."[45] Notice again that there is a Form underlying Paz's understanding of homosexuality: it is grafted onto a heterosexual grid or template, whereby the "active" agent remains unmarked and heterosexual, and the passive agent "opens up" like a woman, and is wounded, raped, *chingado*. Freud has taught us that sexual identity succeeds through an interplay between sexual object choice and aim. Paz's paradigm seems to emphasize the aim in the sexual encounter, the relation between both specific bodies. Male homosexuality is defined here through a relationship that cuts across the bodies. Interestingly, it displaces the importance of the sexual object choice in defining the sexual identity. Male homosexual identity is not simply written on the body, it is not only about how one body relates to another, but rather—more aggressively—it is about how one body traverses the other, how gender and sexuality are written through the body.

I have begun with an introduction to reading through other bodies and cultures. This serves as a prolegomena or an intervention, which might helps us think through some of the pressing questions about gender and sexuality that travel from South to North and North to South. This back-and-forth movement is about opening up a dialogue about the strangeness of categories, about the pleasure-in-difference of these categories, and about translating those keywords like gender, sexuality, and queerness that have yet to be fully analyzed and grasped.

The Body of This Book

"The Avowal of Difference" presents a layered description and analysis of the various social, cultural, national, and linguistic forces that impinge on and anchor down queer Latino American subject formation; it analyzes different discursive modes of literary production—*modernismo*, Neo-Baroque, and other forms of literary writing—to understand how queer subjects are written (or erased) in the social and cultural imaginary. I do not want to create a false sense of literary genealogy or development, rather, I would prefer to consider each chapter as an analysis of various forms that sexual identities—normative and queer—come into being and into narrative. My acknowledgment of those literary moments in Latin American literary and cultural studies—namely, *modernismo*, Boom, and Neo-Baroque—are meant to show that there exists within each movement a set of discursive approaches to the narration of identity, and we should consider how textual and discursive analysis offer us important critical tools to read the Latino American queer body.

In this introduction, I have raised a number of theoretical questions that structure the book; in particular, to what extent do corporeality and visibility figure in queer Latino America? I hope to explore the questions of the body and queer identities, particularly looking at how silences and disavowal emerge as central strategies of subject formation of queer Latino America. Moreover, I will propose some epistemological differences between the narratives used to articulate queer identities in the South versus the North.

This book is structured around four parts or themes: Part I, "Unwriting the Self," examines very specific subject figurations by looking at a series of texts that explore how the self narrates itself in very solipsistic and hermetic ways. Part II, "Interventions," continues a similar exploration of literary works by looking at how the queer Latino American is emphatically presented as other. In this section I explore the limits of heterosexuality and its relation to queer desire. Part III, "The Body Politic," moves from a discussion of the *individual* self to queer *group* formations: by examining certain privileged cultural spaces (for example, the school and the clinic), I look at the deployment of a queer identity in the formation of national, social, cultural, and theoretical differences. Finally, Part IV, "Queer Latina/o

Narratives," looks at Latino writers in the United States to examine how their narratives of subject formation often borrow from two different traditions and cultural languages—South and North—to narrate the queer self. More specifically, I analyze the South–North dialogue that emerges when Latina/o subjects in the United States consider different epistemologies to fashion a transnational queer identity.

Theoretically, this book gauges the potential and limits queer theories to capture the whole of Latino American queer subject formation and experience. More specifically, I propose a reclaiming (or at least a reengaging) of the body in subject formation. However, readers will notice my own theoretical commitment to psychoanalysis—of course, this emphasis allows me to approach very specific articulations of how the queer self narrates or gets narrated. My uses of psychoanalysis are not meant to be prescriptive, but rather by bringing this corpus of queer Latino works in dialogue with psychoanalytic theory, I hope to transform the ways in which we can understand psychoanalysis though a different body of texts.[46]

* * *

Chapter 1, "*Modernismo*, Masochism and Queer Potential in Nervo's *El bachiller*," explores how beginning in the 1880s, *modernismo* inaugurates the earliest moment of Latin America's self-reflection and the conscious literary elaboration of its cultural uniqueness. Amado Nervo's *El bachiller* ["The Student"] from 1895 participates in this project, and introduces us to Felipe, a shy student obsessed with spiritual purity. This chapter explores the ways in which *modernista* discourse shapes subject formation, as well as it explores how its concept of the "reino interior" ["interior kingdom"] becomes a productive way to narrate (and cover up) sexuality in the novella. This notion of radical interiority will play out as a regulating cultural trope throughout this study.

In chapter 2, "Queer Losses in Barbachano Ponce's *El diario de José Toledo*," I present the story of a young man whose obsessive and unrequited love for another man drives him to suicide. The chapter begins with a discussion of Foucauldian relationality, and proceeds to analyze how José's sense of self is structured by a loss of the other;

again, the queer self is narrated as hermetic and solipsistic, unable to enter into any other social bonds. Importantly, both José and his boyfriend Wenceslao depend on the family structures for their well-being—and I add, for creating a sense of gay self. I close the chapter by looking at gay identity *within* the domestic sphere. I try to imagine how gay life within the domestic promotes different versions of homosexuality.

Luis Zapata's 1979 prize-winning *El vampiro de la colonia Roma* represents a new, unapologetic vision of queer identity—and it is the subject of chapter 3, "Adonis's Silence." The protagonist hustler Adonis offers us a queer logorrhea that pictures the ins-and-outs of gay life in the city. What makes this novel so important is that it presents not only an intimate view of gay life in Mexico, but also offers a new grammar to narrate his story. This chapter examines this new queer grammar, and looks at the blank spaces (the silences) that organize the gay subject and scene. This chapter also concludes Part I, and it ends with a discussion of subject formation and the role that different expressions of silence (as the affirmative refusal to name and speak) plays in queer Latin(o) American subject formation.

In the fourth chapter, "Epistemerotics: Puig, Queer Subjects, and Writing Desire," I study Manuel Puig's *The Buenos Aires Affair*. This chapter is divided into two parts: in the first half I look at Gladys, the one-eyed female protagonist and her polyamorous desire; in the second half I analyze Leo's queer desire. In both cases I examine the ways in which each character expresses her or his sexual desires through violence. How does violence in desire (tacitly) structure subject formation? This chapter is about the limits of heterosexuality as a category of identity—and more precisely how these limits rub against the concept of queerness. In this chapter I introduce the concept of "epistemerotics" as a critical tool that accounts for and insists on the centrality of cultural and social context in the articulation of sexualities.

I continue in chapter 5, "La Manuela's Return: Transvestism/Identification/Abjection in Lemebel's *Loco afán*," with an analysis of Pedro Lemebel's essays on transgender identity. More importantly, I read his particular critique of neoliberalism and homonormativity. (In fact, Lemebel's critique of homonormativity is formulated in the 1990s, well before this concept appears in United States academic circles.) Lemebel writes from the global South and looks at "gay identity" as an ideological template imposed by the global North. He asks what kind of identity, and what are the paths of identity formation that result from this kind of northern imposition? Additionally, his chronicles become one of Latin America's earliest explorations of the politics of AIDS. These two chapters form Part II: the principal thrust here is formulating a more capacious understanding of queer identities, specifically, thinking of heterosexuality as just an instant, particular temporality, or a very specialized expression or queer in the broader spectrum of sexual expression.

Part III, "The Body Politic," collects three chapters that reflect on queerness as a group formation, rather than an individual one. In chapter 6, "Homosociality, Disavowal, and Pedagogy in Vargas Llosa's *Los cachorros*," I question what Sedgwick's homosocial triangulation might look like without woman as object of desire and intermediary of the relationship between men. In other words, how do male-male exchanges attain the status of the normal without the heterosexual veneer guaranteed by woman-as-text? This chapter traces a genealogy of male-male relations by reading *Los cachorros* alongside André Gide's *L'immoraliste* and other works. Again I pay special attention to how the queer body helps constitute and guarantee heteronormativity. Indeed, I want to revise the ways in which a libidinal economy circulates, and assess the kind of subject formations it produces in a model similar to Rubin's "traffic in women," yet without a female body present.

Chapter 7, "Sadomasochism in *Paradiso*: Bound Narratives and Pleasure," gathers many of the theoretical questions that inform this book, namely appreciating the role of erasure and silence in the constitution of the homosexual in the latter half of twentieth-century Latino American narratives. I perform a close reading of the famed chapter VIII of José Lezama Lima's novel, and analyze the many significations of the phallus and the role that silence plays in producing sexual, gender, social, and cultural meanings.

"On the Homo-Baroque: Queering Sarduy's Baroque Genealogies" analyzes Sarduy's theory of the Neo-Baroque. In this eighth chapter, I underscore the libidinal economy in the Baroque and Neo-Baroque projects—and I coin the term *Homo-Baroque* to propose a new practice of reading the relationship between queer subject formation and the mechanics of Baroque artificialization. Then I consider how Sarduy's structures of signification reemerge in his last novel, *Pájaros de la playa*, which is precisely about naming and the impossibility of curing "el mal" (read as both illness and evil).

Finally, in Part IV "Queer Latina/o Narratives," I hope to promote a South–North conversation about productive ways in which queer theory may be read in the South, as well as to temper any imposition that queer theories may have as they circulate globally. "The Avowal of Difference" hopes to engage the work of many U.S.-based and Latin American scholars whose scholarship on Latino American sexuality and cultural studies looks carefully at sexual subject formation from the South, that is, scholars who have been attentive to Latin American cultural difference in supplying new epistemologies to describe and theorize gay, lesbian, and queer experiences in Latino America. The final two chapters offer my contribution to such a conversation.

Additionally, I must mention that the question of race has been a theoretical preoccupation throughout the book. However, it is quite complicated to address race in a singular or universal fashion when speaking of Latin America—primarily because the geopolitical concept of "Latin America" contains many different historical and national understandings of racial formations. Racial formations have to account for historical period (colonial versus Independence versus the modern era), region and cultural tradition (Caribbean, Brazil, or Southern Cone), also racial identity (*mestizaje*, blackness, and indigeneity)—and a whole host of forces and movements that have an effect on how race is conceptualized. Furthermore, the engagement with race in Latin America has been at times what might be called "uneven racializations," that is, some regions have profited from such conversations whereas others have even disavowed race as a critical tool of analysis and politics. Thus, the question that I needed to answer more specifically for the majority of Latin American authors is *How does racial discourse get taken up and inscribed in the queer narratives that I analyze?* To that end, I was able to approach some of the particularities of racial formation throughout the book—to name a few, for example, how does the figure of a blonde woman signify European subjectivity in *modernismo*, how do foreignness (and primitivism) and queerness relate in the national imaginary, to what ends does blackness get fetishized, how do transgendered identities get (e)raced, and so on. I should add that racial formations are processes that unfold analogously to queer subject formations—that is, uneven, "messy," and often shrouded in different kinds of silences (the silence of strategically remaining "in the closet" is not the same the silence of "being in the closet" is not the same as the silence of [racial] "passing"). Instead these different mechanics of subject formation inform each other, sometimes working alongside each other, at another times, working against or despite each other.

Indeed given the rich scholarship in queer of color critique that has burgeoned in the United States in the last ten years, and also given how U.S. Latino authors have tackled questions of race in what may seem a much more deliberate way, I have paid more attention to the intersectionality of queerness and race with greater ease in this final section. This does *not* mean to suggest a genealogy whereby race matters only happen in the United States; rather, any "accidental" genealogy that a reader might perceive announces a critical imperative that much more work has to be done in Latin America in bringing race, racialization, and queerness into a fuller conversation. I hope my work encourages such a robust conversation.

Chapter 9, "Queer *Latinidad*: Thomas's *Down These Mean Streets* and Díaz's *Drown*," explores the explicit tension between the traditional U.S. coming-out story and the need for silence in order to have or experience queer sexuality. Both Piri Thomas's and Junot Díaz's texts show how queer exchanges are possible under the mantle of silence. This silence cannot be read as self-effacement (or simply closetedness), but rather as a complex cultural imperative. I then go back to Freud to theorize his idea of "contingent" homosexuality and relate it to silence.

Finally, chapter 10, "Traveling North, Translating Queerness: Rivera-Valdés and the Trouble with Discipline," examines Sonia Rivera-Valdés's *Forbidden Stories of Martha Veneranda*, in particular how queer *practices* become different queer *identities* when viewed from the North versus the South. Few contemporary literary works display such a rich understanding of queer sexuality and identities. Moreover, the text's critique of different disciplinary epistemologies—social sciences and humanities—gives us an important insight to the many approaches to conceptualize and understand Latino sexualities.

This critique of epistemology, of course, becomes central to this book's approach and contribution to queer and sexuality studies.

* * *

Throughout these analyses, I am very interested in a few general questions: How does queer Latino American subject formation happen? What role does silence play in Latin American narratives about subject formation? What are the potentialities and limitations that queer theory offers us in reading Latin American texts and subjects? Conversely, how do Latino American queer bodies and articulations revise Anglo American and European theoretical assumptions about queer identity? This double movement—reading Latino American texts with queer theory (based on U.S. cultural production) *and* questioning the universality of these queer theories *through* the cultural specificity of Latino America—becomes this project's most significant contribution, helping us to arrive at a fuller portrait of queer Latino American sexual identities. It is my hope that others will contribute to this conversation, and may imagine new ways of thinking through sexuality in other words and realms.

part 1

Unwriting the Self

1
Modernismo, Masochism, and Queer Potential in Nervo's *El bachiller*

> Amo más que la Grecia de los griegos
> la Grecia de la Francia...
> —Darío, "Divagación"

> La chair est triste, hélas! et j'ai lu tous les livres
> —Mallarmé

> The habit loves the monk, as they are but one thereby. In other words, what lies under the habit, what we call the body is perhaps but the remainder (*reste*) I call object *a*.
> —Lacan, *Encore*

That moment in Ruben Darío's oeuvre when he declares his love for the "Greece of France" as greater than the "Greece of the Greeks" contains a particular *modernista* affectation, that is, the author is declaring his love for a mediated object rather than the object in its "natural" place or state. Greece as articulated by its citizens is just one form of representation, but Greece as the French would have it becomes an object of greater love and desire. This Darian moment has become a linchpin in Latin American *modernista* art, whereby artifice and mediation become of more value and affect to the poet. I begin by focusing on that particular experience of reading the object and self, mediated or filtered *through* the experiences and visions of others as somehow more desirable. Darío's relationship to France (or Frenchness) has been criticized as being too "afrancesado" [Frenchified], and this quote does not save him. But what is he in fact borrowing from the French? What is that *thing* that incites a greater love? I would argue that it is more than something tangible, a discernable style, but rather a sensibility, a way of looking at the world. Furthermore, this thing cannot be copied exactly, but it is something that Darío approaches, approximates, and transforms, something he plays with, a thing that he makes or keeps unnamable, yet personal.[1] On another note, to say that Darío is *afrancesado* is to call him mannered or "queer"—in the contemporary sense of the word. Some critics of Darío may in fact have been dismissing his writing with such a homophobic characterization—however, thinking of new templates for queer Latino American identities, I would like to take on the question of Darío's (and the *modernistas'*) Frenchness, both as a marker of cosmopolitanism, otherness, and queerness, as something desirable, as one marker of difference that must be avowed.

When writing a book on queer narratives and identities, I choose *modernismo* as a particular event in Spanish American literary history very deliberately, and, in so doing, am quite aware that I am constructing (imposing, even) a critical genealogy for the articulation of queer Latino American subjectivities. As Gerard Aching, along with others, has noted "*modernismo* marked the beginning of a Spanish American self-reflection and the conscious literary elaboration of a cultural uniqueness."[2] Moreover, "the *modernista* movement brought privileged groups in the region into a burgeoning intertextual commerce with similar reading constituencies in Spanish America, Europe, and the United States,"[3] thus, *modernismo* provided a cosmopolitan context for its authors and readers. What draws me to *modernismo*, in general, is that inaugural moment to mark Spanish America's difference along with its cosmopolitan dimension; in other words, that self-figuration accompanied by that outward gaze. In particular, *modernismo*'s linguistic and cultural mediation offer an important site for rethinking queer identities.[4] Indeed, I want to argue that *modernismo*'s mediated representation provides a new model to situate and read Latino American queer identities; additionally, I want to make a critical displacement, that is, to dislodge how Latino American queer identities might too often be read through other hegemonic queer identity formulations, namely Anglo American queer theory. I want to advance the following thesis: what *modernista* language does is appropriate European and U.S. discourses as other—and that appropriation as a strategy of recycling and reinvention becomes an important critical move and figure for Latino American queer identities.

Beyond the question of mediation and artifice, *modernismo* has been read through a series of clichés—from nude bodies and lust, the museum space, overwrought luxury, to the concept of the "*reino interior*" [interior kingdom or realm].[5] I will not try to deconstruct those leitmotifs or images; rather, I want to dwell on the figure of the *reino interior* [interior kingdom] to rethink how the question of queer subjectivity might be productively elaborated out of this literary moment. In fact, I hope to present a series of models to rethink queer identity that are based on or follow from Latin American cultural and artistic experiences, this just being the first one.

"Closet" vis-à-vis *"reino interior"*

I begin by proposing a genealogy for queer Latino American identities based, not on the "closet"—often reduced to a question of positionality, of inside/outside—but rather on the *modernista* notion of a *reino interior* [interior kingdom]. If subjectivity can be understood as an interior dialogue that leads to a particular narration of identity, I would like to put forth the idea that the *reino interior* might offer us a particularly (autochthonous) model of subject formation that inaugurates the modern queer Latino American subject.[6] I would like to examine such a thesis in Amado Nervo's 1895 novella, *El bachiller* [The Student], a story of a sad boy who becomes an even more saddened man.[7]

The story begins with a melancholic description of our hero, Felipe:

Nació enfermo, enfermo de esa sensibilidad excesiva y hereditaria que amargó los días de su madre. Precozmente reflexivo, ya en sus primeros años prestaba una atención extraña a todo lo exterior, y todo lo exterior hería con inaudita viveza su imaginación.[8]

[He was born sick, sick of that excessive and hereditary sensibility that embittered his mother's days. He was precociously reflexive, and early on he paid strange attention to all exteriors, and all things exterior wounded his imagination with unheard of liveness.]

This excessive sensibility gets mentioned again and again throughout the novella.⁹ Importantly, it affects how he is seen by others:

> De suerte que sus dolores eran intensos e intensos sus placeres; mas *unos y otros silenciosos.*
>
> Murió su madre, y desde entonces su taciturnidad se volvió mayor.
>
> *Para sus amigos y para todos era un enigma* que causaba esa curiosidad que sienten la mujer ante un sobre sellado y el investigador ante una necrópolis egipcia no violada aún.
>
> ¿Qué había allí adentro? Acaso un poema o una momia?¹⁰

> [Fortunately his pains were intense as were intense his pleasures; yet *some and others remained silent.*
>
> His mother dies, and since then his silence became greater.
>
> *To his friends and all others he was an enigma* that provoked that curiosity a woman might feel before a sealed envelope and a researcher feels before an Egyptian necropolis not yet opened.
>
> What was inside? Perhaps a poem or a mummy? (Italics mine)]

These opening remarks about Felipe's way of being offer us important insight into the text's discursive linkages to a literary tradition. First, the novella is discursively framed by Latin American *modernismo*. To recap, some of *modernismo*'s central features include a language that is excessively attentive to details and "all things exterior" or superficial, an interrogation of the relationship between surface and the *reino interior* of the subject. To the above quote, we may apply Gwen Kirkpatrick's insightful description of *modernismo* "as closed space, a silent theater in which rituals, gesture, and erotic ceremonies are carried out, with the body of language itself sharing this endless rehearsal of the rites of self-enclosure."¹¹ Felipe's sense of self is expressed through the language of isolation and alienation; also, he is made other—an enigma. Moreover, what this scene reveals is a protagonist whose sense of self gets doubly concealed: a poem in a sealed envelope, a mummy inside a sealed crypt; in other words, a trope tucked inside another trope, provocatively speaking, a metaphor inside another metaphor.¹² The double metaphorics of the trope inside another trope suggest a roundabout mode of representing the object, and do something to the act of deciphering and reading it: on the one hand, the double metaphoric structure produces an insisted-on concealment; on the other hand, I would propose that this structure, in its most absolute simplicity, evokes a desire to maintain or effect the possibility of privacy as part of subject formation. Graciela Montaldo has proposed "una estética del rodeo" ["an aesthetics of circumlocution"] to appreciate the structure of address, with which *modernista* authors articulated their object.[13] By extension, I would argue that this aesthetic of circumlocution becomes a useful tool to read the queer figurations that we might perceive or identify. The private self vibrates inside the surface that we see. In the case of Felipe, it produces an interior monologue—again, a subjectivity—that challenges the surface-self, in this specific case the corporeal chastity that Felipe purports to own.[14]

This dual subjectivity—one interior and uncontrollable, the other visible and *récherché*—is precisely what explains the young man's turbulent social, sexual, and gender vicissitudes. After his mother's death, Felipe goes to live with his "solterón" [aged bachelor] uncle who takes charge of his education; Nervo notes clearly: "Su vida [en el Seminario] transcurrió desde entonces sin más agitaciones que las que su viciado carácter le proporcionaba; su fantasía, aguijoneada por el vigor naciente de la pubertad, iba perpetuamente, como hipogrifo sin freno, tras irrealizables y diversos fines."[15] ["His life (in the Seminary) transpired since then without any more agitation than what his stale character already afforded him; his fantasy life, punctured by the nascent vigor of puberty, moved perpetually, like an unbridled hippogriff, chasing after unattainable and diverse ends."] We see here that Felipe's fantasy world is "punctured" by the corporeal—and we recall the earlier characterization that "all things exterior wounded his imagination." In this passage, I would argue that the penis, in its bulging physicality, rips fantasy asunder; however, this puncturing of fantasy moves Felipe's self-narrative forward as well. It is as if each thump of Felipe's pulsating pubescent body (really, his penis) pokes through his "perpetual" fantasies, propelling them into more outrageous scenarios. If we might return momentarily to the image of the "poem inside the sealed envelope" and try to overlap that image with the relationship between fantasy and the immanence of puberty, we run into some trouble. Whereas the poem-inside-the-letter image is quite clear as to the relationship of interiority versus exteriority, defining the inside-outside structure between fantasy versus the bulging penis is more complex: Is the penis pounding the fantasy world? Is fantasy an escape from the corporeal? Is the penis about to rip fantasy or to enforce it by punctuating it—or both? In other words, in that interior monologue that sets up subjectivity, which thing lies inside the other—fantasy or corporeality? If "all things exterior wounded his imagination," then does this mean the penis gets cast as being *exterior*—or other—to the self? This bodily exodus raises the question as to whether fantasy or corporeality takes priority? And what does this priority signify? Most importantly, what and how this relationship is read and narrated becomes a difficult task for the critic, yet one in which new (queer) narratives might be otherwise possible.

In Felipe's religious and sentimental education, one thing becomes clear: that he worships an ideal. His objectification of the ideal takes on two forms—first, a strange heteronormative need for the perfect woman, and second, an ascetic and masochistic spiritual desire and religious fervor. An example of his attention to women appears early on in the novella, "A los trece años, habíase enamorado ya de tres mujeres, cuando menos, mayores todas que él; de esta, porque la vio llorar, de aquella, porque era triste, de la otra, porque cantaba una canción que extraordinariamente le conmovía."[16] ["At thirteen years of age, he had already fallen in love with three women, at least, all older than him: of this one, because he saw her cry; of that one, because she was sad; of the other, because she sang a song that extraordinarily moved him."] The reasons for falling in love are weirdly uneven: love produced by a crying woman, a sad woman, and a moving chanteuse. Although we may speculate that what leads Felipe to fall in love is not the women themselves, but rather how they make him feel, what emotions they provoke in him. In fact, Felipe's act of loving is one in which the women always get cast as objects, never as subjects: he "loves" them, though he never *is loved* by them. Furthermore, we notice that the commonality among the women is their age difference—"all older than him." Surely this fact points to an Oedipal tension. Whatever affect that comes back to him is narcissistically produced, thereby structuring, effecting and insisting again on a self that is pure interiority, an interiority that reaches outwardly, but refuses to be tampered with or disturbed. The exterior—the body—is ascetically rejected. He longs for an ideal that is described as

[a]lgo grave. Aquel espíritu, sediento de ideal, desilusionable, tornadizo en extremo, habia acabado por comprender que jamás saciaría su ansia de afectos en las criaturas, y como Lelia, la de *Jorge Sand*, sin estar muy convencido en las católicas verdades, buscaba refugio en el claustro. En el claustro, sí, porque no era el ministerio secular el que le atraía.[17]

[(s)omething grave. That spirit, thirsty for an ideal, disillusion-able, fickle in the extreme, had come to understand that he would never satiate his anxiety in the affect of creatures, and like George Sand's Lélia, without being too convinced by universal truths, sought refuge in the cloisters. In the cloister, indeed, because what attracted him was not the secular realm.]

So, if his introspective and hermetic life is not enough, Felipe becomes further withdrawn from a secular life, and begins privileging a spiritual world. Ironically, he compares himself with Lélia, a woman incapable of physical passion, as an example to follow and thus becomes cloistered. This comparison is quite provocative because it "feminizes" his subjectivity; in his logic, he becomes an object without affect, and this anticipates the conflicts that follow.

Una idea capital flotaba sobre el báratro de contradictorios pensamientos que agitaban su cerebro. Tal idea podía formularse así: "Yo tengo un deseo de ser amado, amado de una manera exclusiva, absoluta, sin solución de continuidad, sin sombra de engaño, y necesito asimismo amar; pero de tal suerte, que jamás la fatiga me debilite, que jamás el hastío me hiele, que jamás el desencanto opaque las bellezas de objeto amado. Es preciso que este sea perennemente joven y perennemente bello y que cuanto más me abisme en la consideración de sus perfecciones, más me parezca que se ensanchan y se ensanchan hasta el infinito."[18]

[A key idea floated over the Hades of the contradictory thoughts that shook his brain. Such an idea could be formulated thus: "I have a desire to be loved, loved in such an exclusive way, absolute, without interruption, without shadow of deceit, and I need to love likewise; but in such a way, that exhaustion never weakens me, that weariness never freezes me, that disenchantment never dims the beauties of the loved object. It is essential that this object be perennially young and perennially beautiful, and the more I am humbled (*abismarse*) by the consideration of its perfections, the more these become bigger and bigger to infinity."]

Initially, it would appear that Felipe wants to love and be loved, that is, occupy both position of loving subject and object of someone else's love. However, by the end there is an insistence on defining and controlling the other (object). This inability to relinquish control over the object basically amounts to his inability to want to occupy both positions as subject and object. Rather he wishes to remain active as subject, detailing to the very end the perfections (literally, the completeness) of the object—Felipe will always privilege such an active subject position. Therefore, it makes sense that he would describe this conflict (of being both subject and object) as Hades, a hell for him. Instead of imagining multiple positions from which subjectivity and identity may unfold (this kind of creative imagining that is in essence so much a part of him), Felipe shuts out those qualities such as exteriority, being loved, or allowing the outside world to be part of him, since they are considered incompatible for a greater desire of complete control over the self.[19] This is also a clear instance of rejecting relationality as constitutive of defining the subject in the world.[20] Indeed, we might remember that the very thing that defines our humanity, what saves us, is allowing the contradiction of multiple positions to coexist. As Frank Browning so eloquently reiterates, citing Oscar Wilde: "What the paradox was to me in the sphere of thought, perversity became to me in the sphere of passion."[21] Browning adds that

> Reason cannot order and reconcile the multiple and competing surfaces of identity. Passion cannot map and contain the myriad forces and fault lines of desire. Only the fleeting mask, not some illusory face of permanent inner nature, captures the real. Wilde's writing remains so powerful—and so dangerous—because he celebrates the mask as reality, artifice as nature, just as modern gay culture does.[22]

Indeed, the contradiction, or the paradox of the perverse are structures too problematic for Felipe to hold on to. He seems to be trapped in that dichotomy between the imaginary and the material, thus he shuns one at the expense of the other. Likewise, he seeks to resolve any religious and libidinal conflict through repression of sexual desire, as if that were the sole measure to allow the religious ideal to prosper. He does not realize that both the sexual and the religious operate as drives as well as ideals—and one easily converts itself into the other. We might remember that, throughout the text, the dichotomy imagination/corporeality is grafted neatly over another one, pleasure/pain. Imagination is seen as liberatory and leads Felipe into his more devastating moments of pleasure, whereas the body (or owning a body—in his mind, becoming or being seen as an object) is always considered a source of constraint and pain. The end of this passage in which Felipe expresses his desires presents a new paradox. He must be able to go into the depths (*abismarse*) of his object of desire; this penetrating gaze returns to humble (*abismar*) him. That is, the penetrating and subjecting gaze of the object *subjects* him in turn. This line reverberates with the myth of Narcissus. The gaze into the other devolves into a *mise en abyme*;[23] however, the other's perfections—really, the self's own projections—become mired in an infinite narrative of self-aggrandizement.

These two previous citations from the novella are significant because they show important practices and choices of self-fashioning. Interestingly, all attempts to reproduce a "stable" and knowable self will fail. Although there might be times when the "I" seems imperious, Felipe leaks out his desire to be an object of desire (he wants to be loved). This desire provokes his need to fix—to affix—the self in an enclosed place to secure a sense of subjective integrity.[24] Furthermore, Felipe must guarantee that integrity by rigorously entering a life of rituals and cultural religious performance that promise a certain sense of what may appear familiar. We see how he commits to this ritualized life at the Seminary:

> Desde el primer día, Felipe dióse a la piedad con empeño tal, que edificaba y acusaba una completa conversión. El era el primero en entrar a las *distribuciones* y él último en abandonar la capilla; y el pedazo de muro que a su sitial correspondía, en ella hubiera podido dar testimonio de su sed de penitencia, mostrando la sangre que salpicaba y que se renovaba a diario, cuando durante la distribución de la noche, apagadas las luces, los acolitos entonaban el *Miserere*.[25]

[From the first day, Felipe gave himself to being pious with such zeal, that he edified and showed a complete conversion. He was the first to receive communion and the last to leave the chapel; and the piece of wall by his assigned seat would have beared witnessed to his thirst for penance, showing the sprinkled blood that was renewed each day during the evening communion, with the lights out, when the acolytes chanted the *Miserere*.]

Quickly however, what is familiar (the assigned pew) becomes uncanny (a bloodied wall). Specks of blood on the wall begotten in the throes of prayer and ecstasy mark a place for Felipe, and out of this blood-sign we can read a shifting object of desire, no longer a weeping or sad woman, but rather God himself. How foundational it is that what moves his passion forward is no longer a bulge under his robe, but rather the intonation of the *Miserere*, the opening of Psalm 50 of the *Vulgate*, "Miserere mei, Deus, secundum magnam misericordiam tuam; et secundum multitudinem miserationum tuarum, dele iniquitatem meam" ["Have mercy on me, God, according to your great mercy and your many kindnesses, erase my iniquity"].[26] The chanting gives a context to Felipe's passion. Felipe enters this phase of his life rejecting women as more than distractions, but as sources of evil. For instance, "[e]squivaba aún la mirada de una mujer, y cada vez que algún ímpetu natural conmovía su organismo, acudía a las mortificaciones más terribles; ya hundiendo en su cintura las aceradas púas del cilicio, ya fustigando sus carnes con gruesas disciplinas, ya llevando la frugalidad hasta el exceso."[27] ["he even dodged a woman's gaze, and every time some natural impetus moved his body, he rushed to the most terrible mortifications, whether it meant sinking into his waist the steely pins of a cilice, or whipping his flesh with thick scourges, or taking frugality to an extreme."] Women or rather the emotions provoked in him by them are immediately replaced with self-violence: "Tal mortificación perpetua hacía que su ánima se recogiera más y más en sí misma y que su sensibilidad se volviese más delicada y asustadiza."[28] ["Such perpetual mortification caused his soul to become more and more collected onto itself, and that his sensibility become more delicate and easily frightened."] Again, we notice an alienation of the interior.

In this context of spiritual desire, Felipe declares that chastity is the virtue that he "most loves." Through it, he sees his more direct link with God: "¡Por fin! ¡Ya era todo de Dios; ya había roto por segunda vez el pacto hecho con Satanás; ya podía, como Magdalena, *escoger la mejor parte*, acurrucándose a los pies del Maestro!"[29] ["Finally, he belonged fully to God! He had broken for a second time the pact made with Satan; now he, like Mary Magdalene, could *choose the best role*, huddled at the Master's feet!"] Breaking with sexuality is seen as a break with the demon. Although he seems to break with the devil, ironically, Felipe compares himself with Mary Magdalene—a figure of woman as the humble anointer of feet, the woman weeping at the cross, the first witness of the Resurrection, and the prostitute. It is important that Felipe wishes to "choose the best role," as the one who lays down by Jesus's feet, forgetting the Magdalene's many other roles, most provocatively as a prostitute. What is essential to discern in this passage is that Felipe's appropriation of Mary Magdalene is quite sensational: he opts to identify with she who performs the lowliest job of cleaning the feet of the "Master." Moreover, as we have seen with Lélia, he chooses a feminine self-representation again. Together these acts give him a masochistic persona.

Felipe masochist

In fact, I cannot think of a more exemplary literary work than Nervo's *El bachiller* to read alongside Freud's 1924 essay "The Economic Problem of Masochism." Writing almost thirty years after Nervo's novella, Freud argues with certainty of a primary masochism that does not necessarily reflect the opposite of sadism, yet it is bound to it. He wants to understand "if mental processes are governed by the pleasure principle in such a way that their first aim is the avoidance of unpleasure and the obtaining of pleasure,"[30] how and why self-injury and self-pain result as actual aims, eventually leading into a subject formation. Hence, this constitutes for Freud an "economic problem." *Masochism is an injury of subjectivity that paradoxically produces and culminates in subject formation*. Furthermore, Freud identifies masochism in three forms—erotogenic, feminine, and moral.[31] It is quite striking to see how these three expressions of masochism are contained in Felipe's persona. His sense of self is always being represented *as feminine*; for example, Felipe assumes the role of the selfless woman through his characterization as Lélia, Mary Magdalene, and so forth; *as erotogenic* when he denies sexual pleasure, and in its place he opts for flagellation and asceticism; and, most importantly, *as moral* when he submits completely to the authority of the other and Other, God. Each act of submission permits him to take on a sense of self that is more and more "pure" or rightful. Most importantly, these different masochistic personas flow one into another; one converts into the other easily and seamlessly—most significantly, he never becomes a sadist. This last point is very important to underscore, because it contrasts sharply to Freud's evaluation of the relationship between sadism and masochism, and their potential to convert one into the other.[32]

Freud writes that "[t]he libido has the task of making the destroying instinct innocuous, and it fulfills the task by diverting that instinct to a great extent outwards [...] towards objects in the external world. The instinct is then called the destructive instinct, the instinct for mastery, or the will to power."[33] Freud seems to suggest that the interplay between the libido and the death instinct plays itself out with the dominance of the libido, which diverts the activity of the death drive outwardly onto external objects. This outward expression of the death drive becomes the "destructive instinct." In other words, in Freud's cosmology of instincts, the libido (or sexuality) fends off the death instinct, whose expulsion (performatively) gives a subject the characteristic of the will to power. Moreover, Freud notes that "[a] portion of the [destructive] instinct is placed directly in service of the sexual function, where it has an important part to play. This is sadism proper."[34] This is an important link that Freud makes between the will to power and sexual function. From the outset, sadism is an effect of the externalized destructive instinct expressed *in* and *through* sexual acts. We can extend the argument: some sexual acts contain the will to power; some expressions of mastery may be conceived as sexual. Indeed, this folding of power and sexuality into one another is one of the basic tenets of psychoanalysis.

Freud continues that "[a]nother portion does not share in this transposition outwards; it remains inside the organism, and with the help of the accompanying sexual excitation described above, becomes libidinally bound there. It is in this portion that we have to recognize the original, erotogenic masochism."[35] That is to say, erotogenic masochism is a part of the destructive instinct that becomes libidinally bound. Thus, *as a sexual instinct*, masochism flows without a source, yet it possesses a logic that can only be discerned by observing its effects. Freud admits that

> We are without any physiological understanding of the ways and means by which this taming [*Bändigung*] of the death-instinct by the libido may be effected. So far as the psycho-analytic field of ideas is concerned we can only assume that a very extensive fusion and amalgamation, in varying proportions, of the two classes of instincts takes place, so that *we never have to deal with pure life instincts or pure death instincts but only with mixtures of them in different amounts.* Corresponding to a fusion of instincts of this kind, there may, as a result of certain influences, be a *defusion* of them.[36] (Emphasis mine.)

It is here that Freud stresses that the instincts of life and death work together and suggests that they are inseparable. Out of this collaborative work, emerge sadism and masochism as contrasting expressions of the same mechanics. One more time, Freud gives priority to the libido as the "tamer" of the death drive—and not the other way around. But what if the death instincts cannot be "tamed"? He does conclude by stating that it is impossible to ascertain "[h]ow large the portions of the death instincts are which refuse to be tamed in this way by being bound to admixtures of libido."[37] What happens when the death instincts are negligibly tamed as might be the case with Felipe? Or, what if the destructive instinct cannot be externalized (and become sadism)—and thus remains bound to libidinal pulsions? As I mentioned above, Felipe's masochism never crosses over to sadism, but rather converts itself into different masochistic forms. It is easy to see how his repression of desire flows to take on different representations—sometimes as feminine, other times as moral, finally as erotogenic masochism.

If we return to that scene when "[Felipe] was the first to receive communion and the last to leave the chapel; and the piece of wall by his assigned seat would have borne witness to his thirst for penance, showing the sprinkled blood that was renewed each day during the evening communion, with the lights out, when the acolytes chanted the *Miserere*." This scene also reminds us of Kaja Silverman's analysis of Theodor Reik's distinction of what might be called Christian masochism:

38 *The Avowal of Difference*

She notes that in this particular instance, masochism contains three general elements: first, the masochist requires an external audience encounter; second, "the body is centrally on display; and, third, behind this masochistic scene, we might find a "master tableau or group fantasy—Christ nailed to the cross, head wreathed in thorns and blood dripping from his impaled sides. What is being beaten here is not so much the body as the 'flesh,' and beyond that sin itself, and the whole fallen world."[38] Indeed we may argue that Felipe's masochistic scenario neatly fulfills these three elements: he situates himself as an example to others (the other brothers and choristers are his witnesses); then, his body is rendered in its fleshly physicality, the blood marks in his assigned seat are his signature; and finally, what began as a punishment for desiring a woman becomes a performance of a greater repentance.

Ecstasy

Felipe's delirium rises to a feverish pitch one night of prayer: "haciéndose desfilar por su mente las dolorosas escenas inmortalizadas por el Evangelio."[39] ["recreating in his mind a parade of painful scenes made immortal by the Gospel."] His creative mind, often digresses from these images; however, he always returned to his "rightful path."

> Entonces occurió una cosa excepcional. Ante él se levantó, perfectamente determinada, una figura; pero no la del Maestro; no era la radiante epifanía del Cristo con su amplia túnica púrpura, con su corona de espinas, su rostro nobilísimo ensangrentado y sus manos heridas por los clavos; era una mujer, una mujer muy hermosa, rubia, de aventajada estatura, de rostro virginal y delicadas y encantadoras formas de núbil, que tendían sus curvas castas bajo el peplo vaporoso y diáfano.[40]

> [Then an exceptional thing happened. A perfectly resolute figure rose before him, but it wasn't the Master's. It wasn't the radiant epiphany of the Christ with a full purple tunic, with his crown of thorns, with his most noble face bloodied, and his hands wounded by the nails; it was a woman, a very beautiful woman, blond, taller, with a virginal face, and delicate and charming nubile forms, that spread its chaste curves under the airy and sheer peplum.]

The woman who Felipe conjures up in his mind turns out to be Asunción, the daughter of the foreman at his uncle's estate. We notice that she is characterized as "virginal," "nubile," and "chaste"—triply pure. And, although such a figuration of chastity is what he most prizes, in this scene, such chastity gets inverted and becomes the very thing that awakens his desire. Felipe sees chastity both as something that he wants *in* himself as well as something he wants for himself to possess; chasteness is both an identity as well as a supplement that inaugurates desire for the other.

The woman he desires is Asunción—her name meaning assumption. Not surprisingly, the assumption or spiritual elevation Felipe is looking for is embodied in the name of his object of desire; in other words, his objective—being spiritual—becomes linked with or reified as an object that effects other consequences: "¿Por qué surgía frente a él? Debía, es claro, cerrar los ojos ante la aparición maligna, sin duda, pero ¿cómo, si eran los del alma los que la veían?"[41] ["Why did it emerge in front of him? He surely had to close his eyes before such a malignant apparition, without a doubt, but how, if it were the eyes of his soul that were seeing it?"] The "it," the image that rises before him is this ghostly apparition that he refuses to acknowledge; the "it" is an idealized woman, virginal and blond. Also, the "it" is another erection, so to speak (I repeat, "Why did it emerge in front of him?"). Again, the spiritual elevation he is seeking can only be named with the signifier of a physical erection. So even in his most spiritual of moments, the penis pops up and interrupts that sense of community with the divine. In other words, the process of subjectivity (as that interior dialogue that seeks to transcend the material world) fails. This failure signifies that the arrested development of any interior dialogues—subjectivity or fantasy—is produced by a recalcitrant and ever-present body. The body is that thing which cannot be repressed. Jacques Lacan also reminds us that "the phallus is the conscientious objection made by one of the two sexed beings to the service to be rendered to the other."[42] The phallic erection is a signifier that disrupts and blocks becoming one with the other.

The question—¿Por qué surgía frente a él?—also and perversely asks why did it *flow out* (*surgir*) before him? In other words, does Felipe cum? "Y su terror, desvaneciéndose lentamente, daba lugar a una sensación tibia y suave que llevaba el calor a los miembros rígidos y aceleraba los latidos del corazón."[43] ["And his horror, slowly disappearing, gave way to a warm and smooth sensation that brought heat to his rigid members and sped up the beating of his heart."] Felipe's hysterical reaction to this warm feeling is to cry out, "¡Madre mía, socórreme! ¡No quiero ser malo!"[44] ["Mother, help me! I don't want to be bad!"] One cannot help but notice the cry for the absent mother. Indeed, what is fascinating about Felipe is that his Oedipal narrative is always fractured—for example, his mother is dead, he falls in love with older women, also, the only Woman he wants is highly idealized; there is never notice of a father, we only know of his "bachelor" uncle who raises him. Felipe's real place in the Oedipal triangle is reflected against the real absences of a father and mother; their absences highlight the fantastic nature of the family romance. It is tempting to say that the self is narcissistically or solipsistically rendered and articulated. Later sobbing, he adds, "—¡Te juro que por tu divino Hijo, que está presente, conservarme limpio o morir! ¡Morir!, repitió el eco de las amplias bóvedas, y en la cripta abierta a los pies del altar, las vibraciones sonoras dijeron también: ¡Morir!"[45] ["I swear in the name of your divine Son, who is present, keep me pure or let me die! *Die!* echoed the wide vaults, and in the open crypt by the steps of the altar, the resounding vibrations also said, *Die!*"] In other words, his (physical) *petite morte* prefigures and culminates in an echoing death sentence. The voice of God gets represented as an echo of the self. In this scene we evidence the *nom-du-père*. The name of the (absent) father emerges as the voice of God, that is, as the non-*du-père*, the chastising and condemning voice of the Father's prohibition. I am reminded here of that scene when Echo meets Narcissus and she tries to reach out and touch him:

> "Let's meet" [echoes Echo]; then, seconding her words, she rushed
> out of the woods, that she might fling her arms
> around the neck she longed to clasp. But he
> retreats and, fleeing, shouts: "Do not touch me!
> Don't cling to me! I'd sooner die than say
> 'I'm yours'"; and Echo answered him. "I'm yours."[46]

Like in the story of Narcissus and Echo, a narcissist, Felipe gets caught up in the aural allure of the self as other. What is important to capture here is that the voice always returns *as* difference: Felipe's option to be kept pure or to die returns to him as a singular and devastating command that announces his own death. Felipe appealed to the mother

("¡*Madre mía, socórreme!*"), but in the end it is the Father who speaks. But it is a very special kind of Father who speaks back—it is the Father as Felipe projects him; ironically, it is Felipe's own voice that returns to punish him. It is as if the Father can never truly be other, but rather the Father is always a return and conversion of the self.

I would like to take up here the concept of the "conversion of the object." What happens when the desire for an object (the ideal woman) becomes replaced by (or converted into) a desire for an abstraction (God)? It is evident that the object of Felipe's desire is God; his desire pushes him to such ascetic extremes to mark, to make material, his grasp and comprehension of God; the bodily mutilation suffered during prayer is Felipe's way of making God present, in other words, of making God into an object. What happens in this "exceptional" moment of prayer is a foundational moment. If we consider that prayer is a form of desiring speech through and out of which "miracles happen," we could easily argue that prayer is a type of speech act. It is at this moment of prayer and delirium that "a perfectly resolute figure rose before [Felipe]." However, as we quickly learn, the figure is not the Christ that he so longs to see, but rather a woman. Thus, Felipe's prayer somehow misfires. His conscious desire for God is overwhelmed by an unconscious desire for Asunción.[47] Although it is essential to recognize here that both desires are not so different: if God represents a particular abstraction, so does Asunción as a particular representation of an idealized woman, a "beautiful woman, blond, taller, with a virginal face, and delicate and charming nubile forms," and so on.[48] What I want to show here is that Felipe stops desiring an object, rather he opts for an abstraction—this is what I mean by the object-conversion. An object necessarily implies a certain materiality; the inverse of such materiality generally refers to an abstraction, which when taken to its logical end means the desire for the sublime—whether represented as the divine, Truth, or beauty itself. Desiring an abstraction is really the abstraction of desire. So, in this scheme, it is possible to see that the conversion of the object—as the very institution of desire—leads to a state of indeterminacy, an aporia, to mark the material and the object. Desiring one abstraction is as slippery as desiring another: Felipe's *desire* for God is as understandable as his desire for Asunción, because, for the narcissist, in the end what matters is his desire itself. If I may push this further, the fact of the "conversion of the object" produces an indeterminacy and replaceability of masochisms—from erotogenic to moral to feminine, and back and forth. This conversion of objects also makes it possible for us to read this text's queerness. Queerness refers to those circuits of desire that disobey any imposed normativity; appreciating how these circuits function contributes to how new subjectivities are cast into stabilized identities.

*　*　*

If I have been holding back to talk about the queerness of *El bachiller*, this has to do more with trying to appreciate the textual importance of the novella's debt to literary *modernismo*, which I argue, in the broadest theoretical terms, offers us a discursive entrance to Latino American queer narratives.

Again, *el reino interior* is about a particular obsession with interiority—as a literary sleight of hand, this trope literally turns surfaces and exteriors as means to peek into the inside of the subject. It is about representation that through a greedy centripetal force draws subjectivity. It overlaps in many ways with masochism's *turning inwardly* of the death drive. We remember that another tenet of *modernismo* is its outward gaze, giving Latin America a certain degree of cultural import. I would like to juxtapose the inward turns of the *reino interior* and masochism, and the outward expression of *modernismo* and sadism—what we have is a fascinating dialectic between the interior space of what is Latin American proper and an uneasy cosmopolitanism, which gets read as a will to power.

If, as Jrade argues, *modernismo*'s "mission is to create a spontaneous, natural, fluid, intuitive language that is truer, more authentic, more representative of the native spirit" (33), then that fluid language must work on two separate levels—one to engage with a painful (almost masochistic) meditation into the self, all the while projecting itself outwardly in a will to cultural power. Forgetting that outward gaze is a danger that leads to Felipe's tragic undoing.

Masochism Unbound

Due to his increasing and exaggerated masochistic practices around religious fervor, Felipe's health debilitates—first anemia, then rheumatism of his right leg—so he finally agrees to leave the Seminary and go stay at his uncle's *hacienda* for some sun and fresh air. There he is cared for by none other than Asunción. This of course represents a spiritual and moral crisis for Felipe: it so happens that his ideal woman becomes quite real and, significantly, he discovers that she has an agency of her own. In Felipe's mind the young woman had "exacto el parecido [. . .] con su fantasma."[49] ["exactly the same look [. . .] as the phantasm"]. Asunción's own father draws for Felipe a new image of the woman: The older man notes "—Pero ¿no la ve usted que crecida? Ya no es la marimacho que usted conoció; no, no. ¡Si viera qué hacendosilla se me ha vuelto! Ella barre, ella cose, ella aplancha, y aún le sobra tiempo para cuidar de los canarios and zenzontles, a cuál más cantador."[50] ["But, can't you see how much she has grown? She's no longer the tomboy (*marimacho*) that you knew; no sir! If you just saw what a little hard worker she's become! She sweeps, she sews, she irons, and she even has time to care of the canaries and *zenzontles*, which sing the most."]

Thus, at this moment we witness that the abstraction of desire takes on a particular concreteness. Abstracted desire, repressed by the narrative operations of the Imaginary meets the Lacanian Real; in other words, the fantasy of Asunción becomes quite a Real Asunción, which overwhelms all previous apparitions that Felipe had conjured up of the young girl. Standing face to face with Asunción represents for Felipe an encounter with the Real. I would like to suggest that Felipe now has to define himself *relationally* with the other; whereas before, he had only done so with(in) himself. This encounter with the Real produces an exit from the Imaginary order, and culminates in a horrible evacuation and disappearance of the subject. I have been arguing all along that Felipe's sense of identity has been framed as a very individualistic practice, unable to relate to others. This raises some very important questions about subject formation: What are the implications of subject formation within the realm of the *reino interior*? Is such an individual and narcissistic effort possible? While it has become the prevailing practice to conceive of subject formation as a relational one, what is the significance of Felipe's more narcissistic subject-formation devoid of the presence of the other? To be sure, narcissism has been understood as one approach to theorize the homosexual; however, it might be interesting to revisit this approach. What must have been the delicate condition Felipe found himself in that the presence of Asunción (as the reification of the ghostly apparition) would break him down.

Complaining and whining about his condition, Felipe is bed-ridden. The precocious Asunción comes in and flirts with him. "Ella se le acercaba más y más, y hubieran podido oírse los latidos de ambos corazones agitados."[51] ["She got closer and closer to him, and one could have heard the beating of both agitated hearts"]. Such flirtiness makes him increasingly uneasy—and he asks her to stop and leave. In a whisper, she finally breaks down and confesses "—No te ordenes, no te ordenes ... ¡Te quiero!"[52] ["Don't become a priest, don't become a priest ... I love you!"]. The young girl not only confesses her love for him, but more importantly asks him not to become a priest. *Ordernar(se)*, to become ordained, also can be read literally, "to put oneself in order." Might she be asking him not to submit himself to such a strict set of rules, of imposing on himself a series of "orders" and rules—religious and otherwise—that would exclude him from being with her. Of course this "ordering" of the self represents a disciplinary bond that reminds us of Felipe's masochism. We could even go as far as to say that Asunción wants him "messy," for such messiness is precisely the realm of the human. What does he do?

> Felipe había tenido un momento para reflexionar. Se veía al borde del abismo, y todos sus tremendos temores místicos se levantaban, ahogando los contrarios pensamientos.[53]

> [Felipe had but a moment to react. He saw himself at the border of the abyss, and all his tremendously mystic fears were raised, drowning the opposite (or contrary) thoughts.]

The girl's confession of love leads Felipe to the edge of a great fall. His sensible thoughts (here depicted as "contrary") are drowned out by "mystic fears." In other words, the sense of right and wrong becomes thwarted by Asunción's love confession. The other's love becomes a threat that shatters his narcissism. Later on,

> Felipe se sentía perdido; paseó la vista extraviada en rededor y quiso gritar: "¡Socorro!"
> Había caído en sus rodillas, con sus ropas, el cuaderno que leía, y la palabra *Orígenes*, título del capítulo consabido, se ofreció a una punta de su mirada.
> Una idea tremenda surgió entonces en su mente ...
> Era la única tabla salvadora ...

Asunción estrechaba más el amoroso lazo, y dejaba su alma en sus besos.

El bachiller afirmó, con el puño crispado, la plegadera, y la agitó durante algunos momentos, exhalando un gemido...[54]

[Felipe found himself lost; he looked around disoriented, and wanted to scream: Help!

The book that he was reading fell along with his clothes to his knees, and the word *Origènes*—title of that well-known chapter—was offered as a target to his gaze.

A tremendous idea then emerged in his mind...

It was the only saving scenario...

Asunción brought her loving embrace closer, and left her soul in her kisses. The student grabbed with a clenched fist the paper cutter, and shook it for a few moments, letting out a moan...]

This final scene is the representation of Felipe outside the confines of his imaginary and fantasy world. He feels lost, disoriented; his gaze is lost and he cannot speak ("he ... wanted to scream"). It is at that mute moment of both loss and perdition that he returns to his center, to his "origin" so to speak. The hagiography of Origènes becomes a focal point. Already earlier he had encountered the story of Origènes as if by accident:

Desfloradas todas las hojas del cuaderno, abriólo al azar y se encontró con el principio de un capítulo denominado *Orígenes*, el cual refería la historia de aquel padre de la Iglesia que se hizo célebre por haber sacrificado su virilidad en aras de su pureza, profesando la peregrina teoría de que la castidad, sin este sacrifico, era imposible.[55]

[The pages of his book were deflowered, and he opened it randomly to find the beginning of a chapter entitled *Origènes*, which referred to the story of that Father of the Church who became famous for having sacrificed his virility for the sake of purity, professing the strange theory that chastity was impossible without this sacrifice.]

Felipe had been cutting the pages of his book on church history. The simple act of cutting the pages apart becomes a sexual act, whereby he "deflowers" the book. And accidentally, he comes across the story of Origènes, who was the martyr who castrated himself to remain pure, and not desire his female students. Origènes's story can be understood as a misreading of Matthew 18:8, the Biblical text that also serves as an epigraph to the novella: "Por tanto, si tu mano o tu pie te fuere ocasión, córtalos y échalos de ti; mejor es entrar cojo o manco en la vida que, teniendo dos manos y dos pies, ser echado en el fuego eterno." ["And if your hand or your foot causes you to sin, cut it off and throw it away; it is better for you to enter life maimed or lame than with two hands or two feet to be thrown into the eternal fire."] The Biblical passage warns against temptation—but not necessarily or specifically of sexual temptation. At the end of the novella, Felipe also "deflowers" himself using the paper cutter—again, it is important to underline the "feminized" position in which he casts himself. Importantly, castration is written as a deflowering, a cutting up of an original virginity.

The text comes full circle—beginning with the Biblical warning, and ending with its enactment. The act of castration itself is written quite sexually: "agitó [la plegadera] durante algunos momentos, exhalando un gemido..."[56] ["he shook it (the paper cutter) for a few moments, letting out a moan..."] The act of castration gets signified as masturbation and ejaculation, blood flowing "torrentially." The castration perversely satisfies Felipe's sexual desire as well as it restores his purity. The culminating moaning celebrates a final triumph. Asunción steps back and notices how Felipe's "rostro, que contraído por el dolor, mostraba, sin embargo, una sonrisa de triunfo."[57] ["face, contracted by the pain, showed however a triumphant smile."] Felipe's castration, his self-penetration, leads him to moan; it is a moaning that signifies pain and triumphant pleasure.

Felipe's passion—both as suffering and pleasure—arrives at a moment of jouissance. Lacan argues that

> Nothing is more compact than a fault, assuming that the intersection of everything is enclosed therein is accepted as existing over an infinite number of sets, the result being that the intersection implies this infinite number. That is the very definition of compactness.
>
> The intersection I am taking about is the same one [...] as being that which covers or poses an obstacle to the supposed sexual relationship.[58]

In a turn of interpretation, Lacan reads the "fault"—*faille* meaning shift, lack, break or flaw, and why not as the mark of castration—as a compactness itself. The fault is a graphetic reminder (like Oedipus's scars from eye gouging) that unites different narrative strands. Seen in this manner, Felipe's castration is not so much an opening, but a compactness, one that might be his last-ditch effort to bring together into one those disparate identities—the fantastic, the bodily, the sexual, the secular and the human—that have been at constant battle with one another. With the stroke of the knife, Felipe creates a gash that unites the infinite significations of the self. Felipe's castration can be read, on the one hand, as a punishment for his physical desires, and on the other, as a "deflowering," in effect, a *queer realization* of his sexual desire.

Again, the shake of the knife leads to a moan... If indeed the word *meaning* is closely related to *moaning*:[59] textual meaning is always a moan that excites and seduces us. Felipe's final orgasm is the literal moaning/meaning of his disruption of the interior/exterior dyad he so persistently tried to maintain.

Queer realization

It is this punishing attitude—this masochistic tendency to stick with the critical vocabulary so far—that leads to a "queer realization" with which I would like to conclude this chapter. I would like to propose that silence, a particular representation of castration, is required for the realization of some queer subjects to emerge. We can also return to an early description of Felipe's temperament: "his pains were intense as were intense his pleasures; yet some and others remained silent." The circularity of the text[60] forces us to notice again to reread those silences. Furthermore, I hope to argue throughout this book that silence is a condition for queer Latino American narratives to flourish.

If we take a panoramic view of *El bachiller*, I would like to reread Felipe's castration as a self-penetration. Felipe's story oozes of queer sexuality—the melancholic boy, the Oedipal desires for older women, his asceticism and masochistic practices, his cloistering, his relationship with God, and so forth. All these figurations of his *reino interior*, articulated by a queer meandering of the imagination, would seem to asphyxiate the subject, but I want to read his self-penetration with all its completely paradoxical power. On the one hand, this penetration kills the subject, leading him to an ecstatic death—this penetration allows for a literal entrance into the *reino interior*, a perverse means to access the subject's innermost sense of self; on the other hand, this penetration must be read bluntly as just that, the best fuck of Felipe's life. This queer moment of pleasure becomes that cruelest manifestation of the Freudian *fort-da*, a paradoxical knot that requires analysis, αηα-λγσις literally ana-lysis, to loosen up. To that end, if analyzing a paradox (like getting that curious feeling a woman has before a sealed envelope) propels the critic's imperative to decipher and uncover other knowledges, then the silence around perversion (and the perversion of silence) becomes the site and sight where we might uncover—even, or especially, in its failure—sexuality's most miraculous and queer insights.

2

Queer Losses in Barbachano Ponce's *El diario de José Toledo*

> Mild und leise
> wie er lächelt,
> wie das Auge
> hold er öffnet—
> Seht ihr's, Freunde?
> Seht ihr's nicht?
> —Isolde's "Liebestod"

Self/Other/Absence

I begin with a brief analysis of the centrality of *relationality* in the articulation of the subject. Consider that the self cannot exist without the presence of the other—the self needs that other to differentiate itself, to make sense of itself. If we recall Amado Nervo's *El bachiller*, Felipe's sense of identity is bound up with his desire to be "good" and "pure," either by rejecting the body, assuming the role of the divine, refusing his desire of women or idealizing Woman, among a host of other practices of identification or disidentification. Therefore, we might explore the ways in which relationality opens up a host of complicated questions: How does the self relate *to* the other, *against* the other, *through* the other, *alongside* the other? Or does how the self abandon the other, and so on? In other words, the work of subject formation is not simply a choice of one of either extremes—self in opposition or mirroring the other—rather, it is a process of structuration that deconstructs the either/or positions where the self might find or situate her- or himself. The degree to which and the mechanisms by which the self attaches him- or herself to or ignores the other is always changing—and transforms the design of self-representation.

One issue that we may appreciate in *El bachiller* has to do whether in fact there is a love object there for Felipe to differentiate himself. Felipe obsesses with the spiritual, the physical, the affective to the point that he wants to define himself without having to consider the specificity (materiality) of that other/object. We may review Felipe's subject formation as an exercise in self-absorption or reverie, in Spanish, *ensimismamiento* (literally, into-himself-ness). This hermeticism doubles the series of practices to which he submits his body and mind to achieve that "pure" self that he so much wants to have or be. In other words, we may guess that, for Felipe, the self is sought as a relational meditation *without* the presence of the other (any allusion to masturbation is inevitable). While we envisage Felipe's self-figuration as one that abstains itself from a relational object, an object whether real or phantasmatic is always persistent. I would like to turn to a different kind of relationality, one in which the other itself refuses the status of object and will not allow to be recognized as point of comparison, differentiation or departure.

* * *

In "Instincts and Their Vicissitudes," Freud comments on loving and its antitheses: Loving admits not merely of one, but of three opposites. In addition to the antithesis "loving-hating," there is the other one of "loving-being loved"; and, in addition to these, loving and hating taken together are the opposite of the condition of unconcern or indifference.[1] For Freud, loving refers to a manifold of instincts, the totality of expression of sexual feeling. Loving is precisely a form of attachment that effects how object relations and identifications happen and culminates in identity formation. His three opposites of loving—hating, being loved, and indifference—are importantly linked to conceptualizations of subject and object positions. Loving and hating are emotions that Freud links to activity; love is just the negative of hate. Both "loving" and "hating" point to the existence of a subject, who can exercise a level of agency and consciousness. When the "I" loves or hates, she is positioning herself actively. "Being loved" requires a certain displacement, which presses the "I" to imagine him- or herself as object. This object-formation depends on the subject's vulnerability to become other—or as the other would have him be. Indeed, a great deal of work has been done to explain how subject and object positions relate to identity. Here, however, Freud introduces a third position: self-figuration through indifference or unconcern. If the self can be narrated through subject and object positions and relations, how does self-figuration happen through unconcern and indifference, that is, outside the realm of relationality? This is a question that I began exploring in the previous chapter. Moreover, remaining in the constellation of sexuality, how do sexual subjects—and what kind of sexual subjects—result from or through such indifference?

How does identity emerge out of absence? Is it possible? Through a close reading of Miguel Barbachano Ponce's *El diario de José Toledo* (1964),[2] I hope to investigate the ways in which queer identity and sexuality get articulated through the desire for an absent subject.

Often considered and dismissed as a homophobic work of early gay writing, *El diario de José Toledo* ends with the protagonist's suicide after longing for (and not receiving) acknowledgment from his lover Wenceslao. Barbachano's text documents how José rewrites his obsession in his diary; it is an exteriorization of an internal dialogue. This novel also shows us how the self gets defined relationally to the other, one who is literally "not there." In so doing, it allows us to understand the inner workings of desire, and how these circuits of desire function and contribute to how new queer subjectivities are written and rewritten.

The diary

The structure and framing of the Barbachano Ponce's text is quite interesting—the diary runs with daily entries for about four weeks. Each diary entry is followed by a narrative that completes or complements the story. This omniscient narrative is sometimes in the third person; interestingly, when speaking about José the narrative changes to the second person. The contrast between José's voice and the omniscient narrative is quite stark: whereas José gives us a rather self-involved account of the story, the other narrative tells us what was happening in reality, or what another character may have been thinking distinct from what José has written in the diary, or offers other background information. For instance, the first diary entry ends with Wenceslao leaving José's home, "No sabes cómo pasé la noche," writes José, "pensando dónde estabas y con quién..."[3] ["You don't know how I spent the night, thinking where you might be and with whom..."]. The accompanying narrative part to that entry tells us that Wenceslao grabs a cab and goes to a bar in Garibaldi, where he passes out drunk. This back-and-forth format continues to nearly the end of the text, except for the last six entries of the diary, which do not get commented on.

The central part of the text is framed by an anonymous narrator who announces that "*Un día de agosto, meses antes de que te suicidaras, comenzaste a escribir un diario*"[4] (original italics). ["*One day in August, months before you committed suicide, you began to keep a diary.*"] That same anonymous or disembodied voice ends the novel stating that "El veintiseis de octubre de mil novecientos cincuenta y ocho extraviaste el diario en un camión de segunda clase."[5] ["On October 26, 1958, you lost the diary in a second-class bus"]. The entries appear without a date; we are only given the day of the weeks (Sunday, Monday, Tuesday, and so forth) for each entry. However, if we pinpoint specific historical events related in the novel, we can determine that José begins writing on Tuesday, August 19, 1958. He writes every day for four weeks, except on September 13 and 14, and concludes the diary on Tuesday, September 16.

Furthermore, a second frame structures the novel, it is a news report that serves as a kind of epigraph: In oversized and bold font, the undated headline reads "Quitóse la vida el señor José Toledo" ["Mr. José Toledo took his own life."] The brief news item ends, "Sus padres dijeron que desconocen las causas por las cuales su hijo se arrojó al vacío."[6] ["His parents said that they were unaware of the reasons for which he jumped into the void."] Both framed narratives—what I call the anonymous voice and the news report—attribute a certain meaning to the main text composed by the actual diary and the interlaced omniscient narrative. The central text responds to the news report for it explains *why* José "se arrojó al vacío"—which can be read as both "jumped into the void or abyss" as well as "led a life of perdition." In a different fashion, the central text gets organized by the anonymous notes that announce the beginning of the act of writing and the loss of the diary. I would like to argue that the anonymous notes refunction the diary *as* a body; indeed in classical style, the written text becomes the body of the absent lover.

El diario de José Toledo opens up exactly by recording the last time that José will see his beloved Wenceslao for a long while—in other words, he begins writing the diary on the day he breaks up his lover. In the very first paragraph, José relates a series of lovers' quarrels, really spats of jealousy that become the relationship's downfall:

> me hiciste enojar con tus preguntas diarias: que si no había ido a buscarme el cuate del coche verde, que si no me había encontrado a alguien en el camión; acuérdate que tú también ves muchas cosas en la calle y nunca te lo reprocho, además, sabes que soy tuyo en cuerpo y alma, y lo seré toda mi vida, aunque no lo creas.[7]

> [you angered me with your daily questions: whether that guy in the green car had come to look for me? or, if I had met someone on the bus? Remember that you too see many things on the street, and I never reproach you. Besides, you know that I am yours in body and soul—and that I will be yours my entire life, even though you don't believe it.]

Later on, the jealousy continues, "A veces pienso que tú provocas los pleitos porque ya tienes alguna otra movida por ahí y no quieres decírmelo, ¿qué relajo te traes, Wenceslao?"[8] ["Sometimes I think that you provoke these fights because you already have something else going on there, and you don't want to tell me. What easy ride have you got yourself into?"] That same day, the young men go to the movies, and while returning home, "[en el] camión te miraron en tal forma que sentí unos celos horibles; durante el trayecto discutimos violentamente porque sabía que tú también lo habías volteado a ver . . ."[9] [(on the) bus they looked at you in such a way that I felt horribly jealous; during the trip we argued violently because I knew that you too had turned back to see him . . .]. Part of this argument is overheard by José's father:

> Mi papá oyó los gritos y bajó a ver qué pasaba, con lo que se enredaron más las cosas. No supe más, los oía discutir a lo lejos; cuando subiste al

54 *The Avowal of Difference*

taxi sentí la necesidad de irme contigo, pero mi papá me obligó a entrar a la casa y no tuve más remedio que obedecerlo, después me injurió, me dijo que si te vestía, que si te mantenía.[10]

[My father heard the screaming, and came down to see what was happening. This only made matters worse. I don't know what else happened. I heard you two argue at a distance. When you got in the cab I felt the need to leave with you, but my father forced me to go in the house, and I had no other choice than to obey him. Afterwards, he insulted me, asking me if I dressed you or if I kept you.]

We can read the father's intervention as a kind of setting down of the law—what Lacan calls the entrance into the Symbolic order; the father restores the normative order, and subjects José to the place of the domestic ("me obligó a entrar a la casa"). Wenceslao will not see José again until almost three weeks later—thus from that moment on, in Wenceslao's place, the diary becomes the repository for José's longing and desire for the absent lover. The diary comes to represent the lost body of Wenceslao—and in the end, that diary-body is lost "en un camión de segunda clase," which is exactly where the fighting began and José lost Wenceslao the first time around.

If the last entry is estimated to be on Tuesday, September 16, and the diary was lost on October 26, there is a gap of over a month where we do not know what happens to José. Again, the news report of the suicide is undated: we can only guess that José committed suicide weeks after the loss of the diary.

Lost sight

After the breakup, Wenceslao leaves Mexico City the next day, and José only hears news of his whereabouts—first Guadalajara, then Morelia—through Wenceslao's parents. Wenceslao's loss embodies a series of other losses for José: the loss of the beloved object, of a sense of stability and health, of family harmony, and even the loss of self. The language of loss is evoked throughout the novel; moreover, this loss is accompanied by the classic melodramatic trope, "sin ti estoy tan solo"[11] ["without you, I am so lonely"] stated over and over by José. He also has a difficulty in expressing the meaning of this loss: "te buscaba por todos lados, de repente creía verte y era otra persona, me preguntaba: ¿se acordará de mi? Su silencio me hace creer lo contrario: ¿Estará ilusionado con otro?"[12] ["I looked for you everywhere, all of a sudden I thought seeing you but it was someone else. I wondered: Does he remember me? His silence makes me believe the contrary: Is he smitten with another?"] On one occasion when José tries to write a letter, he observes, "Tardé tanto [en redactar la carta] porque es difícil expresar los sentimientos que guardo en mi corazón."[13] ["It took me so long to write the letter because it is difficult to express the feeling I keep in my heart."] Wenceslao's departure represents a crisis of identity and expression. Moreover, the trauma is so great that José has also lost the language to narrate his feelings.[14] We see the question of loss in the very tedium and repetition of certain daily activities. I quote a series of events that become commonplace throughout the diary:

Hoy me levanté con el rostro descompuesto . . .[15]
[Today I got up with my face broken down . . .]

Llegué a la Secretaría a la hora de siempre.[16]
[I got to the office at the usual time.]

Me levanté muy temprano porque tuve la corazonada de que el destino, ya ves como es, me tenía reservada una sorpresa.[17]
[I got up very early because I had a feeling that Fate—you know how it is—had a surprise in store for me."]

A las siete de la mañana fue mi papá a jalarme los pies, pues todavía estaba durmiendo.[18]
[At 7 a.m., my father went to tug my toes because I was still sleeping.]

Llegué a la Secretaría a las ocho en punto y estuve charlando con los compañeros hasta que de pronto tuve ganas de ir al baño.[19]
[I arrived at the office at 8 o'clock on the dot and spent time chatting with my colleagues until I had to go to the bathroom.]

The formulaic repetition of the quotidian plagues the entire novel: José wakes up sad, gets to work, refuses to go out with this colleagues, he leaves work, sighs hoping to run into Wenceslao on the street (even though he is out of town), sighs listening to Libertad Lamarque records, and of course he cries a lot. Very little action gets recorded in the diaries—each entry follows another one to form an extended yearning and longing for the lost love-object, all the way to the very last scene when José says his final good-bye and, as has been already anticipated, he jumps to his death in a queer Isoldean moment.

I would couple José *inability to write* about the loss, along with *the constant and mechanical repetition* of commonplace throughout the texts (such as the ones I note above) to signal his empty, melancholic subjectivity. Freud notes that, in melancholia, "the patient is aware of the loss which has given rise to his melancholia, but only in the sense that he knows *whom* he has lost but not *what* he has lost in him." He adds, "This would suggest that melancholia is in some way related to an object-loss, which is withdrawn from consciousness, in contradistinction to mourning, in which there is nothing about the loss that is unconscious."[20] Following Freud, we can transpose a general subject for specific one: José knows whom he has lost, but he cannot read or understand what he has lost in himself. All there is left is a sense of emptiness and incompleteness. I would like to propose a queer reading of Freud's insight, that the melancholic is unaware to appreciate "what he has lost *in him*"—not only in himself, *but also "in him" meaning the other*. In other words, José is unable to understand what he has really lost in him, in Wenceslao.

There is blindness that does not let José see the real Wenceslao. Consider the following three moments. First, José bemoaning the fact that Wenceslao is in Guadalajara: "Creéme, Wenceslao, si tuviese manera de ir a Guadalajara, ya estaría contigo, pero verdaderamente me es imposible hacerlo, *no tengo las amistades que tú tienes* y que son capaces de proporcionarte toda clase de facilidades para tus viajes. Me gustaría tener tu suerte..."[21] (emphasis mine) ["Believe me, Wenceslao, if I had a means to get to Guadalajara, I would already be with you, but honestly it is impossible for me to do that. *I don't have the friendships that you have* and who are able to offer you all kind of facilities for your trips. I would like to have your luck..."]. A second scene comes from the thoughts of Wenceslao's own father at the moment that he is chatting at with José: "en su mente cruzaba con rapidez una y mil veces el mismo pensamiento: '[Wenceslao] Se larga de nuestro lado porque necesita dinero, y el imbécil de José no es capaz de proporcionárselo.'"[22] ["the same thought crosses his mind quickly a thousand and one times: 'He [Wenceslao] leaves us because he needs money and that imbecile of José isn't able to provide it for him'"]. And a final third moment involves Alberto, the young man at the end of the novel, who tries to pick up José. When Alberto learns from José that "his love" Wenceslao is on a trip, he replies: "Mire, joven, si de verdad comprende a los homosexuales debe darse cuenta de que todos somos iguales, Usted, yo o cualquiera, al salir de excursión, haría lo mismo que está haciendo su amigo: buscar aventuras."[23] ["Listen, young man, if you truly understand homosexuals, you should be aware that we are all the same, you, me or any other, when I go on a trip, I would do the same thing your friend is doing, that is seeking adventures."] In each of these scenes there is a direct or indirect suggestion that Wenceslao is at the very least a kept man, indeed a hustler, that he relies on *aliena misericordia*—the kindness of strangers—to survive. We remember that at the beginning of the novel, José's own father accuses him of having Wenceslao as a kept man—and it is this argument between father and lover that provokes Wenceslao to go away.

So, José is unwilling to see the complete picture—he does not want to recognize that his lover is not as ideal as he imagines him. In José's mind, Wenceslao must remain perfect because that very idealized perfection reflects back onto him. "What he has lost in him," this Freudian trope of melancholia points in at least two, possibly three, directions. First, José loses something in his own sense of self in the relational process through which he sees himself attached to an idealized Wenceslao: the perfect love object is supposed to mirror him. Second, the idealized love object becomes tarnished—or abjected, at the extreme—and this relationally marks a stain on the self. José's very insistence in a perfect object is his way of retaining a sense of integrity related to his very own homosexuality: keeping the image of a "clean" Wenceslao also keeps the idea of homosexuality as something "clean," and not "*diferente*" or "*anormal*," which is what José's own mother calls her son. "What he has *lost* in him" also point to an economic dimension of the relationship: José has been lending money to Wenceslao all along, and he has been expecting it back, even though Wenceslao never says much about paying it back. We can imagine that were Wenceslao to pay it back it would mean that he is a good "investment"; his not paying it back would mean that he becomes a *chichifo*, a hustler, who

58 *The Avowal of Difference*

has taken advantage of José's goodwill—and who indirectly would demean José's sense of dignity or propriety as a homosexual man. In the end, it would appear that Alberto was right about homosexuals, "we are the same, you, me, or any other (*cualquiera*)." The debasement of Wenceslao as just any other homo, a *cualquiera* (in Spanish, *un(a) cualquiera* suggests a "prostitute"); the possibility that his embraces literally came at a cost robs José of an idealized notion of homosexuality as something that can be perfect—and this reading of his situation sends him into a tailspin crisis. José's injured narcissism is a form of castration that eventuates in his taking his own life.

Wenceslao's gaze

Up to now, I have been focusing on José's actions and reactions to this impossible situation, his impossible love. Now, I would like to turn to Wenceslao's position in all this. The day after their big fight, we learn that "[Wenceslao t]e espiaba, gozaba imaginando que te encontrarías con otras personas."[24] ["Wenceslao spied on you, he enjoyed imagining that you would meet with other people."] So despite readers getting a first impression that Wenceslao does not care about José, we get to see that he too seeks out the other man. However, after following José for a few blocks, he becomes "... jadeante, el sudor le empapaba el pecho y las palmas de las manos."[25] ["breathless, the sweat drenched his chest and the palms of his hands."] Weakened, he leans against a wall, and then,

> Sus pasos resonaron nuevamente en las baldosas de la acera para perderse en el fragor de la cuidad. "Necesito liberarme de eso, no puedo continuar haciendo el papel de policía." Inmediatamente su memoria presentó ante sus ojos una larga procesión de situaciones humillantes. [...] Meses atrás sus celos le llevaron a situaciones degradantes, ahora deseaba escapar ese laberinto.[26]

> [His steps resonated again on the bluestone sidewalks and would become lost in the clashing noise of the city. "I need to get rid of that, I can't keep playing the role of police." Immediately his memory presented before his eyes a long procession of humiliating situations. [...] Months before his jealousy had take him to degrading situations, now he desired to escape that labyrinth.]

What is striking here is Wenceslao's great insight—first, that he is playing police, and that this role puts him in a (previously experienced) path that leads to jealousy, humiliation, and personal degradation. He does not want that for himself. So he makes a decisive choice about José: "¡Qué se vaya al diablo!"[27] ["Let him go to hell!"] This is the break and end of their relationship. From here on, Wenceslao removes himself physically from José—he needs to be away to not allow himself being trapped in a relational "labyrinth" that damages his personhood.

At this point, Wenceslao takes a different route, a surprising one to be sure. He knocks at a random door and asks for old clothes for charity. An old woman gives him a blouse, and he then asks for "intimate apparel," which he did not get. Thereafter he moves on, manages to escape a homophobic gang who comes after him, and arrives at the Cabaret "Raul." There, he changes into women's clothing, and goes out to flirt with clients. We later discover that this is one of his means of employment. And, given that he does not have and cannot find a job, the sex trade becomes for him a limited form of income—and I would also argue a venue to access a gendered and sexual identity.[28]

But what makes Wenceslao's self-figuration all the more interesting to us might just be that it takes place in the streets of Mexico City, where the noises of the crowds make his steps literally disappear. In the city he becomes anonymous, and this affords him a particular condition for self-figuration. José experiences the city otherwise. On particular Saturday, José gets to work, and he remarks that "[y]a nadie me habla ni se acuerda de que existo."[29] ["nobody even talks to me nor remembers that I exist."] The narrative goes on to explain that there are major demonstrations going on in the street, where the State's "feral hatred" is being used to repress teachers and others. The text makes reference to the repression and assault on schoolteachers, and thereby we are able to exact the specific date of the events, September 7, 1958. This is the date of major demonstrations on the part of the Movimiento Magisterial de 1958 (Teachers' Movement of 1958) in Mexico; these protests were carried out principally by teachers and railroad workers who sought better working conditions through unionization.[30] In the midst of this social unrest in the city, especially in the city center where he is working, José imagines that his colleagues are simply not paying attention to him:

Indiferente a los sucesos, retornabas a tu casa; con lentitud, arribaste a la esquina de Bolívar y 16 de Septiembre; a diez cuadras de donde te hallabas resonaban los disparos y el silbido de las granadas, ululaban las sirenas de las ambulancias.

Imperturbable, pensabas en Wenceslao, sin hacer caso a los ruidos del zafarrancho, a tal grado había llegado tu enajenación. Antes de abordar el camion de segunda pasaron frente a ti varios transportes del ejército, los miraste con frialdad, sin tener la inquietud de preguntarte su destino.

A tu alrededor se arremolinaba gente con el rostro pálido, desencajado, ansiosa de abandoner el improvisado campo de batalla; no les diste importancia; por fin partiste sin olvidar la figura de Wenceslao.[31]

[Indifferent to the events, you returned home; slowly you arrived at the corner of Bolivar and September 16 Streets. Ten blocks from where you were standing, the shots and the whistle of the grenades were ringing, and the ambulances' sirens were wailing.

Imperturbable, you thought about Wenceslao, without paying much attention to the sounds of war zone—your alienation had grown to such a degree. Before getting on the bus, several military vehicles drove right in front of you, you saw them coldly, without any sense of worry to ask yourself what was their goal.

All around you, people were swirling with pale and undone faces, anxiously abandoning the improvised battleground; you didn't give them any importance. Finally you left without forgetting Wenceslao's figure.]

This is a stunning moment, not the least for the apolitical detachment that José shows—this entire scene highlights the obsessive solipsism (his *ensimismamiento*) in which he is all wrapped up. José cannot see what is happening in the city; he is oblivious, indeed indifferent, to the events, the social and political forces that shape his citizenship and identity. He only has one focus, Wenceslao, and that object of desire does not—will not—respond to his heed. The textual narrative leaks out a final pronouncement: since Wenceslao the person is not present, José is only left with his *figure* to conjure up—in other words, the text reveals to us that the other is a mere fiction. Hence, perhaps, this explains how the real Wenceslao can become easily transmutated into a diary at the beginning of the novel—and moreover, the figure of Wenceslao as a diary is what permits José to put his beloved in his pocket, that is, to control him as he pleases.

Returning to the space of the city, we see distinctly how both men are attentive to their environs. On the one hand, Wenceslao sees it as a place of anonymity and I might advance cruising and economic advantage; on the other hand, José fully abandons altogether the power of that space to transform his life. This second version of the homosexual in the city is quite impactful given how the cityscape is often privileged as a space for queer identification and coming out.[32]

If the city permits Wenceslao the possibility of anonymity, then it is important to underscore his departures. I suggested earlier that he needs to leave Mexico City to Guadalajara to get away from José so as to not fall trapped again in that "labyrinth" of policing and humiliations. Though he comes back to the city after three weeks, he leaves within days. This second departure is important because José does everything to get him back. In the final scene of departure, we see that both men again respond to their contexts in diametrically opposite ways:

> Wenceslao, aturdido por el incesante traqueteo del ferrocarril, evocaba lo que él creía lejanos momentos felices, pero aquellas situaciones ya gastadas eran incapaces de causarle alegría. "Será mejor olvidar" reflexionó.
>
> Tú, por el contrario, mientras transitabas entre la doble hilera de palmeras que bordea el camellón de las calles de Ponciano Arriaga, aún te recreabas con la cadena interminable de añoranzas.
>
> Muy pronto llegaste a la Plaza de la República, torciste hacia la izquierda, bordeando la paredes del Frontón México. En las calles de Buenavista y Ponciano Arriaga habían quedado el monumento a Colón, el hotel Germano-Americano y las estaciones de autobuses. Fue hasta ese momento cuando el desdén de Wenceslao te provocó una melancholia abrumadora y los ojos se te llenaron de lágrimas.[33]

> [Befuddled by the train's incessant rattle, Wenceslao evoked what he thought were distant happy moments, but those already wasted situations were incapable of bringing him happiness. He reflected, "Perhaps, it's best to forget."
>
> You, on the contrary, while walking down the double row of palm trees that edged Ponciano Arriaga Street, still re-created yourself with an interminable chain of longings.

Very quickly you came to Plaza de la República, you turned left, skirting the walls of the Fronton Mexico. On Buenavista and Ponciano Arriaga Streets, the Monument to Columbus, the German-American Hotel, and the bus terminals had remained. It wasn't until that moment that Wenceslao's disdain provoked in you an overwhelming melancholy and your eyes were filled with tears.]

For Wenceslao, memories are worn out, and cannot spark any enthusiasm. In the end he becomes resigned that "it's best to forget." José, for his part, becomes a flâneur in the city, and walks down the palm-lined street, "re-creating himself," imagining for himself other ways of being in light of Wenceslao's departure and absence. As he leaves, the old Buenavista train station,[34] a symbol of Mexican modernity, and comes to where the Columbus Monument and the bus terminal "had remained." (As an aside, I was able to discover that the old station, which was a project of the Porfiriato as an effort to modernize Mexico, was demolished sometime in 1958 [I have not been able to find the exact dates].) Nevertheless, we can argue that the place around which José is meandering is a place of reconstruction and ruins. And it is here, among the ruins of a growing and transforming city, that he becomes aware of Wenceslao's rejection, and that it all is over.

Narcissistic injuries

All along José has been the purveyor of particular ideology about love: "sin ti estoy tan solo, tan abandonado"[35] ["without you I am so am lonely, so abandoned"]. Whereas for Wenceslao, his relationship to José is less about affect and more about ownership: "Lo único que discernía con precisión era que José le pertenecía, era su posesión, su propiedad privada, y nada ni nadie debería tocarlo"[36] ["The only thing that he would discern with any precision was that José belonged to him, he was his possession, his private property, and nothing nor anyone should touch him"]. Two different ideas about the self's relation to the other can be seen here—José's idea of emotion as relationality encounters Wenceslao's understanding of attachment as ownership—one engages (or tried to engage) the other; the other sees the partner as pure object, who he can grasp or abandon at any time. In the end, Wenceslao can separate from José readily; however, José can only dwell in moments such as this one:

Te esperé un largo rato, porque de esa manera creo que de un momento a otro llegarás y estoy más tranquilo; pero es inútil aguardarte, no sé por qué llegué a querer como te quiero, ya ves para qué me sirvió: para que me abandonaras y quedase más solo que de costumbre, pero en fin, ¿qué le vamos a hacer?[37]

[I waited for you a long while because in such a manner I've come to believe that you will arrive any minute, and thus I am calmer; but it is useless waiting for you, I don't know why I came to love you as I do. You see, what good was it for? So that you would abandon me and I would lonelier than usual, but in the end, what can we do?]

This scene contains many tightly wound up narratives: waiting as a way of postponing the other's abandonment, lingering in that moment of waiting and yearning, of *esperanza*, wondering about why he loves his beloved in such a way, realizing that loving is nothing more than a setup for abandonment, remaining alone at the end, and finally returning to the possibility of coming up with an answer together—what can we do? —reinserting hope into a hopeless situation. This structure, full of conflicting tendencies, places José's diary of yearning into the cultural tradition of melodrama—and as such the text unfolds to its tragic conclusion. Becoming aware that Wenceslao was not going to return, that he was indifferent to his every call, José writes after the second departure, "se me achica el corazón al pensar que ya no te acuerdas de mi y que mis problemas no te interesan; no te importa [mi porvenir], prometiste que tan luego llegaras me enviarías dinero, pero ya ves, tus promesas fueron falsas ..."[38] ["my heart shrinks thinking that you don't remember me anymore, and that my problems don't interest you; (my future) doesn't interest you, you promised that as soon as you arrived you would send me money, but you see, your promises were false ..."] José realizes that the other has no sense of responsibility for (or response-ability to) him; there is no such a thing as a sexual (or even an economic) relationship between the two men.[39] The other has abandoned José completely. "[N]o me escuchaste," ["You didn't listen to me,"] José writes in his final letter, "sufrí mucho mucho porque no me hacías caso, después te perdí, quedándome más solo y más triste que nunca."[40] ["I suffered so so much because you ignore me, then I lost you, being left more alone and more sad than ever."] José expects an answer to feel validated, to be made whole, within that melodramatic logic. He loves, and wants to be loved, but instead he is abandoned. He cannot write himself out of such a position of abandonment and abjection—he cannot imagine himself, if not through the other.

This impossibility to imagine for himself an independent queer life leads José to utter his "Liebestod": "Amor mío, cúrame por favor,"[41] ["My love, cure me please!"], a final cry requesting a response, a cure for a "deep dark pain that is called love" and that will never be healed.

"Who's your daddy?"

In the previous chapter, we note that Felipe goes about his identity formation through a series of domestic and institutional settings—his uncle's home and patrimony, the Seminary school, the Church. It is quite useful to consider how the filiative versus the affiliative spaces (to echo Edward Said) offers a context in and through which subject formation develops.[42] Filiative and affiliative contexts and forces impinge on the ways in which the self imagines himself: that is, the self first begins imagining himself within the space of the family (the rule of the father is taken literally) and when he leaves the family, he can then begin thinking of how he defines his identity through (institutional) affiliations, like the school, the Church, the State, and his profession (the Father is a metaphor of the institutions). In *El diario*, we can see how José becomes aware of the reality that Wenceslao is gone only when he is walking in the ruins of the changing city; that is, his (queer) filiation is gone, and it is replaced by the crumbling buildings (the ruins of an affiliative, institutional modernity) —we might ask more precisely what is it about old buildings that metonymically remind José of his political, social, and affective standing? I raise this question because it falls in line with my contention that the large context of Latin America, in particular the discursive practices available, makes for subject formation to surge and evolve differently. I have explained that *modernismo* (especially, the *reino interior* as a meditation on subjectivity) and hinted that melodrama with its lavish production of absence are two styles for subjects to imagine and write themselves queerly.[43]

* * *

Coda: The meanings of home

I want to end this chapter in a different fashion by introducing a facet of the debate that looks at the relationship among domesticity, filiative relations, and identity formation. One thing that might strike contemporary readers is that both José and Wenceslao live in their parents' home, yet still have a sense of a homosexual identity, and do not just simply engage in private homosexual practice. This situation raises some important questions that sketch out a different history of homosexual identity in the context of Mexican and Latin American cultures.

I would like to consider John D'Emilio's important essay "Capitalism and Gay Identity."[44] He argues that in the history of U.S. sexuality, certain social, political, and economic forces shaped the articulation of a gay and lesbian identity. He notes that gay men and lesbians "are a product of history, and have come into existence in a specific historical era. Their emergence is associated with the relations of capitalism . . ."[45] (468). More explicitly, he adds that

> As wage labor spread and production became socialized, then it became possible to release sexuality from the "imperative" to procreate. [. . .] In divesting the household of its economic independence and fostering the separation of sexuality from procreation, capitalism has created conditions that allow some men and women to organize a personal life around the erotic/emotional attraction to their own sex. It has made possible the formation of urban communities of lesbian and gay men and, more recently, of a politics based on a sexual identity.[46]

In other words, capitalism has enabled a select group to acquire and produce certain conditions and spaces to create networks and institutions around same-sex desire, and these new organizations have centripetally drawn others who identify with their goals, thereby coalescing into communities and defining a new and particular body (and affective) politic. D'Emilio's theory clearly applies to different turning points in United States' history of sexuality from the second half of the nineteenth century to the present day. I appreciate D'Emilio's effort to historicize the forces that shape gay and lesbian identities—and the evolving narratives used to cohere a sense of identity politics and community; moreover, he considers how other facets of human life produce different expressions of gay life: "These new forms of gay identity and patterns of group life also reflected the differentiation of people according to gender, race, and class that is so pervasive in capitalist societies."[47]

To D'Emilio's caveat that gender, race, and class inform gay identity formation differently, we can add culture, nationality, and a host of other social, political, and economic conditions or forces. Indeed, a central effort of this project is to consider the cultures of Latin America writ large as they inform sexual identities and expression. At this point I would like to ask about one single factor—gay identity within the heterosexual domestic space.

Going back to the novel, I asked us to consider the significance of Jose's and Wenceslao's living at home: How does this domestic life inform their gay lives? We might consider generally that Wenceslao defines his gay life through his departures from the home—from the beginning he leaves his parents' home and the novel closes with him leaving again. There is no evidence throughout the novel that he has to leave home in order to become a "gay" man.[48] We might recall that scene between José and Wenceslao's father who thought over and again, "He [Wenceslao] leaves us because he needs money and that imbecile of José isn't able to provide it for him." Wenceslao's father does not seem disturbed as to how his son gets his money; all that matters is that he gets it. One could almost surmise that the father is turning a blind eye to his son's homosexuality as long as there is an economic reward. Perversely, I am suggesting that the father here does not care about homosexuality, just show him the money, period. What are the politics of this position? That is, what does it mean that knowledge of homosexual identity is glossed over completely by some financial reward or return? It is like saying, "I don't care about your being gay, as long as you provide money for the home," or, "I don't care what you do outside the home, just bring money to it." These social constructions are different than the one proposed by D'Emilio. He proposes that gay identity thrives in alternative domestic and social institutions, supported by capitalism: gays create new spaces—gay bars, gay bookstores, gay homes, gay everything—as an alternative to the heteronormative home. Wenceslao's father's attitude represents another political position, something like, "You can do anything you want outside the home, just don't talk about—and I promise even not to ask...." More radically put, Wenceslao can create and practice anything and everything "gay" outside the home; however, he cannot name it. This is an important caveat: homosexuality may exist in some inchoate form, behavior, or sense, but it cannot ever be fully articulated, that is, it must remain surrounded by silences.

José's family situation is somewhat different, though it responds to this issue of silence in its structure. We remember José's reaction as Wenceslao leaves the first time: "When you got in the cab I felt the need to leave with you, but my father forced me to go in the house, and I had no other choice than to obey him. Afterwards, he insulted me, asking me if I dressed you or if I kept you." This scene shows us a more traditional patriarch who does not want his son's affairs out in public, and disciplines him by sending him inside the house. José entire narrative is nothing more than shuttling back and forth between his job and home, occasionally, an outing with his coworkers. Domesticity is presented in the most conservative form. The home conceals and normalizes. We notice that the José's father never asks outright what kind of (sexual) relation José might be having with Wenceslao. Rather, his father asks if theirs is an economic one, one of dependency. Sexuality is elliptically presented here, and only as economic relation: by eliding the obvious, the father seems to insist that there is no such thing as a sexual relation. José feels insulted by such questions. But what exactly is so insulting in the father's words? Is it that he does not call their relation love, or even homosexuality? That he chooses to characterize the men's relationship as nothing more than economic dependency? If the father is euphemistically referring to his son's homosexuality as a financial arrangement, and in fact he is calling his son a homosexual, why would José feel insulted by being identified as such? This is especially odd, since José is not tormented for being gay; more exactly, he spends the entire novel dwelling on a lost love. His suicide is about losing Wenceslao, not about being a homosexual.

I return to D'Emilio's essay, and note again one salient difference between the situation he describes in the United States, and that of Mexico in the late 1950s and early 1960s. At this particular moment in Mexican history, the capitalist transformations that D'Emilio describes are not happening—or at least they are not happening at the same rate—in Mexico compared to the United States. It is not surprising that the men live at home, and that their homosexual identities depend on the rule (or blindness) of the father as well as on the cultural meanings of home. They are still able to enjoy a certain homosexual existence, yet it is demarcated by a series of silence. Gay or queer life, while still living by the rules of home, has never meant that such a life is impossible; rather, it means that its conceptualization and narration must account for certain restrictions and silences.

3
Adonis's Silence
Textual Queerness in Zapata's
El vampiro de la Colonia Roma

> If we are to approach a text, it must have an edge.
> —Jacques Derrida

> Vous avez raison, son mutisme est assourdissant. C'est le silence des forêts primitives, chargé jusqu'à la gueule. Je m'étonne parfois de l'obstination que met notre taciturne ami a bouder les langues civilisées. Son métier consiste à recevoir des marins de toutes les nationalités dans ce bar d'Amsterdam qu'il a appelé d'ailleurs, on ne sait pourquoi, *Mexico-City*.
> —Camus, *La chute*

In this chapter I propose to sketch out the coordinates of a theoretical reading of homosexual identities, queer theory, and blank spaces in Luis Zapata's challenging novel, *Las aventuras, desventuras y sueños de Adonis García, el vampiro de la Colonia Roma* [The adventures, misfortunes and dreams of Adonis García, the vampire of Colonia Roma].[1] Beyond a literary analysis that brings together different narrative strategies of self-figuration, this chapter should also be understood as a social and cultural reading of sexual identities and of the ideological templates that regulate those identity formations.[2] How do we articulate a theory that contains productive ways in which to talk about Latin American sexual identities, in general, and homosexual identities, in particular? Finally, I contextualize my analysis of Zapata's novel as part of a larger meditation on queer subject formation that relates masochism and a theory of Latin American narrative.[3]

Unmarked spaces

The extent of critical and theoretical work being done in the United States on questions of sexuality has been truly admirable. A wide range of debates have installed "gay" and "lesbian" identities as central, while others have discarded identity politics for being too essentialist in its program of describing or naming a gay and lesbian community. Queer theory has come to occupy a privileged site within U.S. academic circles to show the productive politics of sexual and gender fluidity.

In the context of these debates, I insist on the political currency and limitations of claiming a "gay" or "queer" identity in Latin America. I observed in the "Introduction" that the refusal itself to claim such an identity—that is, retain "unmarked" identity or one without labels—would signify on "privileging [of] a fragmented subjectivity." That is, the refusal itself of being called "gay" or "lesbian" may be part and parcel of a history of (postcolonial) resistance in Latin America by not adopting other names for oneself.[4] I also suggested that, perhaps, the *refusal* of "gay identity" as a form of identification shows the movement from "nongay identity" to "gay *non*identity—a gay identity of disfiguration, one that relentlessly enjoys its scars."[5] Here I will seek to describe something different: *grosso modo*, not only how language constructs "subjects," or not just how subjects play with language to construct and reinvent themselves; but rather, how these two activities might be culturally marked and read.[6] I am interested in the *inter*implication among a particular identity figuration, and the textual and cultural spaces negotiated by that figuration.[7]

Theories of subjection (Foucault's term is *assujetissement*) animate subjectivity differently. Judith Butler's work considers such subject formation:[8] there is a paradox that in naming a subject, that very subject is being constituted through a process of being subjected; being a subject implies the acquisition of an identity as well as being taken over (in Spanish, *apoderado/desapoderado*) by a *force majeur*. But for me, at this juncture, what is interesting is not so much the philosophical tweaking into subject formation, but rather the very deployment of terms like *gay, lesbian, queer,* and the like, and, importantly, the effects that those terms may produce in Latino American sexual and cultural identities. I have brought up Butler because of the sympathy that I have for her work. But it is a cautious sympathy, because the "queer identities" that she describes seem to have an uneasy relationship with the historical understanding wherein they are produced. Is it fair to say that the epistemologies of queer identity are the same in all of North America–U.S. and México? Borrowing Butler's maxim that "'subjection' signifies the process of becoming subordinated by power as well as the process of becoming a subject"[9] and replacing its implicitly postmodern underpinning with a postcolonial one, we see that it fails. In the space of the postmodern as well as the postcolonial, we can argue that "'subjection' signifies the process of becoming subordinated by power," all right. However, we cannot possibly, ethically, complete the sentence: subjection "... [signifies] the process of becoming a subject" when talking about the postcolonial. Indeed, the project of postcolonialism has been to throw out the conceit of allowing "he who knows best" to dictate the identities of the oppressed. Postcolonial thinking has been precisely about breaking this paradigm of imposed dependency. From this movement between the postmodern to the postcolonial, here we encounter a critical gap; it is a critical gap that underscores a series of clichés: the ahistorical nature of the postmodern vis-à-vis the precise revisionist historicity of postcolonial discourses. Thus, we see an important caveat to reading Butler's work alongside other literary or philosophical traditions.[10]

As a way of another example of the considerations needed to discuss homosexual identity in Latin America, I return to Paz's "Máscaras mexicanas" ["Mexican Masks"],[11] in which he argues that Mexican identity is most affirmed when it is most closed or hermetically sealed. *Abrirse* (to open oneself up) or *rajarse* (to cut oneself open), thus allowing the other to enter, is in effect the least "Mexican" thing a man can do or be. Throughout his essay, Paz discusses the different ways in which Mexicans (more exactly, Mexican *men* are always the subjects of his narrative) can and should not open themselves up, *abrirse*. Toward the end of his essay, Paz is discussing the extremely "Mexican" practice of *albures* as a game of emasculation.[12] Here we find that especially queer paragraph that almost seems out of place with his argument that far:

> Es significativo, por otra parte, que el homosexualismo masculino sea considerado con cierta indulgencia, por lo que toca al agente activo. El agente pasivo, al contrario, es un ser degenerado y abyecto.[13]
>
> [It is significant, on the other hand, that male homosexualism is considered with a certain level of indulgence as it relates to the active agent. The passive one, on the contrary, is a degenerate and abject being.]

Paz is alluding to the "penetration paradigm" to differentiate between male hetero- and homosexualities. Basically, the paradigm assigns to the one who penetrates (the active agent) the role of "man" (in this cosmology, to say "heterosexual man" would seem a tautology); the subject who is penetrated (the passive one) is a "woman" or "like a woman." This simile—being "like a woman"—signifies the homosexual body. According to this paradigm, what defines the hetero-/homo- divide is a positionality, a spatial relationship of "who's on top" and "who's on the bottom."[14] Of the many criticisms that can be made against this paradigm, the main one is that it always presents male heterosexuality as "unmarked" or "without stain of original sin" versus the homosexual body as always, already excessively marked or oversignified.[15] As I proposed in the "Introduction," Paz offers us—whether we like it or not—a very *different* formulation of how gay identity and self-figuration may be conceptualized. I stress again that this is a very problematic way of defining gay identity; however, Paz presents us with a disfigured act of gay presence, a complex knot that may serve as a starting epistemological point.[16] Though problematic as it may seem, perhaps this paradigm may give us an important insight into the link between homophobia and misogyny. From this link, we may find a political and cultural coalition to address homophobic and misogynist views.

In both readings of Butler and Paz, we can discern the possibilities and limitations of each critic's work. We can revisit and refunction Paz's work to develop new ways of knowledge and political design. We can differentiate at least two readings of the penetration paradigm above: on the one hand, a more "individualistic" reading on how sexual identity is effected would focus on the homophobic convenience of remaining "unmarked" to define male heterosexuality; on the other hand, a broader or more "autochthonous" (I cannot think of a better word here) conceptualization of the paradigm would give it a certain value and expression of cultural, social, and theoretical *resistance* versus other social constructions of sexuality.

I think of Barthes's honesty. "I confess," he begins,

> I am unable to interest myself in the beauty of a place if there are no people in it (I don't like empty museums); and conversely, in order to discover the interest of a face, of a figure, of a garment, to savor the encounter, I require that the site of this discovery have its interest and its savor as well.[17]

Barthes brings together the subject and the place, their histories, to see how they inform each other. It might be possible to imagine a subject without a place or, by extension, without a body or a history, but at what cost? It is this link of face and place—body and context—that provokes an interest, a memory, a particular identification with another.

Thus, and so navigating in a sea of theory, we must beware of the shallow waters where we might get stuck, especially at the beginning of a voyage of gay adventure in the history of Latino American sexuality. I want to chart a course of the ways in which we can approach a gay, lesbian, or queer Latino/a American subject, in his or her terms. I will look at some ways in which these queer subjectivities might be read otherwise in Latin America. My map looks like Luis Zapata's *Las aventuras, desventuras y sueños de Adonis García, el vampiro de la Colonia Roma*.

Adonis's Body

How does this novel help us understand gay identity? Why have I placed the story of a gay hustler in Mexico retelling his experiences at the center of gay identity? The title of the novel gives us some answers. A text of enormous complexity, little has been written about *El vampiro de la Colonia Roma*.[18]

The name says it all ... Adonis, the most beautiful man. García, perhaps one of the most common Spanish last names. Adonis García, a masked man, unknown to all, a *puto*, a hustler. Vampire, living-and-dead figure that lives off others, a figure transfigured. Adventures

74   *The Avowal of Difference*

and misfortunes, hard realities; dreams, absent events. Rome, the long-lost marvelous civilization. The Colonia Roma, once, a center of power, home to the best families in Mexico until the Revolution and, then, a middle-class enclave throughout the 1940s and '50s. By the 1970s and '80s, the Colonia Roma was nothing more than decadence. La Colonia Roma, abandoned and displaced by the Zona Rosa and Coyoacán, became the new home for the underdogs, the gays.[19] (The Colonia Roma would suffer some of the most devastating damages during the Earthquake of 1985.) La Colonia Roma, decadence.[20] Names say it all.

The title of the text serves as a palimpsest of the multiply layered and competing agencies of power; it describes a sight of sites. The many shades or nuances of the title point from the outset to the complexity of the text. This complexity follows in the structure of the novel itself. And indeed, before entering in a closer textual analysis, it is worthwhile to discuss this structure.

The novel is a transcription of seven cassettes, which contain recorded conversations or interminable chit-chat by the protagonist Adonis García—his life, his sexploitations, his dreams, and the like. Only he speaks; although we become aware of the presence of another (an interviewer? an ethnographer? a psychoanalyst? a trick?) by the fact that Adonis is constantly asking questions and making remarks, for example, "Tell you my life?" or "Really?" or "Okay, now turn it off, no?" Each cassette tape begins with a story of a dream that Adonis has had, and then with a discussion of different moments in his life. The seven tapes are presented with the following warning by the author:

NOTA

La forma conversada en que se narra la novela exige una credibilidad fonética *que se opone a las convenciones del lenguaje escrito; por ello, los espacios en blanco sustituyen a la puntuación tradicional y se evitan las mayúsculas. En cambio, se usan otros recursos (comillas, signos de exclamación e interrogación) que en el lenguaje escrito equivalen de algún modo a los tonos de la conversación.* L.Z.[21]

[NOTE

The conversational form in which this novel is narrated demands a phonetic credibility *that is oppositional to the conventions of written language; thus the blank spaces substitute traditional punctuation, also capital letters are avoided. However, other resources (quotation marks, exclamation and interrogation points) are used; in written language these are equivalent in some way to the tones of a conversation. LZ.*]

This initial and marginal note[22] tries to propose a different *textual representation* that will break with any norm, not only opening up a space for how things are being said (grammar), but what is talked about (sexuality for sale). This new grammar (which borrows from ethnography and *testimonio*[23]) is solicited by the very subject that is being treated, in this case, male prostitution.

Zapata creates a tension in his text between writing and orality. The author defines himself not as an author but as an editor; he tries to invent a grammatical and syntactical structure through which he allows language to flow. We detect a certain anxiety by the author before Adonis's presence and voice, especially when he says that "the conversational form ... demands phonetic credibility." The author knows that Adonis, his movements, his orality, his performance demand a new textual space, a new grammar. The *espacios en blanco* (blank spaces) that replace punctuation symbolize an opening in language; the absence of periods and commas gives us the impression that language does not end, and that it comes in a hurry. It is a logorrhea. In any event, the voice of the *puto* (the hustler) goes beyond the conventional and requires a different mise-en-scène, a space big enough to represent himself, without the trappings of the established norms of standard Spanish. Grammatical structure becomes literary poststructure. The breaks with formal structure hint at a new arrangement of knowledge, an epistemological shift, which radically alters the representation of gay identity, whose voice is uneven, full of gaps and silences.

These moments of silence seem quite dramatic in the textual space of Zapata's novel. Moreover, I would also propose that we keep in mind that those *espacios en blanco* (blank spaces; literally, white spaces) might be editions made by the author himself. Thus, substituting blank/white spaces for grammar and punctuation suggests that silences are artificial or invented.[24] On the question of the making(s) of silence, I find Shoshana Felman's reading of Camus's *La chute* helpful. She states that

> Silence here [in Camus's text] is not a simple absence of an act of speech, but a positive avoidance—an erasure—of one's hearing, the positive *assertion* of a deafness, in the refusal not merely to know but to *acknowledge*—and henceforth respond or *answer to*—what is being heard or witnessed.[25]

Silence can be read or interpreted as the act of "not saying" (here as Adonis's resistance to reveal too much) as well as the acts of "not hearing" or "not acknowledging" (as the work of the author/editor in selecting what might be known).[26] I chose the epigraph from Camus's *La chute* very deliberately, asking myself whether the fact of the bar's name, Mexico-City, in the opening scene of the novel might reveal anything for our reading. Mexico City is place of many geographic, cultural, social, and political centers—and throughout its history, these centers have changed and have been displaced. Throughout the twentieth century, the city's borders have been growing and consuming other neighboring centers. Mexico City also refers to a palimpsest of historical cities. Tlatelolco, the Plaza de las Tres Culturas, is an obvious example of the spatial conjunction of three Mexicos, of three histories.[27] Thus, Mexico City is the very space that defies the question of referentiality. Mexico does not name a singular place; it is instead a paradoxical configuration of a nonreferential referent. The narrative event of *La chute* is that the narrator Jean-Baptiste Clamance begins his story in a bar called Mexico-City; this situation problematizes his confession in that he offers a disembodied confession, free of a historical referent. The space from where he speaks and confesses gives form to (or informs) his testimony. Ironically, Mexico-City, the bar where "sailors of every nationality" are entertained, can be seen as a homosocial space, which through deferred reference signifies on the "real" Mexico City where Adonis makes his living as a *chichifo*, a gay hustler.[28]

Throughout the novel, Adonis will reveal those spaces where gay life is enjoyed in Mexico City during the 1970s. His voice traces roads and makes the reader run around a crazy map of the city where "those things don't happen," a phrase often used to deny the existence of gay life.[29] Adonis's gay life in Mexico City is the paradox of the "public privacy" of homosexuality; that is, the struggle to find public and "acceptable" strategies to live that socially and culturally private part of homosexuality.

Picaresque Narratives

More on the structure that Zapata gives to his text: he begins each tape (or chapter) with an epigraph from classic picaresque novels, including el Periquillo, Lazarillo de Tormes, la Pícara Justina, among others. This presentation of the chapter with a picaresque epigraph is significant because the author/editor suggests that Adonis's life is like that of the other outcasts.[30] What is most important is the epigraph that introduces the entire novel; it is from Juan de Luna's Segunda parte de Lazarillo de Tormes (1620):

> Si he de decir lo que siento, la vida picaresca es vida, que las otras no merecen este nombre; si los ricos la gustasen, dejarían por ella sus haciendas, como hacían los antiguos filósofos, que por alcanzarla dejaban lo que poseían; digo por alcanzarla, porque la vida filósofa y picaral es una misma; sólo se diferencian en que los filósofos dejaban lo que poseían por su amor, y los pícaros, sin dejar nada, la hallan. [. . .] [L]a vida picaresca es más descansada que la de los reyes, emperadores y papas. Por ella quise caminar como por camino más libre, menos peligroso y nada triste.[31]

> [If I were to say what I feel, picaresque life is life itself, that other forms of living don't deserve this name. If rich men were to enjoy this life, they would leave their lands for it, as did the ancient philosophers who just to reach it would leave what they owned. I say "just to reach it" because philosophical and picaresque lives are one and the same—the only difference is that philosophers left what they owned for their love, and *pícaros*, without abandoning anything, found it. [. . .] [P]icaresque life is more relaxed than the life of kings, emperors or popes. Through a picaresque life, I wanted to walk as if through as freer road, less dangerous and not at all sad.]

One critic has argued that this epigraph introduces "a structuring element to the complete work by suggesting a philosophical perspective."[32] I find this reading quite superficial: to use a quote that makes reference to a certain "philosophy" does not willy-nilly produce a "philosophical perspective." It is preferable to ask why the author chose to privilege Luna to introduce his text rather than other more "canonical" texts. Or, more simply put, how does the author use the picaresque novel to design his own narrative.[33] Undoubtedly, the author is calling into question the very idea of authority and structure by making reference to Luna, the usurper of the usurper. That is, in the Segunda parte (1620), Luna ventriloquizes and uses the authority of the "original" 1554 anonymous author of the Lazarillo.[34] Likewise, we know that Adonis is not the protagonist's real name: Adonis is a displacing figure of another. And, on another level, through the ventriloquist strategies of testimonio, Zapata too takes over the protagonist's voice. Zapata doubles and perversely parodies Adonis's voice as presence. Luna's and Zapata's texts are different echoes, displaced voices of a lost original. By focusing on the picaresque, the Mexican author is able to reconstruct and to reinscribe a floating voice, a mask as shifter, in his text. Thus, what is summoned is a fragmented gay identity. Furthermore, this is how the author manages to tell a story written by an absent or "unmarked" subject.

Gay Genealogies

con mi papá   en cambio   sí me encariñé más
    era un señor a toda madre   aunque tampoco hablaba mucho   fíjate   ni siquiera sabíamos lo que había estado haciendo en españa antes de venirse para acá   o lo que había estudiado   o lo que hubiera querido ser   o   en fin   todas esas historias familiares   ¿mentiendes?   que todas las gentes saben acerca de sus padres[35]

[with my dad   on the other hand   I did become more involved   he was a real cool dude   even though we didn't speak much   like   we didn't even know what he had been doing in spain before coming over here   or what he had studies   or what he would've like to have been   or   you know   all those family histories   you know what I mean?   that all people know about their parents]

Adonis has lost his genealogy. He only knows that his father came from Spain. I am interested here in the use of the verb "venir(se)," "to come from." In a very similar incident to the one above, Lazarillo de Tormes tells us (in a famously classic passage) that his "viuda madre ... determinó arrimarse a los buenos, por ser uno dellos, y vínose a vivir a la ciudad..."[36] [widowed mother ... was determined to get close to good people, so that she could be one of them, so she came to live in the city.] In both cases the parents went to a city to seek their fortunes. We know that venir means "to arrive." But what calls my attention is the possibilities of the reflexive verb venirse, "to come here," "to install oneself," and, why not, "to reach orgasm." Adonis's Spanish father installed himself in the city, he came to the New World or came to the world anew—a kind of conqueror's reinvention. This critical arrival in effect marks the project of colonialism. The colonial enterprise, we must remember, is more than just arriving at a particular place, it is about installation, the dissemination of (the seed of) authority in the new land. Despite the fact that this particular arrival is sterile (the prodigy became a gay hustler, after all), I would like to offer as explanation that Adonis's telling us about his father's Spanish origin and his arrival in Mexico raises the stakes of Adonis's life story. By telling us that he had a Spanish father (not to mention, his fudging with family details), Adonis might be insisting on his status as a "white" male hustler as opposed to mestizo. His mother's background is never mentioned and mention of her drops out altogether from the narrative. The fleeting mention of his parents, and their eventual dismissal for his story leaves him without a family romance. That is, Adonis has erased (indeed, e-raced) his origins to imagine and identify himself in his own terms, albeit momentarily outside an Oedipal narrative. Nevertheless, by conjuring up a racially privileged image of his absent father, Adonis is choosing a select caste to reinvent himself, a racial identity that will allow him to self-fashion himself otherwise. I am arguing that, rather than speaking of his mother's mestizaje, the father's story as one of (lost) privilege and whiteness brings about the hustler's own privilege of narrating his story. A white Adonis (versus a mestizo or brown one) also comes to represent a more tragic figure that has fallen to sexual perdition. Moreover, we can also add that his whiteness also signifies on the *espacios en blanco* (blank spaces) of the text. Another reading for this paternal dissemination would be to consider the whiteness of the seed as that which itself stains the texts and creates its silences.

Roberto González Echevarría has written that "the process of decolonization always implies a counteroffensive, by and which it rescues not only geographic territories, but also mental ones; not only space, but time; that is: history."[37] Then, if in fact the subject Adonis is subjugated by life's hard blows, his resorting to an absent and white mythology of origins becomes the stuff of projection and the Imaginary. In this context, I would like to reread Adonis's name. Adonis is the name that his friends have given to him; his acceptance of the name represents a self-baptism. To change his name is a way of protecting his identity; this desire to protect his true identity and not reveal his "real" name becomes more dramatic at the end of the novel when we learn that he wants to be a new person and that he wants to walk the path of truth. Furthermore, to change his name is a rewriting of his persona, a rewriting that enables him to say everything, what cannot be said and what should not be said. Adonis's "I" unfolds itself in this renaming. In the narcissistic game of mirrors, the subject's reflection disappears. But also, vampires never had a reflection to talk about.

Confessions

Confession is a way of talking about what is forbidden, what has been marginalized and penalized. Homosexuality and confession almost go hand-in-hand. To confess "I am gay"—those three words that seem to connote a discrete characteristic function strangely enough as a search for acceptance, for penance (I am underlining here the Catholic sense of the practice of confessing). Also, to say "I am gay" conflates the I with the adjective gay—like others, "Republican," "butch," and so forth—thereby, leaving the copula empty. Thus, to say "I am gay" might say little about who I am. Gay identity obviously suffers before this inscribed violence of confession. Furthermore, and sadly, within the social constraints of machismo, to hide rather than to speak those three words, appears to be an "easier" and "safer" practice. I do not want to suggest so narrowly that a gay man or a lesbian should not affirm their sexual identity; what has to be uncovered are strategies to define gay or lesbian experience outside confession. I would weigh in that the capacity to circumvent the trappings of confession via performative acts—the performative is after all about "doing," rather than "saying"—this capacity is what propels much work on queer performativity.

Then, when Adonis's "I" proliferates and disseminates in the text, his confessions are suspended in a space or a relation where he need not be "forgiven," since the confessing subject is virtually absent—what I referred to at the beginning as a gay *non*identity. Homosexuality as defacement seems to be the regulating practice to claim that (disappearing) identity. The performance of multiple subjectivities by Adonis make it unnecessary to expect pardon, that is, legitimation from the outside.

"Don't Talk with Your Mouth Full"

I would like to go back to the *espacios en blanco* (blank or white spaces) of the text. The author insists that they are part of a literary representation of orality. I have tried to suggest that they can be read in many complicated ways: one, editions made by the author; two, sites of effacement or resistance made by the hustler; and three, a metaphor for whiteness as a sign of racial privilege. I would like to add a fourth explanation. I cite from a passage where Adonis talks about his hustling days,

> yo dije   "bueno" y me acosté con él y lo seguí viendo varias veces   lo vi como seis ocho veces y casi siempre de día   iba yo a su departamento por la tarde   me mamaba la verga   le daba su piquete me daba mi tostón y ya me regresaba feliz de la vida entonces una vez que me estaba haciendo un guagüis se dio cuenta   pero casi no le dio importancia   porque las ladillas tampoco se pegan tan fácilmente   total [...]
> pero siguió mamándome la verga   así   como si nada   luego hicimos el sexo igual   como si nada ¿no?   hasta después que acabamos me dice   "oye   ¿sabes qué onda?   tienes ladillas"   "¿tengo ladillas?"   le dije yo haciéndome el inocente   "sí"   dice   "pero no te preocupes"[38]

[I said   "okay" and I went to bed with him and saw him a few more times   I saw him like six eight times and always during the day   I used to go to his apartment in the afternoon   he sucked me off   I would poke him he would give me my money and I would return home happy then one time he was giving me a blow job when he realized   but almost didn't give it any importance because crabs aren't that contagious   well
[. . .]
he kept sucking my cock   like this   as if nothing   then we had sex all the same   as if nothing   no?   until after we finished he says   "hey, how know what?   you got crabs"   "I got crabs?"   I said to him   playing dumb   "yep"   he said   "but   don't worry about it"]

Here Adonis talks about his hustling, explicitly about the economic aspect of the work. Prostitution goes beyond having many sexual encounters; for Adonis and others, it is their only way of survival. Certainly, it would be naive to elaborate prostitution as a melodramatic vindication of promiscuity; the mechanical aspect—almost clinical, at times—with which Adonis discusses his encounters almost suggests a distancing from his work, to the degree that, in the case of Adonis, being a prostitute can be read as a decentering of subjectivity.

What interests me most about the hustling scene is the play in language of giving a blow job, colloquially *hacer un guagüis*. Adonis's partner gives him oral sex and discovers that he has crabs. The indifference with which the two men react point to the mechanization of the sexual act and the objectivization of the subject. Furthermore, Adonis's matter-of-fact attitude shows again a reluctance to acknowledge some consequences or risks of his work. This resistance will remain until the very end of the text, after he imagines getting taken away by gay Martians: "no volvería nunca pero nunca por ningún motivo a este pinche mundo y ora sí ya apágale ¿no?"[39] ["I would never ever return for any reason to this fucking world and now really turn it off, okay?"] The novel ends with a complete negation of the subject.

Another reading of "hacer un guagüis" would follow that Adonis is actually giving a blow job to the interviewer/author/editor. We notice in the passage I quoted when he says, "mamándome la verga (space) así (space) etc." ["sucking my cock (space) like this (space) etc."] What does it mean that the interviewee might be blowing the "author"? The blank spaces can be then read as moments during which Adonis is engaging sexually (orally, in more ways than one) with the author. It is difficult to talk with a penis in your mouth. This scene dramatizes the inability of speaking clearly, fully—and it reminds us of colonialism as a phallic imposition or, if you like, a phallogocentric ramming. Perhaps, it is too late to ask what does it mean? ["*hacer un guagüis*"?]. I cannot give to you a literal translation. Any translation would be necessarily asymmetrical.

I would like to finish with this figure of "*hacer un guagüis*" because writing a history of sexuality is much like wanting to translate this onomatopoetic expression. How do we begin writing a history of sexuality in Latin America where the terms of expression change, or still cause laughter or brutality? Where the subject like a vampire cannot be reflected in any mirror and he privileges effacement as a necessary condition for his self-figuration and self-knowledge? How do we write a history in a place that does not know or acknowledge a queer language?

In conclusion, I have tried to show how content creates new forms of knowing. A new form is always submitted to many interpretations—indeed, readings by a community of readers, who identify part of themselves in a text. The identities produced are as many as can be reflected in the text. I propose reading those white spaces in *El vampiro*, not simply as grammar as the author tells us, but otherwise as editions, failed reflections, spilled semen, racial whiteness, and as moments of sexual practice. These versions of whiteness work alongside and against each other: thus, textuality in *El vampiro de la Colonia Roma* functions as a proscenium that opens and closes, revealing and hiding, identities—Latino American and gay. It has been my intention to show that we can find in those white/blank spaces a new and different place to hear the voices of those who have yet to share in the privilege of speaking openly.

part 2

Interventions

4
Epistemerotics
Puig, Queer Subjects, and Writing Desire

> For me, the only natural sexuality is bisexuality; that is, total sexuality. It's all a matter of sexuality, not homosexuality, not heterosexuality. [...] Just as long as it's not offensive to the other party. I see both homosexuality and heterosexuality as specializations, as limiting matters. I see exclusive homosexuality and exclusive heterosexuality as cultural results, not as a natural outcome.
>
> —Manuel Puig[1]

> The "origin" of auto-eroticism would therefore be the moment when sexuality, disengaged from any natural object, moves into the field of fantasy and by that very fact becomes sexuality.
>
> —Laplanche and Pontalis

Narrative structures

In his monumental work on the Wolf Man,[2] Freud suggests that "memory imprints" represent a particular access and activation of a past scene as a desire for a present "reality." Rather than conceptualizing memory as a knowable, stable, and material image or thing, he privileges the recollection of fragmentary mnemonic images and their assemblages, which are set in motion to reconstruct the event. These memory fragments are rearranged and woven by a metanarrative that bespeaks the present. Without delving too much into the case history, we are struck very early on by that moment when Freud presents a preliminary analysis of the Wolf Man's life. He tells us that "we find before us for reconstruction some such fragments as these: *A real occurrence—dating from a very early period—looking—immobility—sexual problems—castration—his father—something terrible*" (232).³ The interpretation of this material collected from displaced memories, dreams, parapraxes, and so forth, proceeds from what might seem like an archeological project, one of trying to put together a broken object with missing parts, and then trying to imagine it in its completed and original state. These pieces of memory are not meant to be weighed the same, neither is one given a priority over another; rather, they remain in dialectical tension, one alongside the other. These pieces of memory reveal the anatomy of a larger story, which impacts and effects the present. Importantly, for Freud, memories are not about the past, but again about a desire to represent the "here and now." Memories are tools used in a struggle to make sense of the present.

Perhaps more than any other Latin American author, Manuel Puig echoes Freud's critique and deconstruction of "memory." In particular, the Argentine author's narrative experiments as *bricolage* monuments present those parts of the stories that may be told, and leave a series of other stories—from gossipy insinuation to the brutal facts of political repression and violence—he leaves those stories on the side, in the shadows, to emerge later some other way. It is not surprising that Robert Alter described Puig as the "master of occluded narrative." What cannot be said is rendered under erasure, very much like the dashes that connect the memory fragments in Freud's writing of the Wolf Man's case study. The dashes, like a good narrative, both connect those recuperable memory fragments, while, at the same time, refigure the Other's story. I would venture to argue that the connecting dashes or connecting silences of Puig's narratives signify on the political silences or the political disappearances that form the larger context of late-1960 and early-1970 Argentine politics and Peronismo that give context to his novels. The silences and erasures that we read as such in Puig's narrative are the effect of a larger political context. Even further, we could argue that Puig writes the way he does because as a queer-identified Argentine man, he must rely on the irony of silence as part of his language to rewrite history.

An added dimension of Puig's storytelling, which smartly engages the political by deliberately stylizing a fragmentary narrative, has to do with the central role that sexuality plays in his oeuvre. Foucault has taught us that sexuality is paradigmatically the language of elision and power. Alongside that Foucauldian insight, Puig narrates his texts by embroidering them with a sexual dimension that is both hidden and powerful, and thereby he doubly complicates the possibility of accessing a singular straightforward storyline or "official story." Puig's novels are exemplary texts where gender and sexual naming—some would argue, sexual stereotyping—gets formed, only to be readily destabilized. His textuality is laden with sexual personae whose sexuality enters into crisis, a crisis of identification and self-realization.

If memory is not readily available as a knowable event or thing, but rather it is always a process—*in* process—of ascertaining a present; and if sexuality as a discourse is one that by definition names something else, a discourse that cannot fasten down a subjectivity, how then does one remember and narrate one's sexuality? How do we invoke or historicize a sexed subjectivity? Are the results of this effort necessarily a failure? Or might a "successful" articulation of a favorable sexuality, meaning a "healthy" sexual subject in a sexually "progressive" environ, denote an act of violence?

I now turn to Puig and his novel, *The Buenos Aires Affair*, which brings together the complicated ways in which the political, the personal, and the intimate are seamlessly intertwined and capture different forms of violence.[4] I will look at how Puig in his narrative experimentation in general performs a recollection and reassembly that enable a particular subject formation. In particular I will focus on the two chapters on the novel that can be described as "case studies": chapter III, "Acontecimientos principales de la vida de Glady"[5] and chapter VI, "Acontecimientos principales de la vida de Leo,"[6] as well as the masturbation chapter, chapter IV.[7] The two protagonists—Gladys Hebe D'Onofrio and Leo Druscovisch—are sexually queer, in that they do not "fit" in normative definitions of heterosexual identity. In the case of Gladys, Puig looks at the role that masturbation plays in expressing and extending heterosexual desire. Indeed, her heterosexuality can only be defined through female autoerotic self-fulfillment, and not through male penetration or reproduction. In

Leo's case, Puig shows a subject with definite homosexual tendencies, yet who is powerfully homophobic as well. This paradox presses us to examine what the relationship is between queer *assujetissement* and violence. Through these analyses, I hope to speculate what is at stake in conjuring up a sexed memory: How do memory and sexuality traverse one another? Along the way, I will also consider the ways in which space influences the detours of sexual formation.

The Buenos Aires Affair and the Masturbating Woman

Again, *The Buenos Aires Affairs* gives an episodic retelling of an affair between Gladys Hebe D'Onofrio and Leo Druscovisch—and the problems resulting from their sexually queer desires and dysfunctions. Sexual figurations of both characters are quite intricate.

I begin with a rather touchy scene where Gladys masturbates and remembers all her lovers. Her masturbation and pleasure are related as a fantasy-space, which she then uses to recast a new identity. Unlike most traditional sexual experiences, which require the presence of the other, masturbation eventuates in the unfolding of the Self as the Other. This unfolding is a powerful drama, and its sequel is a recasting of sexual and gender identity. Furthermore, the types of fantasies that Gladys imagines—such as sex with many men, men of color, in particular—are important because they perform not just sexual identities, but also racial and national ones.

To begin, Gladys is a rather dowdy art student who wins a scholarship to study in the United States. This move to the States would help her realize her dream of becoming more cosmopolitan: "en Estados Unidos, como extranjera," ["in the United States, as a foreigner,"], she imagined, "su personalidad se tornaría misteriosa y atractiva, y en alguna recepción mundane conocería a un impetuoso director de orquesta sinfónica, húngaro o austríaco, y posiblemente a un novelista ingles, desencadenándose un inevitable drama triangular."[8] ["her personality would become more mysterious and attractive, and in some mundane reception she would meet an impetuous symphony conductor, Hungarian or Austrian, and possibly an English novelist, thus unfurling an inevitable triangular drama."] This was Gladys's way of looking at the world, there is always a fantasy waiting to happen at the very next moment. She likes the idea of being considered a foreigner, as other. In fact, we learn immediately that "[s]u imaginación siempre prefería personalidades europeas, en general prólugos de algún conflict trágico como la segunda guerra mundial"[9] ["(h)er imagination always preferred European personalities, for the most part, exiles of some tragic conflict like the Second World War"]. In other words, fantasy reigns her life's narratives. This life of imagination and fantasy are products of always having felt marginalized; as a young, precocious seven-year-old, and after reading Hermann Hesse's *Demian*[10] and a number of other novels, she identified "la angustia de existir"[11] ["the anguish of living"] as a condition that would torment her. There is no differentiation between objectivity (the outsider world) and subjectivity (her inner drama). Actually, Gladys's very subjective worldview incorporates and recasts the outside, for example: "A su llegada, Washington estaba cubierta de nieve. La ciudad resultaba el perfecto marco para los sueños que había concebido."[12] ["Upon her arrival, Washington was covered with snow. The city was turning out to be the perfect setting (or frame) for the dreams that she had conceived."] Thus, if "fantasy . . . is not the object of desire, but its setting,"[13] Washington becomes the perfect fantasy par excellence. I will return to this idea of fantasy as the setting for desire in different ways later on.

After the fifteen-month scholarship period was over, Gladys decides to stay in Washington. During the next three years she works as a bilingual secretary, only returning once to Argentina for her father's funeral. While in Argentina, she learns about the professional successes of her former classmates, as well as gossip about those who have gotten married. These successes and marriages nag her all the way back to Washington. One night of insomnia, she decides to take a late night walk, when she is sexually assaulted. As she screams for help, the assailant clubs her face, breaking the bone that forms the arch of her left brow, as well as smashing her eye. Gladys refuses to get a glass eye, preferring instead to have her eye closed. This vicious attack transformed her look. We might ask, "How does she look?" Rather than cover up the memory of the trauma with a glass eye, Gladys—like Oedipus—leaves the ocular injury exposed as an overt sign of a tragic memory, occasionally covering it up with a swash of hair or big sunglasses.[14]

Gladys then moves to New York where, at age thirty, she loses her virginity to a married "gentleman" from Chicago. She begins seeing him on a regular basis, but then he stops visiting New York, and takes business trips to Texas instead; though he asks her to follow him, she prefers to stay in the City:

> Dos semanas después notó que pese al relativo éxito de sus encuentros con el caballero de Chicago, su organismo se había habituado al ataque del cuerpo masculino y por la noche ciertos recuerdos, por ejemplo el cunilingus de que había sido objeto, le quitaban el sueño reproduciéndole el mismo tipo de insomnio sufrido en Washington cuando recordaba el éxito de sus compañeros de estudio argentinos.[15]

> [Two weeks later she noted that despite the relative success of her encounters with the gentleman from Chicago, her organism had become used to the attacks of a masculine body. And in the evening, certain memories, like the cunnilingus of which she had been the object, would keep her awake, producing the same type of insomnia suffered in Washington when she thought of the triumphs of her Argentine classmates.]

She becomes an insomniac as a consequence of remembering and desiring to receive oral sex as well as for remembering her classmates' triumphs (read: her "failures"). That is, desire for oral sex and desire for social conformity—two socially and culturally opposed tendencies—produce the same symptom. In the next four years, Gladys has sexual relations with six men: Frank, the Puerto Rican mulatto, married and with three children; Bob, her former boss from Washington; Lon, a black painter; Danny, a youthful history undergraduate, full of innocence and promise; Ricardo, an unemployed Mexican, who she meets while on vacation in Acapulco; and Pete, her neighbor's husband.[16] Each man gives Gladys something different: Frank gave her spontaneity; Bob, the promise of a future; Lon, the ability to speak of art combined with his "African sensual physique," which attracted Gladys; Danny's youth provided her with the possibility of an open future; the Mexican Ricardo gave her the art of seduction; and Pete fulfilled her need to forget Ricardo.[17] I would like to underscore how each man is so clearly marked by his racial or class identity, which in turn is played up to define Gladys's different needs. Each man's masculinity is heightened or lowered by the racial or class adjective.[18] These different

Epistemerotics 93

masculinities are woven into Gladys's narrative fantasies of identification; they appease and supplement her "anguish of living." However, at this time in her life, none of her relations would make her fantasy of marriage come true—on the contrary, by their very marital or social status, the men she chose would never complete the fantasy narrative of "living happily ever after." She then falls into a severe depression. After a bout with drugs and alcohol, Gladys has a nervous breakdown, and returns to Buenos Aires.

In Buenos Aires, she is cared for by her mother, who takes her to rest at a friend's beach home in Playa Blanca. It is here where chapter IV opens up. The structure of this chapter is quite interesting: Puig uses footnotes to describe the actions Gladys is doing throughout the chapter, while in the main text Puig writes out Gladys's fantasy life. The structure of the chapter is a sort of map, which cannot be read in a straightforward fashion. The footnotes, however, if read in a linear fashion, give us the following story:

*Gladys lleva una mano por debajo del camisón y se acaricia los muslos.
**Gladys sube la mano hasta su vello púbico.[19]
*Gladys introduce la yema de un dedo en su sexo, obteniendo sensación de frío.
**Gladys trata de visualizar el sexo erecto del modelo, sin lograrlo.
***Gladys logra un atisbo de placer.[20]
*Aumenta en Gladys la sensación placentera producida por su propio dedo.[21]
*Gladys se ver obligada a detener la acción de su dedo para evitar un orgasm precipitado.
**Gladys en vano trata de retomar el goce interrumpido.
***Gladys no siente ya ningún placer.[22]
*Gladys presiona su uña contra la piel, como lo hizo Bob antes de poseerla.
**Gladys siente desagradablemente filose la uña de su dedo.
***Gladys retira la mano de su sexo.[23]
*Gladys vuelve a introducer un dedo en su sexo.
**Gladys no logra retomar su placer y coloca las palmas de ambas manos a sus lados, contra el colchón.[24]
*Gladys siente que el sudor creciente de sus axilas le irrita la piel.
**Los nervios de Gladys se aquietan después de secarse las axilas con un borde de la sábana.[25]
*Gladys retoma casi inconscientemente su acción.
**Gladys siente un placer cresciente.

***Gladys logra recorder con exactitude la sensación producida por el pene voluminoso de Frank.²⁶

*Gladys siente que el orgasmo se aproxima.

**Gladys siente que el orgasmo se resiste a comenzar.²⁷

*Gladys recomienza a acariciar su vello púbico.²⁸

*Gladys siente que el orgasmo se declara súbitamente y la inunda.

**Gladys exhala un profundo suspiro de satisfacción.

***Gladys retira la mano de su sexo y silenciosamente se dirige al baño.²⁹

*Gladys siente el acostumbrado dolor de cabeza, que se le presenta de mañana cuando la noche anterior se ha sobreexcitado.³⁰

[*Gladys takes her hand underneath her sleeping shirt and strokes her inner thighs.

**Gladys moves her hand up to the pubic hair.

*Gladys introduces the tips of her fingers in her sex, getting a sensation of coldness.

**Gladys tries to visualize the erect member of the model, without success.

***Gladys achieves a smidgeon of pleasure.

*The sensation of pleasure caused by her own finger grows in Gladys.

*Gladys sees herself obligated to stop the finger action to avoid cumming too quickly.

**Gladys tries in vain to recuperate the interrupted *jouissance* (el goce).

***Gladys no longer feels any pleasure.

*Gladys presses a nail against her skin, as Bob did before possessing her.

**Gladys feels her fingernail to be disagreeably sharp.

***Gladys withdraws the hand from her sex.

*Gladys introduces again her finger into her sex.

**Gladys can't regain her pleasure and puts the palms of her hands at her sides on the mattress.

*Gladys feels that the growing sweat of her underarms irritates her skin.

**Gladys's nerves become calmer after she has dried her underarms with the corner of the sheet.

*Gladys takes up her action again almost unconsciously.

**Gladys feels a growing pleasure.

***Gladys is able to remember with exact detail the sensation produced by Frank's voluminous cock.

*Gladys feels that the orgasm is getting close.

**Gladys feels that the orgasm is stubborn to begin.

*Gladys begins to stroke her pubic hair.
*Gladys feels that the orgasm declares itself all of a sudden and it overwhelms her.
**Gladys exhales a deep sigh of satisfaction.
***Gladys removes the hand from her sex and quietly goes to the bathroom.
*Gladys feels the headache that usually appears the morning after she has been overexcited the night before.]

Each footnote links with a fantasy moment in the "main" text. For example, the first time that Gladys loses her excitation, it is because she realizes that the man she is fantasizing about is married and poor: what kind of life would he give her, she wonders. She is able to get aroused again later as she is thinking about Bob's classic WASP good looks, however, his premature ejaculations turn her off; also, she is thinking about a news report about a woman who has cunnilingus performed on her by her dog: this makes her sweat. She then begins thinking about her Puerto Rican lover and his huge penis;[31] this gets her excited again, but she is not able to reach orgasm (it is "stubborn"). Though she never tells us why she cannot cum, I suspect it is again because of his lower-class status as well as to his being married. Then Gladys gets interrupted by her mother who knocks on the door. So she has to start again. She starts thinking about the undergraduate, Danny, and she becomes aroused again and she moves to reading an orgasm. We are told that it was *not* her time with him, walking in the park or making out in a classroom or riding in a scull, "like those of the Oxford style,"[32] that brings about the orgasm, but rather a memory of "un rayo lo que en plena noche negra le encandiló la retina . . ."[33] ["a lightning bolt that in the middle of a dark night dazzled her retina . . ."], that is, of that night she was assaulted. Her happy memories with Danny are interrupted by the violence of the assault, and it is at this precise moment in her fantasy world that she "all of a sudden" reaches climax. Though it might seem strange that Gladys is rehearsing in her mind images of sex on a scull, this image compacts certain images of success and privilege; furthermore, sex on the scull represents that form of privilege, but in a sexy fashion. Although the scull as a phallic symbol might be what sent her over the edge, nevertheless, she begins the actual orgasm with the rape scene, and this brings images in her mind of a volcano, exploding and sighing. She goes to the bathroom to wash her hands; goes to bed and wakes up with a headache. The next morning the fantasy continues; she thinks of Acapulco "[p]orque en Acapulco la naturaleza regala un marco perfecto a las aventuras amorosas más diversas. Algunas con final feliz y otras no."[34] ["(b)ecause in Acapulco nature gives the perfect framework to the most diverse love adventures. Some with a happy ending and other without."] Again, Gladys uses a framed narrative to give structure and meaning to her life. Despite the fact that the rape scene returns at the very moment of orgasm, thereby producing the idea that sex and violence are somehow always linked in her mind, accessing these framed narratives becomes an act of survival.

It is important to reiterate that Puig places the fantasy narrative as the "main" part of the text, while the masturbatory "action" is relegated to a footnote. This narrative inversion is a signature of Puig's oeuvre—think of the footnotes in *Kiss of the Spider Woman*, for instance.[35] But more importantly, this inversion tells us about the author's understanding about the importance of fantasies and how the subject is submissive to or dependent on them—and not the other way around. Puig's masturbating woman expresses the importance for other sexualities to take the upper hand, how pleasure does not necessarily require the presence of another or others. Masturbation is about sexuality that is nonprocreative. Masturbation is important here too because as a sexual act, it necessarily marks an identity: masturbation permits heteroerotic as well as homoerotic identifications to occur. Masturbation allows literally and figuratively for a fluid identification. The very structure of autoeroticism lets one design a multiple set of identities, which one might like to play out.[36]

Let us return to the fantasy scene: it all begins with Gladys's focusing on the locked door and imagining that it opens and a man comes to her: "él pone un dedo contra los labios y pide silencio, ahora está tan cerca que sus palabras no se oyen en el dormitorio contiguo, me está hablando al oído."[37] ["he puts his finger against her lips and asks for silence, now he is so close that his words can't be heard in the room next door, he is speaking to me in a whisper."] She gets up and notices a light table with a map: "the map of America with the itineraries Buenos Aires–Washington–New York–Los Angeles–San Francisco–New York–Mexico–Acapulco–New York–Buenos Aires, marked with a red pencil."[38] This itinerary takes us back to Freud's schematic of the Wolf Man's memory fragments, where each event (here, each city) compacts a larger history, and it is then connected by a dash. The dash is doubly read as a narrative line that has to be provided to bring the different events into relation with each other, or the dash as a mark of deliberate or active forgetting. In either event, I would stress one important difference between Gladys's and Freud's itineraries: his connects events, states of being, people; hers give us cities.

At this point I would like to take a rather extensive detour, and look at another map before I can explain Gladys's more thoroughly. I am thinking of Marlow's maps in Joseph Conrad's *Heart of Darkness*.

Masturbation and the Postcolonial Detour

I want to concatenate a narrative about the ways in which sexuality and colonial discourses may become intimately bound. Rather than talking about masturbation, I want to use instead the critical language of contact zones. Following Mary Louise Pratt's the notion of contact zones as specifically discursive sites, also by accounting for the asymmetrical nature of the encounters that occur within,[39] I want to meditate on how the discourses of sexuality and coloniality do and can inform each other. In other words, how does coloniality and resistance to it become sexualized? Eventually, I will tie this back up to questions of gender agency found in Gladys's storyline.[40]

Thinking about the master narratives which supply examples of different sexual and (post)colonial discourses, I propose to revisit Freud's primal scene narratives. Freud defines the primal scene as the moment when the young boy sees his parents having sex:

> When he [the patient, at the age of four] woke up, he witnessed a coitus *a tergo* [from behind], three times repeated; he was able to see his mother's genitals as well as his father's organ; and he understood the process as well as its significance.[41]

Freud reveals or unravels the significance of the primal scene as an original fantasy of witnessing one's parents during intercourse and readily "interpreting" this event. What is important to underscore here is the question of understanding the process and its significance:

What does the child understand? To what degree does he understand what he sees? Finally, how does his understanding of the event relate to the Self? The understanding of the primal scene is immediate, but never complete. This immediacy of understanding, this initial conceptualization of the event, will be rewritten over and over. Later, the complex significance of the "primal scene" is presented:

> When the patient entered more deeply into the situation of the primal scene, he brought to light the following pieces of self-observation. He assumed to begin with, he said, that the event of which he was a witness was an act of violence, but the expression of enjoyment which he saw on his mother's face did not fit in with this; he was obliged to recognize that the experience was one of gratification.[42]

That is, the patient's witnessing of his parents during sexual intercourse is an act, which he interprets, on the one hand, as an act of violence (classically) by his father against his mother. On the other hand, "the expression of enjoyment which he saw upon the mother's face," that is, the mother's smile, negates the father's violence; the mother's smile as a "process of gratification" is (mis)read by the patient as the mother's castration of the father: every time the father penetrates the mother, his penis disappears, the mother's joy is interpreted as an act of vengeance. Peter Brooks argues that "in the place of a primal scene we [...] have a primal fantasy, operating *as* event by deferred action."[43] In other words, rather than witnessing *and* understanding, the child witnesses and then projects his interpretation, his fantasy, to explain what he is seeing. This projection of fantasies is repeated over time until the child eventually realizes or grasps a normative understanding of the parent's sexual encounter. Freud notes that this process and arrival of understanding happens through "deferred action"—something similar to Derrida's conceptualization of *différance*. Brooks adds that Freud "consider[ed] that such primal fantasies may have a phylogenic inheritance through which the individual reaches back to the history of mankind, to a racial 'masterplot.'" In other words, Brooks concludes that the primal scene signifies "at [a] crucial moment in the case history [of the Wolf Man] an apparent evacuation of the problem of origins, substituting for a founding event a fantasy of fiction on which is conferred all the authority and force of a prime mover."[44]

I would like to rethink Freud's *urtext* of primal fantasies in the context of our discussion of "contact zones." Pratt proposes the term "contact zones" as a site where negotiations happen. The kinds of negotiations in the contact zones involve struggles for territorial power (space) and modernity (temporal dissonance). These zones are not ready-made nor easily identifiable at the moment of contact, but rather they become manifest though the outrage and resistance against cultural, social, and political impositions. Out of this contextual grappling or dialectic emerges what Fernando Ortíz called "transculturation." Ortíz beautifully gives us his idea of transculturation: "And each immigrant [becomes] uprooted from his or her native land in a double movement of disadjustment and readjustment, of *deculturation* or *exculturation*, and of *acculturation* or *inculturation*, and finally, of the synthesis of transculturation."45 That is, if we understand Ortíz's Marxist-laced concept of transculturation as a complex transmutation from one culture into others and as "historical evolution," also, as a strategy by the oppressed to wield some control over the oppressors' forceful imposition, then transculturation transforms the acts of colonialism, thereby circumventing the direct pressures that follow. According to Pratt, locating and defining the ways in which "transculturation" happens in a postcolonial context serves as a critical gesture that enables her "to avoid simply reproducing the dynamics of possession and innocence."46 Transculturation as a process renders visible the asymmetrical relations inherent in an encounter or contact. Pratt recognizes this phenomenon; thus, she states that "[t]ransculturation is a phenomenon of the contact zone."47

Proceeding from Pratt's and Ortiz's notions, we might argue that the Wolf Man's primal scene contains within it two separate "contact zones," if you like. The first contact zone, the Real one, between two subjects, the father and the mother; the second one, between a witnessing subject and an event, that is, the child and the sex scene itself. This second form of contact is the more provocative relation because it mobilizes the fantasy of understanding; this fantasy initiates the projection of the Self caught up in the other scene, as well as marks the beginning of a chain reaction that culminates in a narrative identification with the Other. After all, the child refunctions the primal fantasy *as a mirror* in which he sees the Self. In other words, the child's gaze gathers and constructs a scene that returns to resignify the Self, or put in another way a scene that constitutes the Self at the very moment it is conjured up.

At this point, I turn our attention to another primal fantasy. I am thinking about Conrad's *Heart of Darkness*, which occupies the position of an *urtext* for colonial studies. I cite from a scene where Marlow, the narrator, remembers how he became interested in exploration:

> "Now when I was a little chap I had a passion for maps. I would look for hours at South America, or Africa, or Australia and lose myself in all the glories of exploration. At the time there were many blank spaces on the earth and when I saw one that looked particularly inviting on a map (but they all look that) I would put my finger on it and say: When I grow up I will go there. The North Pole was one of these places I remember. Well, I haven't been there yet and shall not try now. The glamour's off. Other places were scattered about the Equator and in every sort of latitude all over the two hemispheres. I have been in some of them and ... well, we won't talk about that. But there is one yet—the biggest—the most blank, so to speak—that I had a hankering after."[48]

Marlow's passion for maps leads him to look at them for hours "and lose [him]self in all the glories of exploration," to lose himself in fantasy. I would suggest that this is the primal fantasy of colonialism. The young chap sees himself, projects himself onto the blank spaces or the map. If the Freudian primal scene posits the child's gaze as the origins for the construction of the Self, then the Conradian primal scene presents the child's *lurk* as the beginning of the colonial enterprise. A theory of the gaze has been theorized in psychoanalysis, and circulated in gender, film studies and, even, postcolonial disciplines; certainly postcolonial theory has accounted for the power of the gaze through Foucault's discussion on surveillance and Homi Bhabha's work on mimicry as the internalization of the colonizers' gaze by the colonized.[49] However, I would like to theorize "the lurk" as a special kind of looking within colonial spaces and critiques. The lurk is like the gaze, but it is more aggressive, more demanding, more dangerously violent. The lurking subject does not allow himself to be seen, and he remains silent; that is, he does not identify with the Other. I do not want to do away with Foucault's and Bhabha's discussions; rather, I want to add another strategy that occurs in the project of colonialism: consider my conceptualization of the lurk as a matter of asserting power and relating it to the gaze, a continuity of the gaze.

The next thing we notice in Conrad's very suggestive passage is the chap's obsession with the blankness on the map: "At the time there were many blank spaces on the earth and when I saw one that looked particularly inviting on a map (but they all look that) I would put my finger on it and say: When I grow up I will go there."[50] I want to reread the "blank spaces" twofold; on the one hand, the blank spaces (in Spanish, *los espacios blancos*, or in French *les espaces blancs*) are figures of silence and whiteness, more provocatively stated figures of silence as whiteness, the tacit privilege of whiteness not having to express or explain itself. This can be thought to symbolize the idea of unexplored terrain, which then leads us to the question of "unmarked" space and subjectivity as a sign of privilege. Though whiteness and the unmarked are often identified as one and the same: whiteness is not so much the sign of privilege, but rather being unmarked is. The figure of whiteness can be read, on the other hand, as innocence and virginity, which is how the unexplored terrain becomes gendered "feminine." This reading would link closely to Freud's primal scene—and follows the classic trope of conquest as seduction, which is always heteronormative: the explored territory as a woman's body, the explorer/conqueror as man's gaze and phallus.

Marlow ends his memory with the observation "that there is one [place] yet—the biggest—the most blank, so to speak—that I had a hankering after." That place is, of course, Africa. In the next paragraph, this "most blank" space gets transformed into something different:

> "True, by this time it was not a blank space any more. It has got filled since my boyhood with rivers and lakes and names. It had ceased to be a blank space of delightful mystery—a white patch for a boy to dream gloriously over. It had become a place of darkness. But there was in it one river especially, a mighty river that you could see on the map, resembling an immense snake uncoiled, with its head in the sea, its body at rest curving afar over a vast country and its tail lost in the depths of the land. And as I looked at the map of it in a shop-window, it fascinated me as a snake would a bird—a silly little bird. [He ends the paragraph with the line:] The snake had charmed me."[51]

Again, I want to reiterate that we have before us another primal fantasy. Here, the blankness that once charmed the boy has become a place of darkness, a threatening place. If the "white patch" or blankness of the maps represented in his childhood the very site of identification, then, these dark places now represent the mother's genitals, a dark, forbidden and castrating place. From this that the child lays his gaze elsewhere, on the "immense snake uncoiled," the figure of the father penis, which would allow him to enter that "place of darkness." Indeed, the snake had charmed the boy, and propelled him to imagine his life as an explorer.

As a final commentary to this passage, I would like to note the fact that the child is looking at this map in the shop's window. The boy looks at the map, really "the place of darkness" and the "snake," through a glass, which I suspect might very well be reflecting his own image. The reflection of the boy's face becomes overlapped onto the map—he occupies the place of darkness (the mother) and the snake (the figure of the father). This reflective and reflexive moment is so lovely because it is most emblematic and dramatic of the primal scene. To summarize, the primal scenes are really a series of overlapping fantasies, a palimpsest of fantasies, which seek to represent the story of origins and originality. Bound up in this spectrum of fantasies is the Self who, through a series of identifications and disidentifications, narrates his story. The force of these fantasies deconstructs the pretense of originality—that is, who am I? can I ever know?—and makes problematic the question of referentiality—where do I stand? from where do I speak? In the context of sexuality and psychoanalysis as well as theories which explain the motives of colonialism, we see that these questions are central and they overlap. Indeed, the status of psychoanalysis as a master narrative in the twentieth century affects greatly how we think of the colonial subject. Thus, if the colonial subject is clothed by the story of psychoanalysis, and his mission is to rehearse the project of colonialism as an Oedipal narrative within the framework of the primal scene, what is the postcolonial subject to do? In other words, once you have been penetrated, what is there left to do?

* * *

After this extensive detour, I come back to Gladys's map: "the map of America with the itineraries Buenos Aires–Washington–New York–Los Angeles–San Francisco–New York–Mexico–Acapulco–New

York–Buenos Aires, marked with a red pencil." Rather than a map of potential exploration, Gladys's map tracks *previous* travels. Her map tells a history; Marlow's map forecasts future conquests.

Thinking more about the respective maps: whereas Marlow's map as a site of desire, a prescriptive and aspirational landscape, promises contact with others; Gladys's map is descriptive of her travels and adventures, of her failed contacts with others. Marlow stands before a world of possibilities; Gladys stands before history, more precisely, the map documents the very places where she has grown sexually, her history of sexuality. The man's cartography plots out a primal fantasy of individuation versus the Other; while Gladys's map documents her search for the other (a man) to define her. For Marlow, his map represents contact zones, which have yet to be engaged and that, in their fantasy mode, will be central to a long process of identification and individuation. He will become a man by the time he accomplishes his conquests. The future anterior tense is the setting for his identificatory practices, the sign of (male) privilege. Gladys's "anguish of living"—or as Freud would say about his hysterics, "suffering from reminiscences"—is always expressed by the preterite tense; these backward glances regulate Gladys's narratives of identification. I do not necessarily want to universalize along gender lines my reading of how maps and exploration narratives function in both texts; however, it is important to consider how the history of cartography, as well as framed narratives, have played different roles in the lives of men and women.

Now, if Gladys's map opens this chapter, therein signifying her failures and her "unruly" sexuality, the rest of the chapter, the masturbation fantasy narrative, I argue, helps her recuperate a sense of Self. Fantasy allows her to make adjustments and corrections—in other words, to "reset"—the historicizing impulse of the framing and cartography scenes. This allows Gladys to wield an incredible sense of power, to define her own limits or to transgress those limits placed on her.

Gladys memorializes her sense of Self through the performance and pleasure of the masturbating woman. Interestingly, for Gladys masturbation is an act that brings up happy memories of former seductions, whereas for Leo masturbation rarely leads to any memories, but rather it is just a strictly physical experience, followed by a terrible headache. Again, Gladys is able to trace across the map a series of encounters, and through autoeroticism, she can activate the memory of those encounter to rewrite and reposition herself in that history. Gladys's identity emerges out of that retelling of encounters, out of that history. Marlow always stands outside his map; he is situated in a position outside the map's potential histories. It is important to acknowledge that each subject's very situatedness determines the routes of sexual identity formation. Gladys's history of sexuality comes out from movements across the map; Marlow's history of sexuality retold as a rewriting of the Oedipal narrative (the child's image superimposed over the dark continent and the figure of the coiled snake) is predetermined and imposed on the self—there is no space to rename parts of the map, or to think outside the confines of the map. I would like to think about how a story of the Self originates from the subject's situatedness.

Epistemerotics

Laplanche and Pontalis note that primal scenes all relate to the question of origins: "Fantasies of origins: the primal scene pictures the origin of the individual; fantasies of seduction, the origins and upsurge of sexuality; fantasies of castration, the origin of the difference between sexes."[52] I would underline once more the heteronormativity of these primal scenes. Furthermore, as we have seen in Conrad's text, this heteronormative structure, which underlies the primal scenes, eroticizes very precisely the project and politics of colonialism. To wit, politics becomes erotized by the powerful force of primal narratives— actually, the colonial project becomes heterosexualized. I would stress that the sexual is not applied to the colonial narrative, but rather it is implied within that narrative. This is what I meant at the beginning of this chapter that the political turns sexual, that (post)colonial narratives are inescapably erotic and sexual. Though this critical gesture might seem like a twist on the well established Freudian practice, which reinscribes erotics into the realms of the Self and the political, the very implication of sexual structuration as part of the political would suggest a continuum between both poles. The shuttling move from erotics into politics and back is what I will call "epistemerotics."

Epistemerotics collapses epistemology and erotics—ways of knowing and practices of sexuality. Furthermore, epistemerotics refers to the narratives of gender and sexuality that the Self uses to approximate a desired identity. If the Freudian imperative has been to understand the complex relations through which sexuality produces modes of knowledge, then it is important to grasp how other ways of knowing (politics, culture, economics, for instance) enable certain gender and sexual practices and identifications to be realized. Moreover, with this notion of the epistemerotic, I try to pay *deliberate* attention to the cultural context itself and to the technologies to approximate the socially constructed nature of sexuality.[53] Correlatively, do ways of *unknowing* necessarily challenge the articulation and figuration of sexual/gender identity and difference? In other words, to what degree does the awareness of essentialist identificatory categories of sexuality form and inform a subject's attachment and use of that category with regards to the Self. For example, do the terms *lesbian*, *heterosexual*, or *man* signify the same set of experiences across cultures? How do those experiences get expressed? What binds these experiences under those same labels—"lesbian," "heterosexual," and "man"? Wherein lies the difference? How do these sexual terms get refunctioned to mark sameness and difference?

As I have been arguing, Puig's novels are exemplary texts where gender and sexual naming—some would argue, sexual stereotyping—gets formed, only to be readily destabilized. Examples of this strategy abound in his novels: in *El beso de la mujer araña*, the "oppositional" Valentín and Molina become portrayed as the same by the end of the novel. Leni Lamaison's excessive femininity becomes surprisingly heroic. In *Boquitas pintadas*, Juan Carlos's masculinity, exemplified by his enormous penis as cliché of virility, is subverted by his being sick with tuberculosis, a sign of effeminacy. Also, Nené's obsessive heteronormativity gets questioned by her equally obsessive, adulterous desire for Juan Carlos. Similar examples can be found in *La traición de Rita Hayworth*, and other works. In other words, Puig's textuality is laden with sexual personae whose epistemerotic awareness enters into crisis, a crisis of identification and self-realization. These sexual personae are fundamentally unstable and in motion, always on the verge of becoming (un)knowable. Their identities are situated in that "in-between" domain of opposition between subjectivity and objectivity, in other words, in fantasy.

Talking about masturbation is a messy business. And, you might be asking yourself: What does masturbation have to do with the earlier discussion on primal fantasies? Laplanche and Pontalis locate the origin of fantasy in autoeroticism, by showing the connection between fantasy and desire:

> Fantasy ... is not the object of desire, but its setting. In fantasy the subject does not pursue the object or its sign: he appears caught up himself in the sequence of images. He forms no representation of the desired object, but is himself represented as participating in the scene although, in the earliest forms of fantasy, he cannot be assigned any fixed place in it.... As a result, the subject, although always present in the fantasy, may be so in a desubjectivized form, that is to say, in the very syntax of the sequence in question.[54]

Likewise, masturbation is that moment when "the subject does not pursue the object or its sign: he appears caught up himself in the sequence of images." The subject is not caught up with a fixed notion of the Self, but rather in a relation between the Self and a plethora of images. The Self emerges through these images "in the very syntax of the sequence in question." I would like to conclude this chapter by looking now at Leo's sexual sequence.

Leo's Story

In chapter VI of *The Buenos Aires Affair*, we learn the "Acontecimientos principales de la vida de Leo"[55] ["Principal events in Leo's life"]. What is interesting about this chapter is how it is structured around a series of vignettes such that if we string together the subtitles of the different sections, we come up with the following: "Padre e hijo—Olga y Leo—problemas de adolescencia—Juventud de Leo—Actividades políticas—Actividades laborales—Faz estacionaria—Su hermana mayor—Nueva fase—Regreso de Europa—Estado civil—Éxito profesional de Leo." ["Father and son—Olga and Leo—Problems of adolescence—Leo's youth—Political activities—Work activities—Stationary phase—His older sister—New phase—Return from Europe—Marital status—Professional success."] No doubt by now, this series reconstructs something very similar to Freud's retelling of the Wolf Man. Along the way we learn some of the salient

Epistemerotics 107

circumstances that have affected his emotional life, and why he became impotent. Puig unpacks these vignette titles, and in true psychoanalytic fashion begins linking or opposing them. For example, "Padre e hijo" tells us the incident of his father slapping him for making a dirty gesture and cursing in front of his two sisters, but later his father kissing him "good-night" and saying that it was okay to use "bad words, just not in front of women." Ironically, in this scene the seven-year-old Leo does not even know what "bad" words are. In another scene, "Olga y Leo," the two play the game of "la hormiguita" ["the little ant"], which basically is a tickling game that the twelve-year-old sister plays with her little brother. The "hormiguita" manages to find el "ratoncito" ["little mouse"] and then "the campanitas" ["little bells"], which she rings to the boy's delight. However, when he tries to do the same, she calls him "un niño bocasucia" ["a foul-mouthed boy"]. Later Leo discovers that Olga does not have a "ratoncito" or "campanitas," but rather a "plantita" ["a little plant"]—the adolescent girl slaps him. (As an aside, we might say that the Wolf Man also had a similar experience with his older sister, who touched him, but reacted with anger when he tried to touch her.) One might suggest here that for both boys sexual knowledge is always framed as a cause for punishment. However, his father's kindness and assurance that it is okay to use "bad words" will help him out later on. What is important in Leo's early life is his illiteracy, his inability to read social conventions, unable to understand the codes of gender and sexual difference. This sexual illiteracy allows for his sexual identity formation to proceed in other and unexpected directions.

His adolescence is narrated by a series of sexual events; the most notable includes Leo's decision to stop taking communion because he was embarrassed to talk about his obsessive masturbations. Also, "el tamaño de su órgano sexual era admirado y celebrado por sus compañeros, quienes lo obligaban a exhibirse cada vez que llegaba un nuevo inscripto al colegio."[56] ["the size of his sexual organ was admired and celebrated by his classmates, who forced him to show himself off each time a new student enrolled in the school."] Despite (or because of, or unrelated to) the teenage boys' celebration and romance with the schlong, Leo cannot get it up. His first attempt at fucking is a complete failure. At eighteen, he has his first sexual "encounter." Through a set of weird circumstances, he is caught naked in the women's shower room at school:

> ... una jovencita entró desprevenida. Ambos quedaron inmóviles, la jovencita miró el rostro de Leo y contra su voluntad descendió la mirada hasta el miembro viril. En seguida salió... Leo tenía ya el miembro erecto.[57]

> [... a young woman came in unaware. Both were left frozen, the young woman saw Leo's face, and against her will lowered her gaze to see the virile member. She left right away... Leo already had an erection.]

From here,

> ... Leo todas las noches volvía a sentir la mirada de la muchacha sobre su miembro y no perdonarse a sí mismo el haberla dejado escapar. Se revolcaba en la cama arrepentido y para calmarse imaginaba de muchas maneras diferentes el desarrollo de la escena, la cual terminaba invariablemente en una sangrienta desfloración. Leo cerraba los ojos y al rato su semen se mezclaba en el pensamiento con la sangre de la muchacha.[58]

> [... every night Leo would feel again the girl's gaze over his member, and he wouldn't forgive himself for letting her get away. He twisted and turned in bed regretful and to calm himself, he would imagine the many different ways that scene could have unfolded, invariably ending in a bloody deflowering. Leo would close his eyes and in a little while in his thoughts his semen mixed with the girl's blood.]

What I would like to highlight here is how Leo's sexuality is formed by the young woman's gaze; what provokes pleasure in him is *being looked at*, in effect, being an object of desire.[59] This would explain why the homosocial display of his "man meat" among his male classmates was never a cause of stress or even homosexual panic—Leo is after all an exhibitionist. He derives pleasure from showing it off and being "admired." It is the other's gaze that enables Leo's phallic pleasure. This pleasure almost always culminates in violence. We see this sexual violence in each of the different encounters that Leo has with virgins and prostitutes, and of course with the anonymous blond man.

Epistemerotics 109

Although Leo's sexuality is not heteronormative, his perverse sexual subjectivity does have a logic of its own. I propose that this sexual logic that disrupts "normal" heterosexuality can be related directly to the very structure of narrative that is necessarily nonlinear. Any effort to impose a linearity onto the text, to "straighten out" the narrative, represents another act of violence that forbids new expression of sexual and gender difference. I suspect that this is what Puig was trying to avoid when he stated that he saw "exclusive homosexuality and exclusive heterosexuality as cultural results, not as a natural outcome." In other words, the polar extremes in a sexual spectrum represent a cultural product on which it is not useful to rely. Puig insists on the fullness of sexuality as the liberatory choice.

Bareback appeals

Intriguingly, Puig continues his initial comments for a broader notion of sexuality (cited as the opening epigraph for this chapter) with the following insight:

> If people were really free, I think they wouldn't choose within the limits of one sex. At the same time, I believe in the couple, whether heterosexual and homosexual. I think that with one person you can develop things in time, sex also becomes much, much richer, more refined. I don't mean monogamy necessarily, but . . .[60]

I wish to highlight two separate items: first the idea of a couple as necessary for sexual exploration. It almost seems to invite us to consider that the sexual Self can only flourish in the presence of its other—and vice versa. And second, I am captivated by the final sentence, interrupted: "I don't mean monogamy necessarily, but . . ." The ellipsis is never finished; it remains a fragment, like an open question that invites readers to explore. Monogamy would seem to be just one alternative, one that possibly could arrest sexual developments.

Of all of Leo's others, I want to devote the final section of this chapter to an encounter with a blond man in *el baldío* [open field],[61] in what I would translate as the *terrain vague* of sexuality.

Allow me set up the scene . . . as he was studying, Leo got an unexpected hard-on that kept him from reading further, so he decides to visit a prostitute. After a while, she arrives, and refuses to have sex with him. This angers him, and he walks away with a "laguna total en la cabeza"[62] ["complete lacunae in his head."] As he walks, Leo notices that a "delicado" blond man keeps turning back to see him, this gives Leo a hard-on, and they both take the same bus: "el sujeto se pegó al cuerpo de Leo"[63] ["the subject pushed against Leo's body"]. After Leo gets off, and the young blond follows, Leo asks him angrily what he wants. The other man offers to give him a blow job, an idea that pleases Leo, knowing that he would get sexual release. "El sujeto tomó coraje y dijo que también se dejaría penetrar, si así le proporcionaba más goce"[64] ["The subject gathered courage and said that he would allow himself to be penetrated also, if that would give Leo more pleasure."] I pause here momentarily, and signal that the other man is referred to throughout as "el sujeto."[65] His sense of agency is clear from the very beginning, as it is he who turns around to look at Leo, he is the one who presses his body against Leo's. He is the one who wants to blow Leo, and who even offers to get fucked. Just because he is the "bottom" does not mean that he is not in control; on the contrary, the blond is a greedy bottom who dictates the opening of a sexual transaction.

The men find a dark spot—"el baldío oscuro"—and they go in ... the blond begins sucking Leo off, and

> Leo se separó y le pidió que se bajara los pantalones. El sujeto se negó porque el miembro era muy voluminoso. Leo le agarró un brazo con toda su fuerza y le repitió la orden. El sujeto se bajó pantalones y calzoncillos.[66]

> [Leo moved aside and asked him to pull down his pants. The subject refused because the member was too voluminous. Leo grabbed his arm with all his might and repeated the order. The subject/subjected one pulled down his pants and underwear.]

We notice here how under the forceful grasp by Leo, the "sujeto" ("subject") becomes "sujeto" ("subjected"). Continuing,

> Leo trató de penetrarlo. El otro se debatía y trataba de soltarse. En un momento consiguió desprenderse y se tocó el esfínter: mostró sus dedos ensangrentados a Leo. Éste le pidió que se diera vuelta, esta vez tendría más cuidado. El sujeto se negó.[67]

[Leo tried to penetrate him. The other struggled and tried to break free. In an instant he manage to break away and touched his sphincter: he showed his bloody fingers to Leo. He asked him to turn around, that this time he would be more careful. The subject refused.]

After he is penetrated, the "sujeto" ("the subjected one") becomes "el otro" ("the other"), and again when he frees himself, and refuses going on, he becomes again the "sujeto" ("subject"). It is this to and fro of subjectivity—from subject to subjected to other—what may be called a queer *assujetissement*. The reclaiming of his own agency and subjecthood by the blond man ultimately angers Leo, and he goes on to rape him.

Leo no pudo contenerse y recomenzó el vaivén, tapando la boca del otro con una mano. El sujeto se debatía. Leo comenzó a sentir su placer en aumento, le acarició el pelo de la nuca. El otro no soportó más el tormento e hincó los dientes con todas sus fuerzas en la mano que lo amordazaba. Leo desesperado de dolor por el mordisco que no cedía vio un ladrillo al alcance de su mano y se lo aplastó contra la cabeza. El otro aflojó la presión de los dientes y Leo prosiguió el coito, la estrechez del conducto anal le proporcionaba un deleite nuevo, en seguida le sobrevino un orgasmo, murmurando "decime que te gusta, decime que te gusta."[68]

[Leo couldn't contain himself and started up again that back-and-forth struggle, covering up the other's mouth with his hand. The subject struggled. Leo began to feel a growing pleasure, he caressed the hair on his neck. The other couldn't bear any longer the pain and forcefully bit the gagging hand. In great pain from the bite that wouldn't let go, Leo saw a brick within reach and smashed it against the head. The other's bite loosened all pressure, and Leo carried on with the coitus, the narrowness of the anal duct brought him new delights, an orgasm ensued right away, while whispering "tell me you like it, tell me you like it."]

The other man was foaming at the mouth, dead. In the end, Leo's pleasure "ya en las vetas supremas, se empañó muy pronto falto de un ulterior rechazo por parte del otro"[69] ["already in its supreme stages, became foggy quickly by the lack of a subsequent rejection

112 *The Avowal of Difference*

by the other."] Let me try to unpack this scene of horrible violence and pleasure, or as Leo would have it, violence as pleasure. The contradictions of feeling are quite striking—as he rapes the man and his pleasure grows, Leo caresses the other man's neck. This coming together of violence and tenderness only heightens the violence.[70] Also, the tightness of the man's ass provides Leo a new delight, also it gives Leo a new identity. Of course the ultimate perverse moment is when Leo insists "tell me you like it, tell me you like it." Here he is soliciting the affirmation by the other: he wants the other to tell him that he is a good fuck—by extension, a real man. Of course, the other can no longer respond. This lack of response by the other—either as an affirmation ("tell me you like it") or as that inevitable rejection ("un ulterior rechazo")—takes away Leo's fleeting moment of pleasure. I am going to go out on a limb, and claim that this idea of response is precisely what Puig meant when he proposes the figure of the "couple" as an ideal—not monogamy, but pushing the limits, within the realm of consent, he said, "Just as long as it's not offensive to the other party." Puig may be calling for an ethic of sexuality that permits a broader re-creation of sexual identities. Leo's newfound pleasure in the other man's tight hole fails because he is unwilling to respond as well, he is unable to respect the limits set by the other. He cannot bear the other's pain.

Remembering back

In the brief vignette titled "Actividades políticas" we learn more about Leo's anti-Perón politics. He becomes involved with the Communist Party, and gets arrested "en circunstancias comprometedoras" ["in a compromising position"]. The agents torture him, and even threaten to electrocute his groin, and he finally speaks . . . before such violence, he collapses and worries that he might become a "sexual invalid." Then, "[c]uando vio que uno de los agentes volvía a enrollar el cable [de la picana eléctrica], Leo pensó si el sujeto del baldío antes de morir habría sufrido tanto como él"[71] ["(w)hen he saw that one of the agents started to roll up the cable (of the electric prod), Leo wondered if the subject in the open field had suffered as much as he was suffering."] The threat of castration makes him speak. Moreover, when he sees that the prod (a symbol of phallic police authority) is being put away, he thinks of the man he had murdered, and wonders narcissistically if that other man suffered as much as he was suffering at that moment. The directionality of the identification implicit in Leo's question is important here: he asks *not* whether the "I" identifies with the dead man (am I feeling what he felt?), *but rather* whether the other is like him? By extension, Leo does not ask whether he is like the gay man, but rather is the gay man like him. This is the exhibitionist's imperative: does the other identify with me?—not that it would really matter in the end.

What we have here is not a normal sequence of events—which would be stated in such a way that the pain suffered by the young man in the murder scene gets experienced later on by Leo at hands of the police. Instead, in Leo's mind, the relation between the murder scene and the torture is represented in reverse order; that is there is a retroactive rewriting presented here, whereby the earlier event would seem to follow the later one. This is precisely the kind of narrative "adjustments" that describe Freud's understanding of history to the service of the present. More specifically, I would propose that what is at stake in this torture scene is Leo's masculinity. He wonders whether the blond victim suffered as he was suffering at that moment—stated differently, whether the victim "suffered" the pain as he did. Suffering both signifies experiencing pain and *allowing*. To experience the pain and to allow the pain to rescript the Self is a cultural trope for adopting and writing a particular version of masculinity;[72] thus, Leo's torture scene where he reflects on the homophobic crime he committed could never be seen as a moment of repentance for killing the other man, but really and simply is an enactment of masculinity to counteract the violence he is experiencing under the police.

The young man in the empty lot becomes for Leo a memory-fragment, which he activates to make the threat of castration bearable. He needs to recast himself in an empowered and masculine position, literally to make himself a rapist and killer (as particular figurations of *machismo*) again, in order to resist the police brutality. Sexual "memory" gets twisted, and traverses the political—and, importantly, allows the resistance of political reality. This maneuvering is what is at play in Leo perverse reconstruction—and it might help us begin to understand the distorted logic that happens when the fields of sexuality and politics traverse each other.[73]

Scenes of Queer Heterosexuality

I opened this chapter citing Puig's call for a "total sexuality," one in which exclusive homosexuality and exclusive heterosexuality is a "cultural," rather than a "natural," event. That is, sexuality unfolds as a cultural phenomenon, rather than as a strictly biological drive. Moreover, I would add that culture and space impinge on how that sexuality is framed and narrated. I have tried to show that Gladys's masturbation fantasies, as well as Leo's exhibitionist pleasures recast the sexual personae of each, and I would here extend that we appreciate how normative heterosexuality traverses into a realm of sexual queerness. What Gladys's and Leo's experiences reveal is that sexual silences surround "heterosexuality" in much the same ways as the silence around homosexuality. Gladys's autoeroticism (relegated to the footnotes) and Leo's homoerotic criminality (deliberately forgotten and later taken up to activate his masculinity) are instances where sexual identification and identity extend the practices and meanings of heterosexuality—and approach Puig's notion of a "total sexuality." Queerness, then, must be understood as social and cultural (and perhaps racial and class) modulations on those fixed identities that exclusive "heterosexuals" and "homosexuals" fetishistically purport as stable and knowable. Thus, in *The Buenos Aires Affair*, queerness extends the practices of heterosexuality, making it a thing that is at times unrecognizable and uncanny.

5
La Manuela's Return
Travestism/Identification/the Abject in Lemebel's *Loco afán*

> La poética del sobrenombre gay, generalmente excede la identificación, desfigura el nombre, desborda los rasgos anotados en el registro civil. No abarca una sola forma de ser, más bien simula un parecer que incluye momentáneamente a muchos, a cientos que pasan alguna vez por el mismo apodo.
>
> —Pedro Lemebel, *Loco afán*

Primal Scenes: From Illegibility to Illegitimacy

If the ending of José Donoso's masterpiece, *El lugar sin límites* (translated as *Hell Has No Limits*)[1] appears to us somewhat enigmatic, especially as we think about the "death" of La Manuela, the novel's heroine, then the rewriting of the transvestite figure in the essays of Pedro Lemebel would affirm with certainty La Manuela's survival and her ways of being. Let us return to the scene of the crime when the very macho Pancho Vega and his brother-in-law Octavio corner La Manuela, then attack her violently and homophobically:

> ... lo encontraron y se lanzaron sobre él y lo patearon y le pegaron y lo retorcieron, jadeando sobre él, los cuerpos calientes retorciéndose sobre la Manuela que ya no podia ni gritar, los cuerpos pesados, rígidos, los tres una sola masa viscosa retorciéndose como un animal fantástico de tres cabezas y múltiples extremidades heridas e hirientes ...[2]

> [... they found him and jumped on him and kicked and beat him and twisted him, panting over him, the hot bodies writhing on top of la Manuela so that she couldn't even scream, the heavy bodies, rigid, the three one single viscous mass twisting like a fantastic animal with three heads and multiple wounded and hurt extremities ...]

I have already commented on this scene elsewhere, speaking of how La Manuela's transvestite's body functions as a screen on which the men are able to project and impose their identities and fantasies.[3] The transvestite body would be that other space where the subject can play out and play with his otherness. I have argued that once that identificatory fantasy has realized, the subject may then choose to dispose of the transvestite's body, thus producing the "death" of the transvestite. The ending of *El lugar sin límites* is enigmatic, as I've said above, because in the final chapter of the novel we find la Japonesita waiting for her father to return, since he already "[le] ha hecho esto otras veces"[4] ["had done this [to her] on other occasions"]. Despite the violence in the previous scene, given la Manuela's ways and in la Japonesita's mind, la Manuela's return would appear less doubtful. I will argue that it precisely in the works of Pedro Lemebel where we see again the unbridled reemergence of such a transvestite figure and persona, after having been so repressed in Chilean and Latin American letters. It is not surprising that Lemebel himself would have said in an interview that

> lo único que podría interesarme a estas alturas del siglo [veinte] es, de toda esa mugre que leí en el colegio y que no voy a leer de nuevo, lo único—y más como actuación de sujeto, por su teatralidad—es la Manuela, en *El lugar sin límites*, de Donoso. Creo que es lo único que podría interesarme y como construcción de un sujeto teatral.
>
> I think that the only thing that can interest me at this moment is—of all the shit I read at school and that I would not read again—the only thing, and mostly for its theatricality, is Manuela in *El lugar sin límites* (*Hell Has No Limits*), by José Donoso. I think that she is the only one who could interest me, as construction, as a theatrical subject.[5]

It would be fair to say that la Manuela serves as a literary model for so many of the characters in Lemebel's *Loco afán* [Mad Desire],[6] among them: La Regine, La Madonna, la Pilola Alessandri, Loba Lamar, and others. La Manuela is that "theatrical subject" that (in)forms the construction of transvestite subjectivity in Lemebel's work. Theatricality as such is the idea of putting on and removing different masks to effect diverse and possibly new identities. This proliferation of transvestite theatricality to remake new identities blows up in a chapter titled "Los mil nombres de Maria Camaleón"[7] ["The Thousand Names of Maria Chameleon"], which ends with a litany of names and playful nicknames (sometimes even mean-spirited)—names like la Desesperada, la Cuando No, La María Felix, la Fabiola del Luján, la Sui-Sida, la Depre-Sida, and la Ven-Sida. We notice the use of the feminine article "la," which both emphasizes the femininity of the subject as well as it marks the lower-class status of the subject (Maria versus la Maria, we know that in common speech, the use of the article before the name is a class marker). Some of the transvestite names are those of famous Chilean "transformistas" (Fabiola del Luján), others are movie divas (María Felix), still others are comical names like the desperate one and the "when not?" The last three names I have listed are macabre puns—suicide, depression, and defeat. Each of the names is split to highlight a medical condition—SIDA, that is AIDS—and the possible consequences from having that condition.

Yet before examining the many figurations and namings of transvestism in *Loco afán*, I would like to return to Donoso's text and analyze that scene where we find those writhing bodies, one against and with the other. We might begin by this twisting and turning of bodies points toward and signifies a trope (at the expense of being tautological: the etymology of trope signifies twist or turn). In other words, transvestism itself is a kind of trope.[8] The corporealization of transvestism becomes manifest in that indecipherable "sola masa" ["single mass"]. Moreover, this scene becomes more problematic to read as other bodies pile on top of the transvestite, thus creating a "single viscous mass," which we might say represent a primal scene (*Urszenen*). A primal scene is that traumatic event witnessed by a child who can neither comprehend what he or she is seeing nor internalize it at the moment it is happening. A series of events or interpretations are organized around that scene, and out of this organization, the child begins giving meaning to the original event. The classic example that Freud offers to explain primal scenes is when parents are caught in the sex act. This scene presents itself for the child to decipher it, and hence define him- or herself as a subject in relation to this event. This moment signals entrance into the Oedipal drama. What is important to remember about primal scenes, what characterizes them, is their initial illegibility. Allow me to recap and continue with a more in-depth discussion of Freud's notion of primal scenes, which I introduced in the previous chapter. In that scene of witnessing, Freud writes that the Wolf Man:

> He assumed to begin with, he said, that the event of which he was a witness [his parents engaged in the sexual act *a tergo*] was an act of violence, but the expression of enjoyment which he saw on his mother's face did not fit in with this, he was obliged to recognize that the experience was one of gratification. What was essentially new for him in his observation of his parents' intercourse was the conviction of the reality of castration . . .[9]

By witnessing the sexual act, the boy initially thinks that the father is violently attacking his mother from behind; however, her smile of pleasure makes him think that it is she who is castrating the father, since every time that he penetrated her, his penis would disappear, thus making quite real the threat of castration. In such a way, the father's violence becomes reversed, and becomes the mother's violence. These forms of violence become fused and confused, especially since they do not harmonize with the pleasure that both the father and the mother show respectively. Only retroactively through deferred action is how this primal scene will come to acquire its true meaning. What interests me is understanding the process by which these primal scenes get read, and to see which elements are selected by the witness/author/subject in the self-figuration of the "I."

That viscous mass—one single body composed of La Manuela/Pancho/Octavio—represents that palimpsest of bodies that cannot be differentiated or defined clearly, it becomes seen as something "like a fantastic animal with three heads and multiple wounded and hurt extremities." Beyond the bodily illegibility, the actions that these bodies are exerting one on the other also cannot be read with much certainty. That is, the panting and moaning of those "hot writhing bodies" can be read both as acts of violence as well as pleasure. Donoso's text continues describing those three bodies bound together:

... buscando quién es el culpable, castigándolo, castigándola, castigándose, deleitados hasta en el fondo de la confusión dolorosa, el cuerpo endeble de la Manuela que ya no resiste, quiebra bajo el peso, ya no puede ni aullar de dolor, bocas calientes, manos calientes, cuerpos babientos y duros hiriendo el suyo y que ríen y que insultan y que buscan romper y quebrar y destrozar y reconocer ese monstruo de tres cuerpos retorciéndose, hasta que ya no queda nada y la Manuela apenas ve, apenas oye, apenas siente, ve, no, no ve ...[10]

[... looking for who is guilty, punishing him, punishing her, punishing oneself, delighted to the depths of that painful confusion, La Manuela's feeble body that can't resist any longer breaks under the weight, she can no longer howl in pain, hot mouths, hot hands, salivating and hard bodies wounding hers and that laugh and that insult and that seek to rip and break and destroy and recognize that monster of three bodies writhing, until there is nothing left and la Manuela can barely see, barely hear, barely feel, she sees, no, she doesn't ...]

Right away we notice that the language and grammar of this scene requires that we reread the scene to figure out who's doing what. We see how the men want to rip asunder that fantastic and monstrous figure; they want to differentiate themselves from that monster of which they are part, thereby eliminating any implication that can be made of them being with La Manuela. In other words, Pancho and Octavio want to make their identity *as heterosexual men* legible at any cost, even (or especially) at the expense of violence against the transvestite. It is commonplace to say that heterosexual masculinity defines itself through homophobia and transphobia, by eliminating different bodies "until there is nothing left" of what is different.[11] The men (like the boy witnessing the parental scene of sexual and gender unknowing) have to identify and incorporate those elements of the primal scene to self-figure their sense of self and to construct their masculinity. Obviously, the process of picking and choosing an identity also contains a tacit exclusion or expulsion of what is undesired. Again, Freud defines identification as "the earliest expression of an emotional tie with another person."[12] The person may become a model or object choice. As objects, they become introjected into the "I," that is, the object becomes integrated in the psychic orbit of the self by means of the copy, consumption, perversion, or other forms.

Importantly, Freud underscores that "the identification is a partial and extremely limited one and only borrow a single trait from the person who is its object."[13] He recognizes identification as a structure where the "I" consumes the other, and defines itself through this process. It is essential to underscore that identification is a partial practice, through which the "I" identifies with a singular element—or better said, a limited element—of the other—and here I would extend it to the primal scene. If we imagine the primal scene as a type of mirror, the child only reflects on (or sees himself reflected in) certain details of the scene—and not in its entirety, since such a thing would be an impossibility. Out of those discrete identificatory fragments unfolds a new narrative of the "I" that will follow other imaginary paths. The particular identifications blossom into a full-fledged narrative of the self. What Freud does not comment on directly are those parts of the primal scene that are *not* integrated into the figuration of the subject, that is, those elements of the primal scene with which the self does not identity: What happens to those elements? Are they displaced? How? Are they repressed? In fact, it would seem as though that which is not identified with simply disappears—or rather it gets relegated to a passive plane in the constitution of the subject. In a similar manner, Butler notes that "[i]dentifications ... can ward off certain desires or act as vehicles for desire; in order to facilitate certain desires, it may be necessary to ward off others: identification is the site at which this ambivalent prohibition and production of desire occurs."[14] Butler also recognizes that identifications are partial and that they represent a site of ambivalence where desire may be produced and forbidden. In this model the "I" is constituted by a series of drives.

 I would like to comment on the way in which Butler speaks of the role that ambivalence plays within identification. I would argue that the production as much as the prohibition of desire cannot be expressed as mere ambivalence (a casual accidental process), but rather that I would argue that at a particular or determined moment a sense of agency emerges; this agency defines the production and prohibition of desire in a very active and deliberate way. That is, when the subject chooses to identify with a particular object, equally he may want to expel another one. Thus, when Pancho and Octavio beat up on la Manuela, they are expelling her from their psychic configurations.

Expulsion as mode identification would lead us to see that the men are actively identifying with the things that they do not want to be or become. Nevertheless, the act of violence (that masculinist aggression itself) is indeed something with which they do identify. Therefore, we could postulate that the illegibility and ambivalence of the primal scene through which identifications happen are not always considered part of the primal scene in its totality, but rather that illegibility and ambivalence are linked and located deliberately within certain bodies. Elements from this scene are forcefully excluded, thrown out from the individual and social imaginary. In other words, the primal scene is not only characterized for being illegible, but more correctly within it there are elements that are defined as illegitimate since they cannot (or they are not allowed to) have a place in the construction of the "I." We can then move on to understand primal scenes as first being illegible in their totality to having illegitimate components and bodies in their partiality. If we return to the scene of violence where La Manuela is being beaten by the men, we can see that Pancho and Octavio are "looking for who is guilty, punishing him, punishing her, punishing oneself, delighted to the depths of that painful confusion." To conclude, identification can be read as much for its potentiality of celebratory imitation, a (self)recognition and renaming in and through the other, as for a scene of punishment and violence.

The names of *la loca*

Pedro Lemebel's texts try to read and legitimize the transvestite body. It is in this effort that we can see the necessity of naming and renaming to give recognition and legitimacy to those bodies previously excluded from the national imaginary. It is important to underscore how the author conceives this project of naming; Lemebel writes that,

> Así, el asunto de los nombres, no se arregla solamente con el femenino de Carlos; *existe una gran alegoría barroca que empluma, enfiesta, traviste, disfraza, teatraliza o castiga la identidad a través del sobrenombre.* Toda una narrativa popular del loquerío que elige seudónimos en el firmamento estelar del cine. Las amadas heroínas, las idolatradas divas, las púberes doncellas, pero también las malvadas madrastras y las lagartijas hechiceras. Nombres adjetivos y sustantivos que se rebautizan

continuamente de acuerdo al estado de ánimo, la apariencia, la simpatía, la bronca o el aburrimiento del clan sodomita siempre dispuesto a reprogramar la fiesta, a especular con la semiótica de nombre hasta el cansancio.¹⁵ (Emphasis mine.)

[Thus, in the matter of (transvestite) naming, it can't be easily fixed with the feminine of Carlos. *There is a great Baroque allegory puts feathers on, dolls-up, cross-dresses, disguises, dramatizes or punishes identity through the sobriquet.* An entire popular narrative of queendom (*loquerío*) chooses pseudonyms based on cinema's star system. The beloved heroines, the idolatrized divas, the virginal maidens, but also the evil stepmothers and the envious witches. Proper names and adjectives that re-baptize continuously according to the state of being, the appearance, the charm, the anger or the boredom of the sodomite clan, always willing to reschedule the party, to speculate with the semiotics of naming until exhaustion. (Emphasis mine.)]

Naming the queer or the transvestite can't be accomplished by simply exchanging the masculine name or ending for a feminine one—from Carlos to Carlota, from Mario to María), a simplistic exercise of putting the letter *a* at the end to denote the Spanish feminine. Rather, as Lemebel point out, it's a matter of engaging with a Baroque allegory, the act of extending the name metaphor *ad infinitum*, to twist and turn the name so that it gets baptized continuously. In other words, the drag queen's (or the drag queer's) name never stops signifying (or resignifying itself) until exhaustion. We remember Harold Bloom's insight about poetic language: "The word *meaning* goes back to a root that signifies 'opinion' or 'intention,' and is closely related to the word *moaning*. A poem's meaning is a poem's complaint ..."¹⁶ If we take into account that the metaphor represents poetic language par excellence, we must also think that its meaning is expressed as a moan, a complaint (a calling and folding together). An allegory defined as an extended metaphor comes to represent that moaning, an endless gasp that aspires interminably to other significations.

Going back to Lemebel's quote, we notice that that "great Baroque allegory" does a lot of work: it "puts feathers on, dolls-up, cross-dresses, disguises, dramatizes and punishes identity." *Emplumar*, "to put feathers on," is the mark of homosexuality, but also *emplumar* gives us the sense of "putting into writing." The Baroque figuration continues, naming "dolls-up, cross-dresses, disguises" identity; this gesture is an allusion to Severo Sarduy.[17] Finally, the Baroque allegory of giving a sobriquet or nickname "dramatizes or punishes," that is, the naming becomes a performance, a cause for celebration, or a punishment that both frees and disciplines the subject. By defining the queen's or queer's sobriquet as a Baroque allegory, Lemebel would seem to be advancing that identification is much more dynamic than previously imagined. Here, I would argue that Freud and Butler zero in on the language of identification as a constative approximation and not overtly as a metaphor, whereas Lemebel's model seems to engage with the process of identification in a more outlandish Baroque and metaphoric language. Lemebel highlights this dynamic and over-the-top identification in a quote that serves as epigraph to this chapter: "La poética del sobrenombre gay, generalmente excede la identificación, desfigura el nombre, desborda los rasgos anotados en el registro civil."[18] ["The poetics of the gay sobriquet, generally speaking, exceed identification; these poetics disfigure the name, they overflow (or unweave) the recorded information in the civil registry."][19] The name of the father (predominant in the civil registry) becomes disfigured under the poetic mark of the sobriquet: to name oneself or another differently is a gesture that exceeds the general economy of identification—this has to do with the fact that for Lemebel the sobriquet is always understood as a metaphor. This new form of identification, that is, identification through metaphor, "[n]o abarca una sola forma de ser, más bien simula un parecer que incluye momentáneamente a muchos, a cientos que pasan alguna vez por el mismo apodo."[20] ["not only encompasses a single form of being, but rather it mimics an appearance that includes many at the same time, hundreds of images that go through it with the same nickname."] In other words, the primal scene constructed by the tangle among la Manuela, Pancho and Octavio is no longer a matter of identifying the one singular version of the self, of identifying that thing of and in la Manuela, which the men want to get rid of. Rather in that primal scene, it is about identifying the many metaphoric significations—explicit and tacit—that hide in the name and body of la Manuela. The process of identification through and against the transvestite (metaphoric) name leads us to consider that the "I" is attracted by the multiple meanings or signifieds under the transvestite sobriquet/signifier. These other meanings are tucked away—and it's the identifying subject's privilege and pleasure to uncover them. Moreover, thinking about the language of identification explicitly as a metaphor allows the possibility of the subject to acquire many strategies to become other or many others. For some identifying subjects, this multiplication and dispersion of identity might just be a strategy of survival. And why not? After all, survival takes on an important and central sense of urgency in the Lemebelian oeuvre, since most of his transvestite subjects in *Loco afán* are facing poverty, death, and AIDS.

Writing (from) that no-place

Up to now, we have been discussing how the "I" gets formed through a complex process of identification. The "I" creates a bond with the object, in that very relational bonding what is deployed is a process of actively affirming and integrating certain parts of the object while actively excluding others. I would like to insist that those exclusions in identification are cultural gestures that point toward the production of what is illegitimate. If initially identification stems from an initial illegibility, a misreading, of the primal scene, then throughout the deferred process of identification a new topography of the self is drawn out that not only identifies an official and integral "I," but also contains the other whose illegibility gets cast as illegitimacy. That illegitimate figuration is never a simple discrete object as such, since all that is illegitimate clamors to be recognized and also written.[21]

The self gets narrated—and clears out all messiness in an effort to getting centered and being anchored. Following Lemebel's critique of drag and queer naming, I have propose that the language in identification is not always constative, but metaphoric instead. This is the place where Lemebel makes his most trenchant critique. In the same interview, he comments on gay Latin American literature, especially on the gay subject that this literature tends to configure and promote:

> Bueno, acá en Latinoamérica hay una vuelta de mano de este marco redecorado del barroco, y también—por ese lado—este barroquismo coincide en su forma medio burguesa con cierta literatura gay neoliberal de ahora, Jaime Bayly, por ejemplo, que escribe desde el lugar más

repugnante de la sociedad limeña, desde esa burguesía heredera de virreyes y toda esa mugre, en un país donde la pobreza es tan violenta. Ahí mi corazón está a ese lado, mi corazón de una loca se tiñe con las tristezas del pueblo, hay un gesto de generosidad que dobla el narciso del homosexual que se adora a sí mismo en el espejo. Como dice Puig, el amor homosexual siempre pasa por un verse a sí mismo en el otro, claro, te encanta ese hombre metro ochenta porque es lo que quieres ser, te adoras a ti mismo en ese otro, tú no construyes un otro. La película basada en la historia de Manuel Puig me pareció genial, genial. O sea, no hay una construcción de un otro. En *El beso de la mujer araña* de alguna manera está esa tesis, cuando se descoloca la marica por la guerrilla, a pesar de. Entonces, *a mí me interesa eso, sobre todo en estos juegos de sujetos, me interesa hacer brillar ese lugar ausente en la homosexualidad latinoamericana porque es un travestismo pobre.* (My emphasis.)

Well, here in Latin America there is a new twist on this, performed with baroque flair and also—along these lines—this baroque has the same sort of bourgeois style as some neoliberal gay literature that we see in Jaime Bayly, for example, who writes from the position of the most disgusting social class in Lima, that bourgeoisie whose ancestors were viceroys and all that crap, in a country where poverty is so aggressive. In this case my heart is on this side, a fag's heart shaded with the sadness of the people. It is a feeling of generosity that supersedes the narcissism of the homosexual who admires himself in the mirror. Like Puig says, homosexual love always goes through a stage of seeing oneself in another. Of course, you love that six-foot-tall man because he is what you want to be, you love yourself in the other; you don't construct another. I think the film they made based on Manuel Puig's story was wonderful, just wonderful. The thing is that there is not a construction of another. In *El beso de la mujer araña* (*Kiss of the Spider Woman*) that's the thesis you find, where the fag gives up who she is to become a guerrilla, in spite of everything. *So, that's what interests me, especially in these games of subjects; I like to make that absent place in Latin American homosexuality shine because it is the place of a poor transvestism.*[22] (Translation modified; my emphasis.)

I begin with the end of this quote, above all noticing how the author defines his social and political space, and situates himself therein. That trope of "hacer brillar ese lugar ausente" ["making that absent place shine"] dovetails perfectly with the practice of identification whereby what is sought is the very thing that is left unsaid, what cannot be seen—that is, to recognize what is illegitimate. Importantly, Lemebel does not speak of the absent place *of* homosexuality, but more exactly he speaks of the absent place *in* homosexuality. In other words, he identifies (with) what is marginal to the margins, what can be properly called the abject. "Poor transvestism"—or really, the locas that star in *Loco afán*[23]—is that doubly marginalized figure, twice forgotten, that he wishes to rescue from oblivion. Lemebel is trying to displace that object of desire that looms six feet tall next to the Latin American gay "I." That object of desire, "tall and handsome," that traffics in the global gay male imaginary is a narcissistic distortion of the Latin American gay self. We might be able to extend Lemebel's critique and imagine that he is suggesting that, by desiring the "tall and handsome" gay ideal, the gay Latin American subject is always already in a position of inferiority before his desire.[24]

Therefore, if the Latin American gay subject cannot see himself in the other, what are the role models available for self-figuration? Furthermore, continuing with Lemebel's suggestion that it is necessary to find "that absent place in Latin American homosexuality," it also essential to recognize and acknowledge other homosexual expressions that get excluded from the project of gay self-figuration, thus, avoiding further marginalization of those who have always been marginalized. That is to say, it is fundamental to question the normalization of the neoliberal gay subject who wishes to accommodate himself inside mainstream culture—this is what Lisa Duggan denominates as "homonormativity." She defines homonormativity as "a politics that does not contest dominant heteronormative assumptions and institutions but upholds and sustains them while promising the possibility of a demobilized gay constituency and a privatized depoliticized gay culture anchored in domesticity and consumption."[25] Homonormativity is part of a neoliberal gay agenda that promotes such values as gay marriage, being "just like everyone else" (that is, "normal"); however, in order to realize such a stabilization of the gay subject, the gay "community" and its politics have had to resort precisely to making certain "exclusions" that it feels do not represent its interests. It is at this juncture that Lemebel introduces "poor transvestism" as a figure of double marginalization, as a space from which he can articulate and launch his cultural analysis and critique.

It is not surprising to hear his criticism of Peruvian author Bayly.[26] Lemebel has already criticized other rarified tendencies in Cuban and Argentine gay writing that ignore certain social realities in Latin America.[27] Having said this, I do not want to fall into a trap and claim (or reduce) Latin American homosexualities as being poorer, and thus move on to a description of homosexuality that only focuses on matters of class.[28] A class analysis of homosexuality might be quite be quite valuable indeed, but immediately one would have to add another layer of critique that accounts for questions of colonialism. Let us not forget that *Loco afán* has the following epigraph: "La plaga nos llegó como una nueva forma de colonización por el contagion."[29] ["The plague came to us like a new form of colonization through contagion."] Accordingly, it would be necessary to consider how coloniality impinges on the construction of gay subjects in the Americas. Thus, my reading of Lemebel tries to discern and articulate theoretically those spaces and subjects that represent a type of (sexual) gap or ellipsis in the sexual cartography of the Latin American gay subject—I am interested in those no-places of identity, those nonbeings (imagined by Lemebel as "poor transvestisms") or those *sujets-manqués*, where what is abject emerges as a new kind of subjectivity.

Strategies for other histories of sexuality

I would like to use the figure of the palimpsest as an analytic tool to help us understand that multiple layers that form gay identity in Lemebel's work. I will consider the queers' HIV-positive status as a detour from homonormativity and as means to understand how they construct their identities. In these final two sections of this chapter, I would like to read two memorable chronicles—"La noche de los visones" ["The Night of the Minks"] and "La Regine de Aluminios El Mono"—to explore how the Chilean author forges and narrates that *loca* identity that puts into play the different layers of that subjectivity.

"La noche de los visones" takes us to a December party in 1972 in front of the UNCTAD, a building constructed months earlier by the Chilean government for a meeting of the United Nations Conference on Trade and Development (UNCTAD). This structure now serves as a background where the locas are zigzagging around "con miradas lascivas y toqueteos apresurados" ["with lascivious stares and rushed fondling"] among "esos músculos proletarios en fila, esperando la bandeja del comedor popular."[30] ["those proletarian muscles waiting in line of the mess hall.] The mise-en-scène is ironic without a doubt, given that months earlier the meeting of delegates and representatives of the United Nations was characterized as wasteful and corrupt.[31] Thus, after the UN parties, comes the glaring political reality of Chile in 1972, and what strikes us is poverty and hunger. It is here where la Palma had promised the other queens a party to welcome the new year. At this party arrives la Pilola Alessandri, who shows up putting on airs with a mink coat from the House of Dior in the middle of the summer. La Chumilou joins her, along with many others. The party is a great hit even though by the time that la Pilola Alessandri and la Chumilou arrive all the food is gone. The queens had begun gathering all the bones to create "una gran pirámide, como una fosa común que iluminaron con velas" ["a great pyramid, like a common grave that they lit with candles"]; someone put a small Chilean flag at "el vertice de la siniestra escultura"[32] ["the apex of sinister sculpture"]. This detail angered la Pilola Alessandri who "indignada dijo que era una falta de respeto que ofendía a los militares que tanto habían hecho por la patria"[33] ["indignant said that it was a lack of respect towards the military who had done so much for the country"]—she wanted to leave, but could not find the mink coat.

The following morning, in the new year, only traces of the previous night were left: "Como si el huesario velado, erigido aún en medio de la mesa, fuera el altar de un devenir futuro, un pronóstico, un horóscopo anual que pestañaba lágrimas negras en la cera de las velas, a punto de apagarse, a punto de extinguir la última chispa social en la banderita de papel que coronaba la escena."[34] ["As if the lit bone collection erected in the middle of the table were an altar of a future becoming, a diagnosis, an annual horoscope that blinked black tears on the candles' wax, flickering about to go off, about to extinguish the last social spark left on the little paper flag that crowned the scene."] That monument prefigured the arrival of AIDS in the lives of the queens in the 1980s. Lemebel is juxtaposing here a series of monuments, the bones and the UNCTAD building which after the 1973 Chilean coup d'état becomes home for the military government, and only with time it becomes a social space where "la democracia fue recuperando las terrazas y patios" ["democracy started to recover the terraces and gardens"] and "los enormes auditoriums y salas de conferencias, donde hoy se realizan foros y seminarios sobre homosexualidad, SIDA, utopías y tolerancias."35 ["the enormous auditoriums and conference rooms, where forums and seminars on homosexuality, AIDS, utopias and tolerances take place nowadays."]

With nostalgia, the author remember that "[d]e esa fiesta sólo existe una foto, un cartón deslavado donde reaparecen los rostros colizas lejanamente expuestos a la mirada presente. La foto no es buena, pero salta a la vista la militancia sexual del grupo que la compone."36 ["from that party, there is only one picture left, a worn-out cardboard where the queer faces reappear distantly exposed to the present gaze. It isn't a good photo, but what jumps out is the group's sexual militancy."] Here we have the first gesture of recuperation and rewriting of the archive. Lemebel seems to be searching for another history of sexuality when he assertively points out the group's sexual militancy. I wonder, what images or figures are contained in this photograph to render visible and legible such militancy? What are the specifically cultural homographetic markings that suggest queer militancy? Perhaps more than the photograph's own details, it is a matter of how the author reads it or wants it to be read: "Enmarcados en la distancia, sus bocas son risas extinguidas, ecos de gestos congelados por el flash del último brindis. Frases, dichos, muecas, muecas, conchazos cuelgan del labio a punto de caer, a punto de soltar la ironía en el veneno de sus besos."37 ["Framed at a distance, their mouths with extinguished laughter, echoes of frozen gestures by the flash of the last toast. Phrases, sayings, grimaces, snide remarks (*conchazos*) hang from the lip and are about to fall, about to unleash the irony in the venom of their kisses."]38 I must point out that for Lemebel as author and reader of this particular picture (and of Chilean queer subculture, in general), he is giving a voice—a kind of prosopopeia—to the queens. It is a voice that cannot be heard, but that nonetheless must be remembered: it is imperative that we make memory of those voices, imagine those voices, before "la bruma del desenfoque alej[e] para siempre la estabilidad del recuerdo"39 ["the mist of the blur drive off forever the stability of memory], that is, before the image's distortion affects too much or outright erases the language to tell their stories. Lemebel seems to link image and voice in a necessary relation, in an urgent grammar to capture that no-place of homosexual representation. He gives another turn of the screw to this concept of voice-image, and adds: "La foto es borrosa, quizás porque el tul estropeado del SIDA, entela la doble desaparición de casi todas las locas."[40] ["The photo is blurry, perhaps because the damaged tulle of AIDS drapes the double disappearance of almost all the *locas*."] AIDS becomes another veil that erases the possibility of listening-seeing the image and of understanding what the *locas* want to say in and through their militant stance.

From here, the author goes on to tell us how each of the queens in the picture contracted AIDS: la Pilola Alessandri "se compró la epidemia en Nueva York, fue la primera que la trajo en exclusiva, la más auténtica, la recién estrenada moda gay para morir"[41] ["bought the epidemic in New York, she was the first to bring it exclusively, she was the most authentic, the most recently released gay fashion to die"]; la Palma "se le pegó en Brazil" ["caught it in Brazil"]; la Chumi "[p]or golosa" [por] "tantos dólares que pagaba ese gringo"[42] ["for being gluttonous" (in exchange) "for all those dollars that gringo paid"]. Each one has her story. Interestingly, la Pilola Alessandri and la Chumilou are infected by men from the United States—one in New York, the other by a rich sexual tourist. These are examples of what Lemebel meant that the disease is "a new form of colonization through contagion," a physical colonization that becomes psychic.

In a rather melancholic gesture, Lemebel comments that "[t]al vez, la foto de la fiesta donde la Palma, es quizás el único vestigio de aquella época de utopías sociales, donde las locas entrevieron aleteos de su futura emancipación"[43] ["perhaps, the photo of la Palma's party is the only vestige of that epoch of social utopias where the queens had a glimpse of flutters of their future emancipation."] Here again, the idea of "entrever"—that signifies literally "to see between things" as well as to have an insight of a radical vision into the future—gets introduced as a strategy to recover and enhance those stories of queer existence that are being lost or that are about to be erased from the social imaginary. Also, Lemebel reworks the meaning of the photograph:

> Antes que el barco del milenio atraque en el dos mil, antes, incluso, de la legalidad del homosexualismo chileno, antes de la militancia gay que en los noventa reunió a los homosexuales, antes que esa moda masculina se impusiera como uniforme del ejército de salvación, antes que el

neoliberalismo en democracia diera permiso para aparearse. Mucho antes de estas regalías, la foto de las locas de ese año nuevo se registra como algo que brilla en un mundo sumergido.[44]

[Before the coming of the Millennium ship, even before the legalization of Chilean homosexuality, before the gay militancy of the 1990s brought homosexuals together, before that masculine fashion imposed itself as a uniform for the army of salvation, before neoliberalism gave permission in the name of democracy for partnerships—much before these rights, the queen's new year photo is a record of something that shines in a submerged world.]

In other words, before the institutionalization of gay identity and of homonormativity, the queers had already made history. And if in fact homonormativity is successful today, this is the result that one can trace (albeit tacitly) its history back to that underground world of the drag queens. Lemebel adds, that "[a]ún, en la imagen ajada, se puede medir la gran distancia, los años de la dictadura que educaron virilmente los gestos. Se puede constatar la metamorfosis de las homosexualidades en el fin de siglo . . ."[45] ["even, in the tattered image, one can measure the great distance, the dictatorship years that manfully educated each gesture. One can observe the metamorphosis of homosexualities at the turn-of-the-century . . ."] Again, the queen's image serves as a barometer of the fluxes of history—how some ways of being gay oppress and others ease queer life. Theoretically, we come face to face with the problem of referentiality: When is the category "gay" used in Chile (or any other Latin American country, for that matter)? In 1972, or in 1996 or 2009? What is "gay" referring to in each historical instance? How deeply penetrating is our gaze—or how much of ourselves are imposing—by naming something or someone "gay" in a particular place and culture, and in a specific historical moment? The dislocation of any referent (whether it is "gayness," "Chilean-ness," "*locura*," and so forth) and applying it willy-nilly to any layer of History's archeology tends to damage the referent. The particular referent becomes something else once it has been universalized—and it is for that reason that Lemebel depends so heavily the metaphor of the sobriquet and on the elasticity of language to identify his queer subjects and their histories.

Sexual Ellipsis

If "La noche de los visones" inaugurates a Lemebelian critique that seeks to rescue lost voices so that they may participate in the figuration of a gay cultural and politically democratic "I," then "La Regine de Aluminios El Mono" seeks to represent other sexualities, however, this time through silence and ellipses.

What matters to me in this chronicle is not so much the hagiography that gets drawn of la Regine, but rather the portrait of her shy lover Sergio. When all the military men enter the palace of Aluminios El Mono, where la Regine reigned, the young Sergio always avoided the drag queen's games—"prefería quedarse [afuera] . . . cagado de frío . . . , antes que encularse a un maricón."[46] ["he would prefer to remain outside . . . frozen shitless . . . before butt-fucking a faggot."] One night he and la Regine spoke. After that night, no one would ever separate them. And that friendship continued until the death of the queen. The chronicle ends thus,

> Del Sergio nunca más se supo, la acompaño hasta el último día, en que la Regine pidió que los dejaran solos una hora. Desde afuera, las locas pegadas a la puerta, trataban de escuchar, pero nada. Ningún suspiro, ni un ruido. Ni siquiera el crujido del catre. Hasta que pasaron meses después del entierro, cuando una loca limpiando encontró el condón seco con los mocos del Sergio, y lo fue a enterrar en la tumba de la Regine.[47]

> [Nothing was ever heard from Sergio again. He joined her until the last day, when la Regine ask the other to leave them alone for an hour. From the outside, the queens glued to the door tried to listen, but nothing. Not a breath, not a noise. Not even the squeak of the cot. It was until some months after the burial, when a queen cleaning the room found a condom with Sergio's dried up jism, and she went to bury it at la Regine's tomb.]

It appears that during this last encounter la Regine and Sergio made love, perhaps for the first time. What is important in this scene is the silence that surrounds the relationship between the two of them. That relationship with no language to define it had no name for the military men: "Mucho después que pasó la dictadura, el teniente y la tropa iban a entender el amor platónico del Sergio y la Regine"[48] ["Long after the dictatorship, the lieutenant and the troop were to understand the Platonic love between Sergio and la Regine."][49] The relationship is characterized as Platonic love, affectionate love between men that can easily lack a physical component. Nevertheless, la Regine was a *loca* and as such a woman—and she would have protested that anyone thought that she was a man having a relationship with another man. Therefore calling what was between the two "Platonic" is nothing more than an incomplete approximation. There is no vocabulary to define their relationship—that is, there is neither identification nor referent. I would argue that the silence around this relationship between a queen and a heterosexual man serves a double purpose: on the one hand, it maintains Sergio's heterosexuality; on the other hand, it "heightens" la Regine's femininity. Silence about the specifics and details of the relationship guarantee a certain narrative of heterosexuality.

Nevertheless, that silence that surrounds the supposedly "heterosexual" relation (like the quotation marks around the term) also frames and delimits the borders of what is considered heterosexual. That is, silence allows that the "heterosexual" man may have relationships with locas, transvestites or homosexuals, and that he remain unmarked by that very sexual object choice or object relation.

In strictly theoretical terms, silence is part of the anatomy of the ellipse as trope. The ellipse is a figure that insinuates something else; however, for this figure to work properly, the ellipse contains a hole in its structural logic. Silence is that hole or blind spot that has to be activated so that the ellipsis may come into being as figure. Insofar as there exists a relation between ellipses and sexualities, we can appreciate how this trope makes certain sexualities possible. This helps explain why the drag queen goes at the end to bury the used condom: she is aware that this trace would betray what may be considered a "homosexual" history between Sergio and la Regine. The queen buries the secret of Sergio's possible homosexuality, thus, creating a sexual ellipse that creates and satisfies Sergio's desire for public heterosexuality, while keeping any homoeroticism (not to say homosexuality) private. The burial of the condom, the disavowal of the abject, instantiates the conceptualization of the ellipse—and, importantly, it allows that Sergio's sexuality get constituted in the imagination of the "queens glued to the door [trying] to listen, but [hearing] nothing," as well as in our own imagination. Thus, the secret remains.

* * *

The histories of sexuality are full of secrets that complicate their archive and narration, but also enable the imagination and imaginary. *Loco afán* meanders through a *terrain vague* of nonofficial sexualities, ones without a history. *Loco afán* offers us a series of strategies of sexual and cultural representation—and also a series of suggestions in how to approach and acknowledge sexual difference. Lemebel's essays document the lost histories, marked by the erasures imposed by heteronormative violence, restricted by the neoliberal gay desire to make gay "normal," and of course shrouded and transformed by silences. Lemebel's text gathers its critical and political strength from his effort to rethink how new and other sexualities are conceived, articulated, and narrated. His critical effort becomes a model for us; it is a political imperative to uncover and imagine and rewrite the histories of all sexualities, of other realities.

part 3

The Body Politic

6

Homosociality, Disavowal, and Pedagogy in Vargas Llosa's *Los cachorros*

> Y si quieren saber de mi pasado
> es preciso decir otra mentira
> les diré que llegue de un mundo raro
> que no sé del dolor
> que triunfé en el amor
> y que nunca he llorado.
> —"Mundo raro," José Alfredo Jiménez

The singularity of the voice

One finds in the narratives of the second half of the twentieth century, particularly in the Latin American "Boom" and its vicinities, texts that capture a snapshot of school scenes.[1] These scenes have different purposes—moments of pedagogy and discipline, creation of community, and so on. If we consider that the "Boom" represented that totalitarian text, obsessed with the *grandes familias* of the nation, another instance of the family romance as an allegory of the nation, then it makes sense that the education of these families also enters the literary imagination and reveals paradigms of cultural authority. I am thinking of classic works such as José Lezama Lima's *Paradiso* (1966), and Mario Vargas Llosa's *La ciudad y los perros* [*The Time of the Hero*, 1963], for example.[2] Indeed Vargas Llosa's representation of the school is marked in a very specific ways: not only to delineate a social group, but to render visible the process by which class privilege is maintained as well as to showcase the education of the nation.

In this chapter, I look at one such work by Vargas Llosa, *Los cachorros* [*The Cubs*, 1967],³ to examine how class privilege, sexual identity, and pedagogy intersect. I want to consider how the school functions a site of social formation, how it deliberately operates to create a social "we" rather than an individual "I." This articulation of a social persona that responds to the name "we" opens up a series of questions about inclusion and ostracism. Also, this articulation goes further in assuming and promoting a particular kind of pedagogy that is considered the "proper" one by a privileged class. Conversely, how does a certain education sustain class and political privilege? These are old issues and questions; however what interests me here is understanding how these sites of social privilege bring together rather inchoate and conflicting social and sexual identities, and furthermore how these sites and the individuals who inhabit them normalize any excesses and difference. Let us recall that famous scene from the *Symposium* when Socrates refuses Alcibiades's sexual forwardness (lines 216c–223d) as a mode of sublimation and thereby learning takes place—that is, the old teacher holds sexual satisfaction at a distance, he disavows sexual needs, thereby letting sexual desire exist as a sexual bond that becomes a pedagogical attachment. Here in *Los cachorros*, nonnormative sexuality is refused altogether, but not as a Socratic pedagogical maneuver, rather as something that brings about a greater social (class) attachment and formation. This refusal even to acknowledge queer sexualities is analogous to the ways in which nations also displace and reject the queer (the sick, the different, the nonnormative) in order to establish a healthy version of citizenship.

Vargas Llosa's novella *Los cachorros* details the life of Cuellar, from the moment he arrives to the Colegio Champagnat, his adventures with his classmates, until his death in an automobile accident. The novel is squarely set in the upper-class neighborhood of Miraflores in Lima, Peru, and constantly represents the manners and conceits of this social class—Which country club to belong to? Where to hang out? What music to listen to? Very much the same way that Carlos Fuentes gives us insight into the Mexican upper-class in his early work *La region más transparente*, Vargas Llosa presents us with a very specific picture of how Lima's miraflorinos work and play every day. These novels were important because they no longer represent or romanticize a rural or autochthonous Latin America, rather they are clearly set in an urban and quite modern context. The 1960s represent for Latin American narrative a major shift from the rural to the urban space.

Although *Los cachorros* follows closely the life of Cuéllar, we would be hard pressed to call this text a *Bildungsroman*. The novella rather than capture the coming-of-age narrative of just this protagonist, it gives us instead the portrait of a whole generation, a group of friends at the Champagnat. It portrays a class—more specifically, a class-consciousness. The experimental narrative voice of the novella makes this point quite well:

> Todavía llevaban pantalón corto ese año, aún no fumábamos, entre todos los deportes preferían el fútbol, y estábamos aprendiendo a correr olas, a zambullirnos desde el segundo trampolín del "*Terrazas*," y eran traviesos, lampiños, curiosos, muy ágiles, voraces. Ese año, cuando Cuéllar entró al Colegio Champagnat.[4]

> [They still wore shorts that year, we hadn't begun smoking, among sports they preferred soccer, and we were learning to body surf, to jump from the second diving board at the Terrazas Club, and they were naughty, barefaced, very agile, bold. That year, when Cuéllar entered the Champagnat School.]

Vargas Llosa signature style of changing narrative voice, which we first saw in his monumental *La ciudad y los perros*, makes for a polyphonic chorus—"they" becomes "we," then "they," and finally "he." The story continues along, introducing and silencing new characters and voices, blending direct and indirect speech. This narrative technique produces the effect of a speaking community, a "we" rather than a singular subject narrates. If we consider that a "we" is simply an "I" speaking on behalf of others, Vargas Llosa's "we" represents the author's struggle to capture that totality, the voice of a group, a "we" that chants in unison tendencies and desires, a sense of cohesion and coherence to a class structure that sees itself as politically and culturally uniform, always promoting the "right" class consciousness. That "we" is a persona that weaves a set of relations and interrelations: in this context, an individualistic "I" cannot survived, it needs to be sustained by a history of family names, social institutions, and other cultural and political attachments that allow that "I" to rise to the status of a national citizen, *the* only way of being a citizen.[5] They all wore the uniform, played the same sports, learned and performed the same activities, and most importantly went to the same school. Cuéllar meets his four friends, who are referred to by their nicknames: Choto, Chingolo, Mañuco, and Lalo. The boys' names reflect both familiarity and affection. Family status, neighborhood relations, and school spirit all work to bring the boys' lives together, and fuse them into one experience, "una vida de mamey,"[6] a carefree life of pleasure, as more than one of the boys would describe it.

The voice of others

Although it is fairly straightforwardly clear that Vargas Llosa's narrative style is trying to capture a symphony of voices that meld into a social or national singularity, I propose that we may read his narrative style somewhat differently. I would like to consider it as a perversion of the long tradition of a Platonic dialogue, a voice that zigzags among different characters, and gets molded and transformed. I am interested in that zigzag, that wiggling and adjusting of a social voice and perspective. As I have been arguing, this multiplicity of voices expresses a class ideology. Moreover, the text becomes the social and political *context* that frames Cuéllar, and against which he must fight to claim a sense of independence. However, that independence will never be achieved because, as we shall see, the text/context will always see him as a monstrous other. Despite the fact that Cuéllar might want to claim a sense of agency, his story will be—must be—told by others, otherwise.

* * *

We hear in *Los cachorros* intertextual echoes of two separate texts: André Gide's *L'immoraliste*,[7] and a scene titled "Aparición del inmoralista" from Jaime Torres Bodet's memoir, *Tiempo de arena*.[8]

We begin with Gide's text: Michel's story is recollected as a framed narrative and retold to and by his friends. While on his honeymoon in Tunis, Michel gets sick. He returns a "new man," and chooses to experience a very physical life rather than the academic one that he had been leading. This cleavage between the physical (or the sensual) versus the intellectual aspects of Michel's story gets retold and rewritten in *Los cachorros*. However, whereas Michel's disease is tuberculosis, Cuéllar suffers a very different fate: castration. I would venture to say that both Michel and Cuéllar become feminized differently—one through the contagion of consumption that has been historically gendered feminine; the other through a narcissistic injury to his manhood.

The other scene that echoes in *Los cachorros* is a chapter from Torres Bodet's autobiography, "Aparición del inmoralista" ["The apparition of the immoralist"]. Obviously, the title of the chapter points to the appearance as well as the ghostly presence of Ricardo Arenales [Colombian author, né Miguel Ángel Osorio Benítez][9] in the *tertulias* [salon meetings] held around canonical Mexican writer Enrique González Martínez. An open homosexual, Arenales scandalized the other young authors at the *tertulias*. Torres Bodet notes "Le encantaba asombrar, especialmente a los jóvenes, con la exposición de teorías heterodoxas en moral, en política, en arte; pero no en literatura o en religión."[10] ["Arenales loved to astonish, especially the young men, with his presentation of heterodox theories on morality, politics, and art—but not in literature and religion."] Arenales's figure is interesting here because of how Torres Bodet himself assimilates him: "No tardamos en comprender que entre ambos se levantaría constantemente una barrera insalvable. De prejuicios burgueses, creía él. De sensibilidades opuestas, pensaba yo."[11] ["It did not take us long to understand that an unsurmountable wall would be constantly raised between us. One made of bourgeoisie prejudices, he believed. Of opposing sensibilities, thought I."] This coming face-to-face with such a queer persona stresses Torres Bodet; indeed, this scene in the text reminds us of another encounter between José Martí and Oscar Wilde. In her seminal essay "Too Wilde for Comfort: Desire and Ideology in Fin-de-Siècle Spanish America,"[12] Sylvia Molloy uses the Martí-Wilde encounter as paradigmatic: She notes that Martí's obsessive gaze on and critique of Wilde's flamboyant body is more reflective of Martí's own preoccupations with his body. She thus argues that, through such a reflection on the excess of the other's body, the Latin American author might really be obsessed with such control and authority over his own body—or more precisely, with the belief and sense of entitlement that one can even exercise such an authority

142 *The Avowal of Difference*

over one's body. We see in Torres Bodet a similar practice reading the other's body in order to avoid thinking about his own: He creates an "unsurmountable wall"—and then chooses to distinguish himself not along class lines ("bourgeoisie prejudices"), but rather, "sensibilities," a code word for sexual difference.

In a powerful moment, Torres Bodet cites Proust by memory, "casi siempre los 'aunque' son en verdad 'porque'"[13] ["almost always the 'even thoughs' are in reality 'becauses'"]. This would seem to betray Torres Bodet's own sensibilities: "He admires Arenales even though he is a homosexual" becomes "He admires Arenales because he is a homosexual." The exception becomes the rule. More provocatively, we learn that "[l]a aparición de Arenales en las tertulias ... coincidió con el descubrimiento que hice del Inmoralista de Gide."[14] ["Arenales's arrival in the salon meetings ... coincided with the discovery I made of Gide's *L'immoraliste*."] Arenales's body and persona is first read through Proust and then Gide—and of course this reading of the other reflects back to the self.[15] (Ironically, like Gide's Michel, Arenales would also die of tuberculosis.) Bodet's own homosexuality can only be mediated, reflected, or refracted through the other's queer presence and body.

Both Gide's text and Torres Bodet's autobiography present us with the problem of reading the other's body. This practice of reading is similar to the one that Molloy analyzes between Martí and Wilde. For Martí's reading of Wilde only reflects back onto his own persona; while what we discover from Bodet, reading the other's body is both an individual and a group reflection—throughout the chapter, Bodet talk about how the other members of the group respond to Arenales's "apparition." We will see that in *Los cachorros*, reflecting (as an act of debasement and exclusion) on the other is about group formation.

* * *

Thus, let us see how this process of diffentiation takes place in Vargas Llosa's novel. Looking back, as Cuéllar becomes part of the group of friends, he shows that he is an excellent intellect, as well as a very able soccer player. One of the brothers at the Champagnat reminds the boys: "mens sana in corpore sano."[16] His friends' initial jealousy is replaced by their support—after all, his individual talent on the field leads *all of them* to become major contenders for an interschool soccer championship. One day after a practice game, Judas, the Great Dane, breaks into the showers, and attacks:

> . . . guau guau guau, sólo Lalo y Cuéllar se estaban bañando: guau guau guau guau. Choto, Chingolo y Mañuco saltaron por las ventanas, Lalo chilló se escapó mira hermano y alcanzó a cerrar la puertecita de la ducha en el hocico del danés. Ahí, encogido, losetas blancas, azulejos y chorritos de agua, temblando, oyó los ladridos de Judas, el llanto de Cuéllar, sus gritos, y oyó aullidos, saltos, choques, resbalones y después sólo ladridos . . .[17]

> [bowwow, only Lalo and Cuéllar were bathing: bowwow bowwow. Choto, Chingolo and Mañuco jumped out of the windows, Lalo shrieked he escaped watch out brother and he was able to close the shower door on the Great Dane's snout. There, huddled, white tiles, drips of water, shaking, he heard Judas's barks, Cuéllar's cry, his screams, and he heard the howling, jumps, crashes, slips and afterwards only barks . . .]

The trauma of castration is never witnessed by anyone, it is only heard. In the aftermath of the attack, the bathroom is entirely covered with blood. The boys can only deal with this trauma by talking about it, though they worry that talking about it too much might consititute a "sin." The boys are saddened by their friend's fate: "y Mañuco pobre Cuéllar, qué dolor tendría, si un pelotazo ahí sueña a cualquiera cómo sería un modisco y sobre todo piensa como sería un mordisco . . ."[18] [and Mañuco (added) poor Cuéllar, how painful it must have been, if getting hit by a ball there makes anyone see stars, imagine a bite"]. This event profoundly changes the boys. First we notice that they sympathize with pain that Cuéllar must have felt when he was bitten. That pain is never explained by the injured subject—he screams—rather it is articulated by the classmates, meaning that the castration injures more than the body of Cuéllar, but also affects the body of the group. Moreover, it so happens that that soccer tournament for which they had been practicing and preparing was about to begin the next day, and they were the favorites to win—they certainly had been bragging about it. And now with their best player on the injured list, they make a strange pact: "hay que rajarse si no queremos quedar a la cola."[19] ["We have to take back what we've been saying (or what we've been bragging about) otherwise we will end up looking foolish."] In other words, there is a change of how the sense of community and group consciousness is achieved: no longer are the boys bragging assertively about how good they are, but instead they must resort to an act of disavowal, so that they do not end up looking bad. An unbridled projection of who they think they are (or what others must think of them) gets curtailed, withdrawn, and disavowed. Or, said differently, the "we" is constituted selectively, and with a particular attachment to blindness. Notice the deliberate choice of words, "rajarse," to cut or slit oneself, an act of ethical masochism, becomes de rigueur in order to belong to something greater.

This horrible incident also marked a "rebirth" for Cuéllar. Before that traumatic moment he was always known by his last name, he did not have a nickname like his friends. However, now some of the other boys in school begin calling him "Pichulita" ["Little Peenie"]. The name of the father that designates his privileges gets embodied in the weakened figure of a flaccid and injured penis. This alias angers Cuéllar enormously, to a point where his father comes and threatens the brothers at the Champagnat. It may also be argued that the brothers' warnings to the other boys did nothing to keep the name from sticking—even his close four buddies began calling him that, eventually Cuéllar accepts the name and starts introducing himself to other boys as "Pichula Cuéllar."[20] Another transformation took place in him, he came back to school more assertively as a sportsman rather than as a good student, and his studies begin to deteriorate. The equilibrium of a healthy mind in a healthy body promulgated by the brothers is completely disrupted. I do not want us to think of this as a simple case of overcompensation, but indeed the body—an overworked, overdone, and even overdetermined body—takes precedence over everything else. The developed body masks a fault or lack. The newly acquired musculature hides the original injury as well as overshadows the intellectual promise that was once there. Opting for the physical over the intellectual parallels with Gide's Michel.

Then comes another period that marks a change for the boys: before they were interested in sports and movies, now as they start their middle school years they preferred "girls and dancing." In fact, the text closes the first chapter of the young men's lives thus,

Ya usaban pantalones largos entonces, nos peinábamos con gomina y habían desarrollado, sobre todo Cuéllar, que de ser el más chiquito y el más enclenque de los cinco pasó a ser el más alto y el más fuerte. Te has vuelto un Tarzán, Pichulita, le decíamos, qué cuerpazo te echas al diario.[21]

[They were already wearing long pants, we combed our hair with gel and they had beefed up, especially Cuéllar, who used to be the smallest and weakest of the five he became the tallest and strongest. You've become a Tarzan, Pichulita, we'd tell him, what a body you take on everyday.]

This paragraph contrasts to the opening one: the boys are no longer wearing shorts, rather they now wear long pants. I would argue that this simple change—from shorts to pants—reflects the boys' entrance into adolescence and adulthood in a very particular way; that is, wearing pants marks an important relationship between maturation and the body: getting older means having to cover up more of the body, making the body less visible. Nevertheless, Pichulita becomes a different kind of man, a Tarzan. This renaming is quite provocative because it hints that Pichulita qua Tarzan is beginning to be removed from the space of "civilized" society, and relocated to nature. Metaphorically, Pichulita gets expelled into the wilderness—and this expulsion, I would argue, hints at others to come. It is an ironic representation of Pichulita. We could expand our analysis here to suggest that Tarzan's relation to race, nature, and class signifies powerfully on Pichulita's identity—he becomes more "brute" so to speak, and this will weigh in how his gender, above all how his hypermasculinity gets constructed by himself and celebrated by the other boys. If we consider that Tarzan wore less clothes: so while the boys were starting to "wear pants"—notice the masculinist imperative implicit in the idea of "wearing the pants"—Pichulita gets portrayed as someone who is losing his attire, in effect, his masculinity. So on the one hand, the focus on the body itself and the body's strength adds to Pichulita's masculinity; on the other hand, the loss of clothes as a marker of losing one's "civilization" also detracts from Pichulita's masculinity. As a Tarzan, Pichulita is caught in a double bind: his new body gives the illusion of a new masculinity that hides a secret wound—the metaphoric renaming suggests a loss of clothes, which in turn diminishes his "civilized" masculinity. Thus he is disinvested of belonging and authority. Calling him Tarzan causes a gender fluctuation; furthermore, the renaming also inaugurates a process that destabilizes his class positionality and identity (progressively the other boys question whether he is "one of us"). Likewise, I would argue that the gender and class shifts also hint at a national and racial difference. Most importantly, from all this, it will be an obsession with the body that regulates and scripts the next stage in the men's lives.

Embodiments

As I mentioned earlier, the boys become interested in girls—and Lalo is the first to declare his interest for a girl, Chabuca Molina. This romance becomes grounds for celebration; however Cuéllar reacts quite negatively to his friend's new attraction. Then, he gets quite drunk, throwing up all over the place and on himself. His friends try to calm him down, and all he can do is call Lalo a "traitor" and a "maricón," that now he would spend Sundays with Chabuca and forget about his friends. Lalo's response is quite important: "qué ocurrencia, hermano, la hembrita y los amigos eran dos cosas distintas, *pero no se oponen*, no había que ser celoso"[22] (italics mine). ["what a crazy idea, brother, the little lady and friends are two different things, *but they don't oppose each other*, you don't have to be jealous."] Later on, things just become more complicated for Cuéllar: Choto begins dating Fina Salas, and Mañuco, Pusy Lañas. This only alienates Cuéllar all the more, and he spends his Sundays with Chingolo, until Chingolo meets China. Throughout this time Cuéllar becomes quite difficult and very misogynistic.

I would like to digress a bit and mention that Lalo will date China later on, while Chingolo will be with Chabuca; however, in the end Lalo will go back and marry Chabuca. I make mention of this exchange of girlfriends because it underscores the fact the young men can only date within their social group, and it signifies the traffic in women, neatly illustrating what Sedgwick calls homosocial bonding through the exchange of women.

Now, returning to the scene of disgust, when Cuéllar throws up after learning of Lalo's love interest: as I mentioned, Lalo's response is quite interesting: "the little lady and friends are two different things, but they don't oppose each other." Lalo's comment would seem to support Sedgwick's idea about homosocial bonding: the presence of the woman does not disrupt male-male relations, her presence does something else. In *Between Men*, Sedgwick argues, rightly so, that it guarantees heteronormativity, and displaces any homosexual anxiety and panic that could possibly be read into any male-male relationship. I would like to read Lalo's comment much more literally, underscoring the separate realms—the one with "the little lady" and the other of male friendships. What if there is no relation between the traffic in women and male-male friendships? That is, that the traffic in women and male-male friendships are things in and of themselves. What would this theoretical separation between the traffic in women and male bonding do to the restricted economy of the triangular relation of homosociality that Sedgwick theorizes? First, separating the two things would change the very status of homosexual panic; that is, if the presence of the woman (embodied in the naked presence of the courtesan of Manet's *Le déjeuner sur l'herbe*) is not required to make the male-male interaction into something that is approvingly heteronormative, then homosexual panic has been revalued (not necessarily devalued) and changed into something else. Any form of homosexual panic would then be allowed to free flow and traverse through male-male relations in other unrestricted ways. I want to argue that this kind of free flow (or free association) of homosexual panic might be expressed as a homophobic surplus, most specifically in the context of Latin America as a kind of homophobic language (*albures*, *choteo*, and other sexual punning).

I want to theorize the idea of a homosocial bonding that does not necessitate that third position to guarantee male heterosexual normativity and authority. The world of these boys is a male-male world where women are easily interchangeable, to the point of appearing superfluous: they are not necessarily that object choice that relationally defines heterosexual identity. Women here get relegated to a different social, economic and political role: they become purely decor (a French pun: *des corps*, many bodies, or *dé-corps*, disembodied). I want to propose that this situation that disregards or diminishes the positionality of women as unnecessary or irrelevant gets reflected here in *Los cachorros* as a Latin American difference that modifies Sedgwick's conceptualization of homosocial bonding.

This difference also points to and describes a cultural phenomenon of male-male privilege that makes certain agreements and disavowals about its sense of self. Importantly, this male-male romance (or more colloquially, their "bromance") offers a queer national allegory that accentuates the place of masculinity in the conceptualization of the nation, all the while it dismisses any possible feminist inclusion or intervention in the writing of the nation.

Integrating the body

Given Cuéllar's testy behavior, integrating the girlfriends into the group proves to be quite difficult for the young men; however, they all agreed that they have to help Cuéllar find a girl of his own, "even if she were a little bit ugly."[23] Even the girls—Chabuca, Fina, Pusy and China—wanted to help out, and they constantly asked their respective boyfriends as to why Cuéllar did not have a love interest. The guys were paranoid, and would ask each other if their girlfriends suspected about Pichulita's unnamed "condition": "Tal vez no saben pero cualquier día van a saber, decía Chingolo, y será su culpa, ¿qué le costaba caerle a alguna aunque fuera sólo para despistar?"[24] ["Perhaps they don't know but any day now they will, said Chingolo, and it will be his fault, how difficult was it to ask any girl out, even if it was to dissimulate?"]

I would like to tie up some loose ends about how the boys (now, young men) have been responding all along to the Cuéllar's trauma. From the beginning, the boys saw themselves implicated in the castration—it was not only an injury onto Cuéllar's body, but an injury that affected them too. The castration is a narcissistic injury directly on the body, and also on the body politic. The boys have been saying all along something like, "He is one of our own, we've been injured." Furthermore, the young men have been trying to maintain the integrity of Cuéllar's body intact because what they are also protecting in the social bonds that unite them and give them their sense of privilege and entitlement. In other words, the young men are able to disavow castration.[25] What we hear leak out for the first time above are hints that Cuéllar may not be "one of them"—and that it is his fault for not dissimulating and "playing along" with the conceits of their social class.

Homosociality, Disavowal, and Pedagogy 149

The difficulty that Cuéllar faces is that he cannot disavow castration in the same way his friends can. For Cuéllar, castration is quite real; it is an overwhelming event that cannot be conveyed fully to others. For his friends, castration initially gets thought of on the order of the Imaginary, a series of projective fantasies. Later on, the friends see castration for its Symbolic value, castration as the figure and the threat of the *nom-du-père*. Cuéllar is no longer under the influence of the name-of-the-father, for it was Judas (the dog) who robbed him of the penis/phallus, hence, of his ability to symbolize. Cuéllar's body becomes a weakened, flaccid penis, a *pichulita*. This bodily marker is far too powerful to overcome.

It is in the first year of college that Teresita Arrarte arrives in Miraflores. Cuéllar is very taken by her. Teresita responds positively to Cuéllar, however, the slow pace with which he moves to make their relationship official is exasperating to their friends. His friends even go as far as asking Teresita directly if she is interested in Cuéllar; she says yes. When they encourage Cuéllar to pursue her, and all he answers is that "le podía decir sí pero ¿y después?"[26] ["she can say 'yes,' but what about afterwards?"] Cuéllar seems to suggest that his relationship with her (or any woman, for that matter) will always have its limitations. He insinuates that his injured body places limits on the possibility of heterosexuality. This all seems to be of little concern for his male friends—all they care about is that he make formal his relationship with Teresita. They would take care about moving the relationship forward:

> Y Lalo ¿cómo podía dudar? Le caería, tendría enamorada y él ¿qué haría? y Choto tiraría plan y Mañuco le agarraría la mano y Chingolo la besaría y Lalo la paletearía un poquito y él ¿y después? y se le iba la voz y ellos ¿después?, y él después...[27]

> [And Lalo, how can you doubt (that she will accept)? You would ask her out, you'd have a girlfriend, and he, what would I do? and Choto would draw out a plan and Mañuco would hold her hand and Chingolo would kiss her and Lalo would sweeten her up, and he, and then? and he would lose his voice, and they, well afterwards, and he, what comes next...]

Again we see how the friends "help out" Cuéllar—they so much want the relationship to work that they are even willing to seduce her in his place. They offer their own bodies to consummate the relationship. This raises the question of interchangeability to a whole new level. Before we saw that the girls in the relationships were easily exchanged; now the very fact that the men can help each other out, that they can offer their bodies in the place of another, means that the social and sexual relationships do not need to have a specific physical attachment. What matters most is that the relationships exist *in name*, that is, discursively. What happens concretely—that is, in practice—under those discursive arrangements would seem to matter very little. After ten beers, Cuéllar finally agrees that "hermanos, teníamos razón, era lo mejor: le caeré, estaré un tiempo con ella y la largaré."[28] ["my brothers, we are right, that is the best: I will ask her out, will be with her for while, and then will dump her."] He agrees with his friends that what matters most is to articulate a particular identity that jives with the desires and interests of his social group; what might happen "outside" the relationship will be happily overlooked.

Nevertheless, before Cuéllar can get his courage up to ask Teresita to be his girlfriend, another character, Cachito, moves in and becomes her boyfriend. His name is significant, as all of Vargas Llosa's characters names are. "Cacho" means a "horn"; therefore, this signifies Cuéllar becoming a cuckold of sorts. "Cacho" also means a small fragment, a broken off piece of something; therefore, Cacho also represents what has been fragmented off, the return of the repressed. I must also comment on Teresita's last name, Arrarte, which is a homophone for *ararte*, literally "to plow you." If she represents another castrating figure, she is paired off with "cacho," the fragmented, the castrated object.

In the end, the friends' effort to keep Cuéllar whole, to keep him a part of the group by making him perform the social part that has been prescribed for him, fails. It would seem that the castrated body can never be made whole again. And Cuéllar returns to his old shenanigans.

Queering the body

Cuéllar becomes bolder in his effort to display his physicality and masculinity. He rides dangerously high waves to show his friends how fearless he is—in other words, just how much of a man he remains being. Over and again, his physical life overwhelms the intellectual

Homosociality, Disavowal, and Pedagogy 151

and the social. If he is unable to establish his heterosexuality, then performing a very assertive masculinity has to suffice. His buddies become more concerned about his not having been with a woman, and take him to a bordello; of course, this adventure fails miserably. He comes out crying, and his friends can only encourage him, "Corre Pichulita, pícala, el fierro a fondo ... Pichulita, demuéstranos que se te pasó, otra risita: ja ja."[29] ["Run back, Pichulita, fuck her, your steel rod deeply ... Pichulita, show us that you are over it, another little laughter, hee-hee."] Importantly, the encouraging words offer us two important details. First, the friends want him to fuck the prostitute "el fierro a fondo": the friends want him to prove his masculinity, not through excelling in sports, but through penetrating a woman. And second, his friends want proof that he is over "it," the ellipsis here point in at least two directions: Pichulita comes out from the prostitute's room crying, so he must get over his "sadness." But that ellipsis also signifies on Pichulita's "queerness," as if the boys were saying, "show us that you are over that which cannot be named." In the end, they need proof that he is "like them." Whereas before, they were willing to cover up for his "inadequacy," to make up stories about his sexual identity, now they want to see proof positive that he is one of them.

He fails to become the man others want him to be, and his life seems to spiral out of control:

> ... en el dia vagabundeaba de un barrio de Miraflores a otro y se lo veía en las esquinas, vestido como James Dean (blue jeans ajustados, camisita de colores abierta del pescuezo hasta el ombligo, en el pecho una cadenita de oro bailando y enredándose entre los vellitos, mocasines blancos) ...[30]

> ["... during the day he wandered from one Miraflores neighborhood to another and he could be seen hanging out on the corners, dressed as James Dean (tight blue jeans, colorful shirt unbuttoned from the neck to the belly button, on his chest a gold chain danced and would get tangled up with his chest hair, white slip-on shoes) ...]

Later on, we learn that he is hanging out in his new Volvo with younger boys, teaching them how do drive and how to surf. He gets singled out by his friends—"mírenlo, mírenlo, ahí está..." ["look at him, look at him, there he is..."]. He has become no longer one of them, but the other. Finally, they all agree "Ya está, decíamos, era fatal: maricón."³¹ ["That's it! we used to say, it's fatal: he's a faggot."] The "we" in this final and scathing pronouncement is different from the previous ones. This "we" excludes Cuéllar as the queer body, dressed à la James Dean, a queer body that is surrounded by young boys to insinuate pedophilia. Equally important, Cuéllar is seen here as dressing as a foreigner. The queer body cannot be part of the larger national one. And despite a small amount of sympathy for him, the distance between the men and Cuéllar grows:

> Y también: qué le quedaba, se comprendía, se le disculpaba pero, hermano, resulta cada día más difícil juntarse con él, en la calle lo miraban, lo silbaban y lo señalaban, y Choto a ti te importa mucho el qué dirán, y Mañuco lo rajaban y Lalo si nos ven mucho con él y Chingolo te confundirán.³²

> [But also, what did he have left, it's understandable, he could be excused but, brother, it's more difficult each day getting together with him, on the street people looked at him, he got whistled at, and he was pointed out, and Choto you care a lot what others say, and Mañuco they cut him off, and Lalo if they see us much with him, and Chingolo, they will confuse you as being one like him.]

First, the affectionate *hermano*, which was used throughout to name Cuéllar is no longer directed at him. And also there is concern for getting together with Cuéllar, for they too might be "guilty by association," implicated as queer. Thus ends the friendship among the men. Afterward they all marry, and Cuéllar moves to Tingo María at the foot of the Andes Mountains. All encounters thereafter are accidental, and the hellos are perfunctory. The novella ends announcing in a matter-of-factly fashion that Cuéllar died in a car accident. But more importantly, the final lines of the text return us to the beginning:

> Eran hombres hechos y derechos ya y teníamos todos mujer, carro, hijos que estudiaban en el Champagnat, la Inmaculada o el Santa María, y se estaban construyendo una casita para el verano en Ancón, Santa Rosa o las playas del Sur...³³

[They were men of good already and we all had wives, a car, children who studied at the Champagnat, the Immaculate or the Santa Maria, and they were building a small summer house in Alcón, Santa Rosa or the southern beaches . . .]

Again, the novella ends with a repetition of the social practices that have defined them all along. Significantly, it is now their sons who are attending the Champagnat: they will be performing the same rituals as their fathers, learning the same lessons on how to become men, on how to deploy their privileges.

As I have argued, the ways of masculinity and authority are inculcated through a series of alliances and disavowals. Disavowal—"yes, there is such a thing as X, but I am not X"—is a curious double figure of universal affirmation and particular negation. I would argue that disavowal offers an important figure to read and understand Latino American sexuality; it sustains the idea that in theory heterosexuality is a desirable thing, but in practice "anything goes." Disavowal facilitates a gesture of authority that says something like "these values are essential for the continuation of culture, although they may not necessarily apply to me." I would like to propose that more than just a psychic device, disavowal becomes a pedagogical imperative that is performed by the upper-class bourgeoisie in Vargas Llosa's text to outline the limits of their privilege. I give it the connotation of a pedagogy, because this form of social disavowal gets used to instruct *celui-qui-ne-comprends-pas* their place within society.

Conclusion: Vargas Llosa on high culture

In the July 2010 issue of *Letras libres*, Vargas Llosa wrote what many would consider a tired, even desperate, essay titled "Breve discurso sobre la cultura" ["A brief discourse on culture"].[34] In it he bemoans the fact that "we" have lost a sense of high culture—and that this represents the loss of a moral compass for society. The essay rehearses the common debates about the disappearance of standards, how anthropologists obsessed with the "horizontal equivalence of cultures" destroyed hierarchies, how the spectral confusion between high and popular culture blurs any lines of distinction, and so on. He argues that "[q]ueríamos acabar con las élites, que nos repugnaban moralmente por el retintín privilegiado, despectivo y discriminatorio con que su solo nombre resonaba ante nuestros ideales igualitaristas"³⁵ ["we wanted to end with the elites who repulsed us morally with their privileged, derogatory and discriminatory tone that clashed with our egalitarian ideals"]; however, he concludes that "un remedio que result peor que la enfermedad: vivir en la confusion de un mundo en el que, paradójicamente, como ya no hay manera de saber qué cosa es cultura, todo lo es y ya nada lo es."³⁶ ["a remedy turned out to be worse than the disease: we have to live in a confusing world in which, paradoxically, there is no way to know what is culture, everything and nothing is culture."]

Vargas Llosa argues that culture was "un denominador común, algo que mantenía viva la comuncación entre gentes muy diversas" ["a common denominator (that) kept alive the communication among diverse peoples"]; it was, according to him, "una brújula, una guía que permitía a los seres humanos orientarse en la espesa maraña de los conocimientos sin perder la dirección y teniendo más o menos claro, [...] las prelaciones, lo que es importante de lo que no lo es, el camino principal y las desviaciones inútiles."³⁷ ["a compass, a guide that allowed human beings to orient themselves though the thick tangle of knowledge without losing direction and having more or less, (...) a sense of priority, of what is and is not important, a principal route and unnecessary detours.] He laments that we no longer appreciate T. S. Elliot's understanding of culture as a "spiritual attitude and sensibility." And he calls for instituting hierarchies to express diversity in the most comprehensive sense, all the while, of course, "rechaz[ando] de todo lo que envilece y degrada la noción básica de humanidad y amenaza la supervivencia de la especie."³⁸ ["rejecting everything that debases and degrades the basic notion of humanity and threatens the survival of the species."] Finally, he calls for the formation of "una élite conformada no por la razón de nacimiento ni el poder económico o politico sino por el esfuerzo, el talento y la obra realizada y con autoridad moral para establecer, de manera flexible y removable, un orden de importancia de los valores..."³⁹ ["an elite composed, not by birth right nor economic or political power, but created by effort, talent and by hard work, and with moral authority to establish a ranking of values in a flexible and renewable manner..."]

I do not want to rehash the many kinds of criticisms that have been

Homosociality, Disavowal, and Pedagogy 155

launched against the position that Vargas Llosa is embracing; rather, I want to underline that the textual and political maneuver that Vargas Llosa engages in is that of replacing one form of elitism for another. The structure of hegemony remains in place. This replacement reminds us of a similar sleight of hand advocated by Cuéllar's friends with regard to his sexuality: retaining the big picture (or universals), and worrying about the particularities later on.

In a stunning misreading of Michel Foucault's work, Vargas Llosa goes on to note that education, like sexuality, psychiatry, religion, justice, and language—he recites the numerous stages of Foucault's oeuvre—education is a "structure of power." He continues that unfortunately the collapse and loss of prestige given to education has made schools into chaotic institutions. His essay continues talking about how the radical calling into question of authority by the student movements of 1968 had thus failed. What exactly does that failure look like? It is important to note that Vargas Llosa defines authority in a very specific way: He wants to claim the existence an elite class, whose idea of prestige is what gives it authority over others. Using the *Diccionario de la Real Academia Española* as a source no less, he defines *auctoritas* as "[el] prestigio y crédito que se reconoce a una persona o institución por su legitimidad o por su calidad y competencia en alguna material"[40] ["the prestige and credit given to a person or institution for his legitimacy or quality and competence in a particular field"]. Prestige is what Vargas Llosa argues has been lost. Authority as power remained, however, Vargas Llosa mourns the loss of this sense of authority as prestige (or prestige as authority). This sense of authority, which he links to culture, died for him in May of 1968 (I would add, one year after the publication of *Los cachorros*).

In a troubling rewriting of Foucault's life, Vargas Llosa argues that Foucault's idealism also died, and this led him "creer que era más factible encontrar emancipación moral y política apedreando policías, frecuentando baños 'gays' de San Francisco o los clubes sadomasoquistas de Paris, que en las aulas escolares o las ánforas electorales."[41] ["to believe that it was more feasible to find moral and political emancipation throwing rocks at police, hanging out in the 'gay' baths in San Francisco or the S/M clubs in Paris, than in the classrooms or the ballot boxes."] In other words, Vargas Llosa redraws Foucault as another Cuéllar, in fact, he castrates him, by devaluing his sexual practices and noting that he did not follow through with his idealism and the promotion of "Culture" with a capital C.

I do not want to apply Vargas Llosa's later and more conservative views on Culture to reduce and resolve the aporia about sexual identity and authority that *Los cachorros* may be articulating. I see the novel as a reflection on the complexities and challenges that sexual difference brings to social and political identity: moreover, the novel presents how sexual difference pressures the heteronormative context, and how the latter represses sexual queerness in return in an interminable chain, generation after generation. If, in fact, the structures of authority are insurmountable, what are ways in which we can politically transform those structures so that they deliver a greater and more open democratic ideal? How do we make wounded bodies a part of a body politic that purports "to know better"? Is this task even a desirable one? These questions—and similar other ones—become our political and pedagogical imperative.

7

Sadomasochism in *Paradiso*

Bound Narratives and Pleasure

> Thus, it is not through sexuality that we communicate with the orderly and pleasingly profane world of animals; rather, sexuality is a fissure—not one which surrounds us as the basis of our isolation or individuality, but one which marks the limit within us and designates us as a limit.
>
> —Michel Foucault[1]

José Lezama Lima's *Paradiso* undoubtedly signals a watershed moment in the (literary) history of (Latin American) sexuality. Certainly the political discussions in *Mundo Nuevo* and elsewhere among Latin American writers and intellectuals about the status of the novel as a queer masterpiece framed the reading of this text greatly; this debate tiptoed around the now (in)famous "capítulo VIII." In this chapter, I propose a close reading of a seminal scene in the novel (Farraluque's weekend sexual escapades) as well as of those debates surrounding the Farraluque episode to capture a moment in a history of sexuality. Such a reading will highlight *Paradiso*'s function as a receptacle of exclusion and inclusion of what will be deemed a "normative" sexuality, both within the confines of a national imaginary and an aesthetic space.

Chapter VIII, or, the Unspoken Scene

I would like to begin by shaping a critical narrative of (sado)masochism to underscore some important points. First, sexuality is a means of knowledge; it provides a peculiar epistemology. Thus, subjectivity is animated through narratives of sexuality. Second, masochism is a difficult case of how subjectivities are formed—socially, politically, and culturally—that permits the emergence of narratives that effect different identities. Nonetheless, I hope to argue that this very difficulty enables us to consider the very scene of sadomasochism (S/M) as a space wherein identifications may occur on both personal and political levels.

I would like to sketch here some of the signposts and critical contours that make *Paradiso* so interesting to read and useful to theorize about sadomasochism, and masochism in particular. From within, the work shows us several places where corporeal violence, aggressive sexuality, and sexy power trips are at play. It also displays how identities (master/slave, teacher/disciple) are set up. I intend to read the spectacular masochism of *Paradiso* as a symptom of Neo-Baroque tendencies, and alongside Foucault's paradox of *assujettissement*. Additionally, I would like to look at the metatextual reinscriptions of the novel by Vargas Llosa and Rodríguez Monegal in *Mundo Nuevo*, and Cortázar in *La Vuelta al día en ochenta mundos*, reinscriptions that impinge a certain cultural capital on *Paradiso* and show how sadomasochist aesthetics function at multiple levels.

These many layers of signification address both the inner and outer workings of masochism as a strategy for self-figuration—(auto)biographical, literary, national, postcolonial, and cultural, to name a few—in Lezama Lima's oeuvre. It is my contention that masochism as a regulating strategy of self-figuration exerts centrifugally a powerful rethinking of the Latin American subject and his disciplining at this moment of the Latin American literary "Boom."

* * *

The whole mess regarding what degree *Paradiso* really is or is not a "homosexual" text began with a review by Mario Vargas Llosa, where he omits reference to the "homosexual episodes" in the text. Emir Rodríguez Monegal writes another letter where he expresses bewilderment as to the "inexplicable omission of all reference to the clearly homosexual aspect of the novel," especially "as we know, Lezama Lima dedicates a good fourth of his book describing in the most deliriously metaphoric manner the characters' heterosexual and homosexual relations."² Then Vargas Llosa proceeds to give a whole series of reasons for the "omission": "The truth of the matter is that I do not find this silence a low blow in any way; it was a deliberate product of a sense of irritation." Irritation, which Vargas Llosa goes on to explain, was caused by "tens of opinions" which "almost all alluded—in praise or criticism—exclusively to the already legendary eighth chapter of *Paradiso* ..."³ Furthermore, he argues that

> Hearing all these presumptive readers of Lezama, I had the impression that this was a novel centered essentially on a homosexual theme, one that does not seem to me more or less legitimate than any other. My surprise was great in reading the book and realizing that this theme in truth occupied a relatively modest space in the novel ... This complex work, arduous to read, and for the same reason hard to "interpret," can be considered many different things, as all mayor works may be, but, under *no* case is this a treatise, a manual or a defense of homosexualism.⁴ (Translation mine)

Rodríguez Monegal takes this and returns to his point that any reviewer cannot dismiss the homosexual element in the work; thus, he follows up with a "page-by-page" catalog enumerating the main episodes and homosexual allusions in *Paradiso*.⁵ Before engaging with Rodríguez Monegal's critique, let us read carefully Vargas Llosa's "irritation," which has to do with the emphasis that critics and others have given to chapter VIII of the novel. Vargas Llosa seems to assume that reading the work as possessing a homosexual theme somehow makes the work appear commonplace. That reading, he states, is "one that does not seem to me more or less legitimate than any other." What he forgets is that homosexuality as a theme functions just like any other, for it marks the very notion of difference—and more so in the history of Latin American writing, where that difference has remained largely silent or has been absented. Thus the loudness with which homosexuality emerges in the text irritates Vargas Llosa (as it will others) because it is a double figure: an inscription of difference as well as the *resistance* to the very erasure of that difference. Furthermore, Vargas Llosa's cavalier dismissal of the homosexual theme reminds us over and again of the ways in which certain themes are imagined as central while others are represented as marginal.⁶

In *Paradiso*'s chapter VIII, we learn the story of a certain Farraluque, son of a Basque man and a Havana woman,[7] "un leptosomático adolescentario con una cara tristona y ojerosa, pero dotado de verga enorme" ["a leptosomatic adolescent, with a sad and baggy-eyed face, but endowed with an enormous cock"]. He was quite proud of his tool. While performing his duties as bathroom monitor of the younger students at the school, he showed it off:

[Farraluque] alzaba los brazos como para pulsar aéreas castañuelas, manteniendo siempre toda la vera fuera de la bragueta. Se la enroscaba por los dedos, por el antebrazo, hacía como si le pegase, la regañaba, o la mimaba como a un niño tragón.

[(Farraluque) raised his arms as if beating on aerial castanets, always keeping his cock outside his zipper. He used to roll it in his fingers, on his forearm, pretending as if he were hitting it, reprimanding it, or caressed it as if it were a hungry child.] [8,9]

One of these "ceremonies" is witnessed "from the Miami windows of the second floor" by a lazy maid who reports him so that he will be appropriately disciplined. During his absence from "service" we learn about Leregas, a classmate of the novel's protagonist, José Cemí. Leregas's member was equally impressive in length, like "un antebrazo de un trabajador manual"[10] ["the forearm of a manual worker"]. Unlike the rows of students who would stare at his massive phallus, I will forgo discussion of Leregas's powerful dick, which could hold up three books, and focus on Farraluque's. What is important for my argument is that Leregas represents Farraluque's double; his presence introduces this idea of doubleness that I hope to elaborate on throughout this essay.

As part of his punishment, Farraluque is not allowed to leave the school grounds for three consecutive Sundays. On the first Sunday, he meets with the maid who had accused him. Unaware that she is responsible for his fate, Farraluque agrees to help her "white-wash" the walls of the director's house. While supposedly helping her, he notices in a room next door the director's cook, a "nineteen-year-old *mestiza mamey*," apparently sleeping. Her luscious back and buttocks become an invitation: "La sal depositada en cada una de esas hondonadas de su cuerpo, parecía arder. Avivaba los reflejos de las tentaciones"[11] ["The salt deposited in each of her body's crevices seemed to burn glowingly. It awakened the reflections of temptations . . ."]. The young man strips and he jumped into a *tableau vivant* of delights (*saltó sobre el cuadrado de las delicias*), at which time, the young cook turns over—still sleeping—and offers her pubis, "the normality of her body," to the newly arrived man.[12] Once finished, he goes and peeks in the second bedroom where he finds the maid, *la españolita*, who had brought him there. She is exposing her breasts and her "arachnid mound," which requires "the carnal cylinder of a powerful adolescent . . . to split the aracnid through its center."[13] When Farraluque goes to jump into "the feathery *tableau* of the second room (*el cuadrado plumoso del segundo cuarto*), the rotation of the *españolita* was the inverse of the mestiza's turn."[14] By giving herself anally, she was caring for her virginity "theologically." Anal penetration protected her honor and against pregnancy. This was a felicitous encounter because "la configuración fálica de Farraluque era en extreme propicia a esa penetración retrospectiva, pues su aguijón tenía un exagerado predominio de la longura sobre la raíz barbada."[15] ["Farraluque's phallic configuration was extremely propitious for this retrospective (that is, anal) penetration, since his spear had its exaggerated predominance (thickness) on the length closer to its bearded root."] She proudly takes control of the situation and handles the massiveness of the young man in a heroic divide-and-conquer fashion, first taking the glans, then the shaft, finally, she enters "permanent undulation" which continues until after he withdraws and leaves; in effect, she experiences an endless anal orgasm.

I would like to look momentarily at the first set of encounters. The *mestiza mamey* begins by seducing him with her back and then turns to offer him the "normality of her body." Really the first tableau into which Farraluque enters is one of heteronormativity.[16] The second tableau with *la españolita* represents its literal turn, perverse heterosexual desire, as well as entrance into the realm of phantasy, here manifested as a "permanent undulation" or quiver. *La españolita* sexually *rides* the overly endowed youth; she *writhes* in the *jouissance* provoked by a phantasy of anal eroticism.[17] Indeed, this fantasy signifies on the young man sexually, she *writes* him as other. The scene of riding/writhing/writing is a magnificent moment in the Lezamian text where pleasure and pain and marked identity meld into the throes of a permanent undulation.

The next day, the cook tells a servant across the street what happened. And she tells her bored mistress about the youth's massive gift. The lady of the house presses her servant for details. The following Sunday, Adolfito—referred to as a *miquito*, the monkey-boy—comes to look for Farraluque to inform him that the lady across the street from the school also needed her house painted. "Painting the house" or whitewashing has become, thus far, the euphemism for fucking. When he gets there "as if in a stage set," he discovers that "the mature Madonna faked without skill a sensual drowsiness." She stretched her arms to form a square with her index and middle fingers, a square which was broken by the proximity of the "phallic Niké." Again, we notice, as before, the arrival and entrance into each staged setting: "Farraluque jumped into the foamy *tableau (el cuadrado espumoso) . . .*"[18] This time however, the sexual act involves a more aggressively active participation by the sleeping beauty: she specializes in "two of the eight parts of which oral sex consists." First she engages with talent in the "biting of the borders," then, in "whirling the carpet of her tongue on the cupola of the head."[19] When she thought his orgasm was immanent, she drew him toward her vagina only to have the young man yank her away from the hair so that she could see his orgasm, "la arrebatada gorgona, chorreante del sudor ocasionado en las profundidades."[20] ["the excited gorgon squishing the sweat produced in its depths."] This encounter had left him a bit unsatisfied, he felt that "his energy had not manifested itself freely."[21] As he haughtily leaves the room, he anticipates what would come next, and sure enough in the next room is Adolfito, the monkey-boy, waiting for him: "Fingía el sueño, pero con una malicia bien visible, pues con un ojo destapado y travieso le daba la vuelta al cuerpo de Farraluque, deteniéndose después en el punto culminante de la lanza."[22] ["He feigned sleep, but with visible malice, since with one uncovered and naughty eye he wandered around Farraluque's body, stopping afterwards on the culminating point of the spear."] Indeed, the phallus is the very point (the *telos*) of every encounter with Farraluque. And again,

> Antes de penetrar Farraluque en el cuadro gozoso, observó que al rotar Adolfito [. . .] mostró el falo escondido entre las dos piernas, quedándole una pilosa concavidad, tensa por la presión ejercida por el falo en su escondite. Al empezar el encuentro, Adolfito rotaba con incredible

sagacidad [...] Pero el placer en el miquito parece que consistía en esconderse, en hacer nacer una invencible dificultad en el aggressor sexual. La búsqueda de una bahía enloquecía a Farraluque...[23]

[Before Farraluque penetrated the joyous *tableau* (*el cuadro gozoso*), he notices that, while turning, Adolfito [...] showed the phallus hidden between his legs, leaving behind a hairy concavity, tense by the pressure produced by the phallus in its hideaway. Upon beginning the encounter, Adolfito turned with incredible sagacity [...] But pleasure for the monkey-boy seemed to consist in hiding himself, in reproducing an invincible difficulty in the sexual aggressor. The search of a bay made Farraluque crazy...]

Finally, in the process of finding the hole, Farraluque squirts over the boy's chest, who then spins over to show his "diabolically spread-eagle legs" and to smear the useless cream over the sheets.

I would like to review certain elements from this dance. We notice again that Farraluque "penetrates" a *tableau jouissant*, but not the boy. This is an important moment because it signifies an initiation to the scene of S/M, for as we know pleasure in sadomasochistic act is located in the very setting and choreography of the event, not in the *telos* of an orgasm. The boy presents himself but hides his penis and turns over and over to prevent Farraluque from penetrating him. So, strangely, the boy's turns come to signify his sexuality differently. He turns obsessively to figure as "castrated," thereby seducing a presumptive heterosexual gaze, and then he re-turns to anal eroticism, thus confusing and infuriating the other youth. Adolfito's body allows for an erotic and sexual refunctioning, which destabilizes the identificatory practices involved in possessing the other. Furthermore, we learn that for Adolfito pleasure consists in hiding himself, "in reproducing (*en hacer nacer*) an invincible difficulty in the sexual aggressor." Pleasure is enacted via a provocation; it is elicited by making the other perform as you want him to perform. This very notion of provoking the other would then call into question the status of the "sexual aggressor." It seems that the boy, seen from outside as the masochist, is in control—but, then again, the masochist is always in control.

Now if we can plot out Farraluque's sexcapades we can see a pattern develop: First, he has sex with the cook, your basic heterosexual framing of "man-on-top." Second, comes the *españolita* who offers her bottom,

164 *The Avowal of Difference*

as a way to protect a particular imaginary of virginity. Third, Farraluque gets blown (away) by the "mature Madonna." What is important in this scene is that his orgasm is accompanied by his violently yanking her hair and making her watch the flow from his "man meat," thus demonstrating that the scene is all about the man's pleasure. This leads us to the scene with the boy, who hides his penis to provoke the other. With each scene we see a modulation of erotic perversion, and we see Farraluque's sexual identity change depending on the *tableau* he enters. We could imagine that he begins identifying as heteronormative, having sex with the nineteen-year-old, followed by a perverse heterosexual connection with *la españolita*. Then Farraluque's sexuality is no longer about penetration as we witness in his encounter with the Madonna; finally, Farraluque ends up in a homosexual scene with Adolfito. With each encounter his sexual identity shifts—he covers a wide spectrum from heteronormative to homoerotic. What unites these scenes is the trope of waste, because each time he reaches orgasm outside the erotogenic zone.[24] Also, each first encounter (the cook, the Madonna) has a double (*la españolita* and Adolfito—each a diminutive) that deconstructs the first. For instance, in the first set of encounters, the security of heteronormativity (the normality of sexual penetration with the cook) is problematized by the promise of anal eroticism (which is always bisexual).[25] In the second set, heterosexual identity (as visibly manifested with sex with a woman) becomes further destabilized by the change of the object of desire (sex with the boy). Even between the two sets there is a change. Penetration as the paragon of genital sexuality (the aim of the first two encounters) is complicated by fellatio (in the third encounter). If we trace Farraluque's experience in a linear fashion, we discover that what began as an imitation to heteronormative sexuality ends in a complex whereby he is made other, unable to be neatly classified into any one sexual identity.

Narratives of Masochism

The third Sunday also takes Farraluque to another realm, fully into a scene of sadomasochism. Before we enter it, let us survey what sadomasochism means socially, culturally, and theoretically.

Readers of Freud know that one of his most important impasses is the question of masochism as a strategy of self-figuration. In his early writings, Freud discusses masochism as derivative of sadism; he would not conceive of a primary masochism until much later.[26] In

"The Economic Problem of Masochism," Freud gives his most complete analysis of masochism, erotogenic ("pleasure-in-pain"), feminine, and moral.[27] Freud seeks to read masochism as a perplexing "economic problem" within the principle of constancy:[28] "For if mental processes are governed by the pleasure principle in such a way that their first aim is the avoidance of unpleasure and the obtaining of pleasure, masochism is incomprehensible."[29] In other words, he asks: How does subjectivity emerge in the scene of masochism? How does the "I" claim agency through its very debasement.

In a completely different manner, Foucault meditates on this paradox in his discussions of *assujettissement*, the process of becoming a subject and the process of subjection.[30] Although I am aware that I am linking the Foucauldian notion of "discipline" with a distinct practice of sadomasochism, I do this deliberately, by placing momentarily the differences aside, with the intention of showing a continuum between both practices and theories. I want to create a critical slippage between "the strategic use of power differentials to produce effects of pleasure instead of domination," which is how David Halperin sees a major difference between sadomasochistic eroticism and discipline in Foucault's work.[31] According to Halperin: "Foucault emphasizes that what goes by the name of 'domination' in S/M is a strategy for creating pleasure, not a form of personal or political subjugation."[32] So, in effect, Foucault presents separate fields—pleasure and domination—which are enacted differently through a variety of practices of relational power. I am interested in the perversion of the question of pleasure as form of domination, not just domination as pleasure (the classic definition of sadism). I want to keep in mind this idea that by acknowledging pleasure, the subject controls, resists, stops the flow of domination. One way to begin looking at this question would be to ask, whether or not the fields of pleasure and domination also operate and implicate one another *metaphorically*. If so, how is the metaphor written and read, meaning: What are the consequences of the act of metaphorization, especially in relation to subjectivity?

The Masochist's Pleasure

If the scene with Adolfito suggests the initiation of Farraluque into the space of S/M, "[t]he third Sunday of punishment"[33] certainly shows S/M in its plenitude.[34] On that morning Farraluque is met by Adolfito and given a key to a place where he is to meet a nameless "*someone, seduced by his art of white-washing.*"[35] Farraluque is already well able to read into what "whitewashing" meant. However, we could add further that the white of his semen writes the *tableaux* in which he is invited to participate. He is given a key and an address, where late that afternoon Farraluque goes to visit. We are told that:

> ... había llegado a un bosque de niebla. ¿En qué profundos había caído? Después de que su vista se fue acostumbrando, pudo darse cuenta que era una carbonería en donde se encontraba. Las primeras divisions que rodeaban todo el cuadrado, estaban dedicadas al carbón ya muy dividido ... [36]

> [... he had arrived to a forest of fog. In what depths had he fallen? After his sight became more accustomed to its surroundings, he realized that he was in a coalhouse. The first partitions that surrounded the entire square were full of coal already separated ...]

The mise-en-scène is quite different from the earlier two scenes. We are no longer in the comfort of domesticity, but rather in the darkness of a coalhouse. The scene, which is thought of as a hell, is described as dark and difficult to see through. If he was, in effect, going to whitewash the place, this particular space presented quite a challenge. As he walks through the coal bins, he comes to a small room barely lit. There he finds a man of around fifty who is naked, wearing only his shoes and socks—and a mask.[37] The man quickly and ceremoniously begins stripping the young man, and immediately takes him.

> La maestría en la incorporación de la serpiente era total, a medida de que se dejaba ganar por el cuerpo penetrante, se ponía rojo, como si en vez de recibir fuese a parir un monstruoso animal.
> El tono apopléctico de este tan poderoso incorporador del mundo exterior, fue en *crescendo* hasta adquirir verdaderos rugidos oraculares. Con las manos en alto apretaba los cordeles que cerraban los sacos carboniferous, hasta que sus dedos comenzaron a sangrar.[38]

> [The mastery of the serpent's incorporation was complete; as (the masked man) allowed himself to be won over by the penetrating body,

he became red, as if, instead of receiving, he were giving birth to a monstrous animal.

The apoplectic tone of this so powerful incorporator of the outside world grew in a crescendo to the point of acquiring truly oracular roars. With his hands up high, he gripped the ropes that fastened the carbon sacks until his fingers began to bleed.]

There is no effort to flirt with Farraluque here. I would suggest that this flirtation had already happened *narratively* through the stories that were circulating around the priapic one. Rumors and phantasies about Farraluque's dominion had been circulating around the school playground; and, when they reached the masked man, these narratives had acquired the form of a speech act that would attract him to Farraluque. In other words, the seduction of the masked man was accomplished *performatively* by the circulation of rumors about the big boy, through his imagining of the boy's body.

What is most important here is seeing who is given and who claims agency in the sexual act, not the endowed man, but the one who gets fucked, "the powerful incorporator." The older man merely puts this scene or fantasy of masochism into motion. What we witness here is a classic S/M erotic narrative—the mask, the darkness, the raw sexuality, the blood. It is a scene of sexual domination that has been enacted *for pleasure*. Again, pleasure lies not in the graffiti of the orgasm or the blood, but in the prior narrative that frames the scene—as well as in the spin-off narratives that the scene will evoke. In other words, pleasure had already been accounted for in the old man's construction of the S/M fantasy narrative, a narrative that had been told prior to the encounter and that gets retold over and over after the event. The enactment and totality of this event is articulated "in *crescendo* to the point of acquiring truly oracular roars." The true narrative of the event at the very moment of its realization is (dis)articulated, it cannot be told, and this marks the entrance into the Lacanian Real. It is that moment of "dreams-come-true," where the subject cannot fully comprehend the overwhelming nature of the event nor does he possess the language to begin speaking of it and to start symbolizing the event.[39]

Read *from outside*, this scene produces the kind of devaluation through horror and panic that exemplifies Vargas Llosa's commentary as well as the uneasy superficial catalogs that Rodríguez Monegal presents,[40] when in actuality, it is imperative to underscore that this scene of masochism obeys the law of Lezamian poetics or his *eras imaginarias*—a series of image worlds that flow across time and space. Furthermore, this reading from the inside is what makes Julio Cortázar's 1967 reading of *Paradiso* so brilliantly relevant: he proposes "that *Paradiso*'s characters always speak *from inside the image*, since Lezama projects them from a poetic system that has its key in the potentiality of the image as a supreme secretion of the human spirit in search of the reality of an invisible world"[41] (original emphasis). The idea of speaking *from within* the literary image is very compelling when thinking of Farraluque, who constantly enters the *tableaux*, sees himself, and projects an identity from inside the visual. This entrance into the *tableau* has connections with Foucault's discussion of the panopticon. Foucault notes that "a real subjection (*assujettissement*) arises mechanically from a fictitious relation."[42] Within panoptic institutions—and I would define these in the broadest sense possible as not just the prison, but the school, the house across the street, exhibitionist relations, and so on—Foucault finds:

> He who is submitted to a field of visibility, *and who knows it*, takes again into his account (realizes) the constraints of power; he allows them to play spontaneously upon him; *he inscribes in himself the power relation in which he simultaneously plays both roles* [subject and subjected]; he becomes the principle of his own subject-formation/subjection (*assujettissement*).[43] (Italics mine.)

Foucault's brilliant insight helps us to see that Farraluque positions himself inside a scene and from there projects outwardly: he becomes a subject by submitting to the place of the other. The difference that we can see between both authors is that Foucault focuses on the simultaneity of the *assujettissement,* thereby producing a relational vision of power, whereas Lezama places and *displaces* (really, oscillates) *the degree of priority given to the subject versus the image-world*. In other words, the Lezamian subject and his image-worlds clash and transform each other violently, producing a distinctive voice in narrative.

I want to return and listen a bit longer to the *rugidos oraculares*—oracular moans or roars—as the struggle by *someone* to say something. We should remember that earlier, when the maid was telling her boss (the mature Madonna) over and over again, "the fever in the ecstasy in receiving such a huge spear," she finally says "with extreme humility":

> Señora, eso únicamente se puede describir bien cuando lo tiene delante, pero, créame, entonces ya uno se olvida de todo y después no puede describir nada en sus detalles.[44]

> [Madam, that can only be described well when one has it before oneself but, believe me, then right away one forgets about it all and afterwards, one cannot describe anything in detail.]

The story of the phallus is also the story of a trauma ("such a huge spear") that cannot be completely described. What follows this trauma is a repetition compulsion, the circulation of the story as well as everyone's desire to receive or incorporate that traumatic event. This compulsion to repeat (the many dualities in the chapter) produces a restricted economy of the traumatic event. Repetition is then a formula containing the violence of the traumatic spear. The narrative of repetition (compulsion) produces the very broken, fragmented, incomplete structure it is trying to repair. Sadomasochism is a structure, which tries to contain a phallic trauma, which of course exceeds the confines of this S/M narrative. The power of the Real thus deconstructs reality as fiction.

"Who's Your Daddy?":
The Absent Question that Structures the Subject

In the last section I looked at the S/M scene between Farraluque and the masked man; however, I shifted the focus of my reading from the visual inflection of the tableaux to a more linguistic inflection. Also, the critical narrative I constructed suggests that the duality of the earlier encounters (cook/*la españolita* and Madonna/monkey-boy) no longer continued on the third Sunday. In this section, I want to return to the visual dimension of my reading and "round off" my narrative by reading the scene of Farraluque's final orgasm, the impossibility of repetition—and the repetition of an impossibility.

Just before reaching orgasm, Farraluque noticed with humor and laughter the penis of the "receptive subject"; the masked man's penis is "concealed by indifference, disdained flaccidity."[45] At that point:

... su falo acostumbrado a eyacular sin el calor de una envoltura carnal, se agitó como impulsado por la levedad de una brisa suave ... Introdujo la vacilante verga en una hendidura de carbón, sus movimientos exasperados en los momentos finales de la passion, hicieron que comenzara a desprenderse un cisco. Tiraba los cordeles, le daba puñetazos a la concavidad de los sacos, puntapiés a los carbones ... Esa sanguínea acumulación de su frenesí, motivaría la hecatombe (sic) final de la carbonería.[46]

[... his phallus, accustomed to ejaculate without the heat of a carnal envelopment, became agitated by the levity of a soft breeze ... He pushed his vacillating cock in a crack in the coal, his exasperated movements in the final moments of passion caused coal dusk to scatter. He yanked the ropes, punched the concave sacks, kicked the coal ... His frenzied hardness caused the final fall of the coalhouse.]

As the men run to safety from the falling coal, they are marked by "irregular black stripes on [their] bodies."[47] This scene brings up again important issues regarding Farraluque's virility. I would like to suggest that penetrating the carbon is a desire to return to the origin. Rather than display the money shot, as he has done before with the Madonna, it appears as though Farraluque is trying to give his semen to the organic matter, thus reenacting another beginning of life, where semen and carbon become the *materia prima* of creation. I am tempted to return to Cortázar's (masculinist) rendering of the Lezamian image-world—"the image as a supreme secretion of the human spirit in search of the reality of an invisible world." Cortázar's description of the Lezamian image-world is just like the figure of Farraluque trying to penetrate the mystery of the origin of life. However the disturbance of this act, literally *contra natura*, ends up in a disaster which leaves the two men's bodies beaten and marked (or written on).

Indeed, the lighter-skinned bodies get marked by the blackness of the carbon—might this not signify something else? Another interpretation of this scene—of semen and carbon, of whiteness and blackness—might be that Lezama is rewriting Fernando Ortíz's metaphor of transculturation. However, rather than thinking about the economies of sugar and tobacco as racial, social, and cultural metaphors that dialectically form the Cuban nation, Lezama is creating a queer sexual origin for the nation, whereby semen and carbon symbolize the whiteness and blackness to rewrite the nation. Throughout chapter VIII, there is constant reference to the skin tone and bodies of Farraluque's partners, so it makes sense to consider this allegorical reading of whiteness and blackness as pertinent here. Again, the two men leave with their bodies marked by the blackness of the carbon, that is, marked by a racial rescripting of their bodies. Jossianna Arroyo has astutely reread Ortíz's allegory of transculturation as an enactment of "cultural transvestism," that is, rather than creating a dialectic or dialogic theorization of nationhood, Ortíz in fact through his privileged status appropriates blackness as a strategy to then define the nation. In other words, in Ortíz's theorization of *cubanidad* there is no synthesis; instead there is a performance—he enacts black masculinity, displaces femininity to then engage in a definition of Cuba's "national character."[48] Therefore, if we consider how the coal marks the bodies of Farraluque and the masked men, we can read this allegory as a writing of blackness onto the lighter-skin bodies—this provides us a different allegory to understand Cuban national formation.[49]

The masked man leaves the scene of the crime, and Farraluque follows a bit later. Outside, he meets Adolfito, who reveals the identity of the someone, that *someone*: "'Well, behind the mask you would have found the husband of the lady across the street from the school. The one you had to pull by the hair . . .' Thus Adolfito finished, smiling."[50] Revealing the identity of the masked man also reveals the circular knowledge that has emerged around Farraluque's member. We discover that Adolfito had witnessed Farraluque and the lady, and that he may have been involved in constructing the fantasy for the masked man. Thus, we learn that every encounter with Farraluque was already predetermined by a particular narrative about the phallus, and this narrative is repeated in an incomplete manner in the afterthoughts of those who seek to come close to him. There appears to be a symmetrical narrative before and after the phallus. This symmetry between the stories before and after the scenes of encounter frames and, in this sense, also closes up the narrative and the circulation of desire for the phallus. But the containment or possession of phallic power is, nevertheless, made impossible because the multiple narratives produced by the phallus become increasingly ungraspable.[51] Even sadomasochistic eroticism, and especially its aggression, cannot contain the fantastic narrative.

Earlier I suggested that this final erotic scene has a double. The chapter ends, and in the critical edition, we find a felicitous footnote: "In the text's manuscript, a larger space between the last sentence of this paragraph and the beginning of the next indicates the end of a section and the beginning of another; this was not taken into consideration in either the *Unión* (1966) [the first edition] or the *Era* (1968) [the previously authoritative] editions."[52] This blank space that follows Farraluque's erotic scenes is the visual performative double of the S/M encounter with the masked man. It brings together a textual reconciliation and Lezama's representation of the Real. It is at once the failure of language to capture the Real, as well as the success of silence, as an affirmation of muteness, to represent (visually) the Real. The blank space is Farraluque's final painting, the whiteness of his semen, the whiteness of his excuse. The whiteness of textual representation is pure image, pure meaning: ungraspable, yet knowable; unknowable, yet narratively and visually graspable as a restricted economy.

8

On the Homo-Baroque

Queering Sarduy's Baroque Genealogies

> Y ahora, en medio de cojines rubendarianos y cortinajes, con fondo de biombos y valses—entre pajarracos y pollos—, sólo reino yo, recorrido por la simulación, imantado por la reverberación de una apariencia, vaciado por la sacudida de la risa: anulado, ausente.
>
> —Severo Sarduy[1]

If everything is about sex, except *sex* which is about power, then Lezama Lima's *Paradiso* teaches us is that sexual identity is always a metaphoric, and can only be approximated and never pinned down. In this chapter I look at the theoretical work of Cuban novelist and theorist Severo Sarduy to understand how he conceives eroticism and sexuality, especially in his structuralist analyses of the Baroque. I also analyze his last novel, *Pájaros de la playa*, to look at other theorizations of the queer body, some of which overlap with his essays on the Neo-Baroque in Latin American writing.

Baroque and Neo-Baroque Genealogies

One of the most succinct expositions of the Latin American Neo-Baroque as a rewriting of a European Baroque expression appears in Severo Sarduy's 1972 essay "El barroco y el neobarroco."[2] Here the author traces a structuralist genealogy of the Neo-Baroque as an particular Latin American artistic movement, offering important insights about the practices of reading the Baroque aesthetically, socially, and culturally.³ What follows is an *explication de texte* of his essay, in particular, teasing out the theoretical moves that Sarduy performs to situate the Neo-Baroque in the context of French post-structuralist theory, particularly Lacanian psychoanalysis.⁴

Traditionally, the European Baroque introduces questions of the spectacularity of the image, the overwrought details, the transformation of perspective, the repositioning of the artist in relation to the work of art, among others. Sarduy's most direct way of understanding the literary Baroque is by taking the algorhythmic formula of a metaphor to the second power (or metaphor squared): (metaphor)². Specifically, he traces a genealogy back to the Spanish Baroque poet Luis de Góngora. He states, "La metáfora de Góngora es ya, de por sí, metalingüística, es decir, eleva al cuadrado un nivel ya elaborado del lenguaje, el de las metáforas poéticas, que a su vez suponen ser la elaboración de un primer nivel denotativo, 'normal' del lenguaje."⁵ ["Góngora's metaphor is always, already metalinguistic, that is, it is an elevation to the second power of an already elaborated level of language, of poetic metaphors, which at the same time presuppose the elaboration of a first denotative 'normal' level of language.] Sarduy goes further to tease out a literary and artistic Baroque *as an act of artificialization* which may follow three different forms or "mechanisms"—substitution, proliferation, and condensation. I shall proceed and elaborate each of these mechanisms briefly.

Making reference to José Lezama Lima's naming of a virile member as "el aguijón del leptosomático macrogenitoma" ["the stinger of the leptosomatic macrogenitome"], Sarduy offers a rather provocative example of how Baroque substitution works: "el significante que corresponde al significado 'virilidad' ha sido escamoteado y sustituido por otro, totalmente alejado semánticamente de él y que sólo en el contexto erótico del relato funciona, es decir, corresponde al primero en el proceso de significación."⁶ ["the signifier that corresponds to the signified 'virility' has been switched and replaced by another, totally separating it semantically, and it only functions within the erotic context of the story, that is to say, the new signifier corresponds to the signified though a process of signification."] Sarduy represents this substitution as follows:⁷

$$\frac{\cancel{S}}{s} \dashrightarrow S^1$$

Sarduy argues that the distance between the signified (represented as lowercase, italicized *s*) and the (new) signifier[1] (represented by uppercase S^1) marks an "[a]pertura, falla entre lo nombrante y lo nombrado y surgimiento de otro nombrante, es decir, metáfora. Distancia exagerada, todo el barroco no es más que una hipérbole, cuyo 'desperdicio' veremos que no por azar es erótico."[8] ["aperture, a gap between the naming and the named, (as well as) the emergence of another name, that is, a metaphor. Exaggerated distance, the entire Baroque enterprise is nothing more than a hyperbole, whose very 'wastefulness' is not by accident erotic."] What Sarduy seems to propose is that the newly formed signifier (S^1) both replaces an "original" signifier (S), as well as it establishes a particular aperture or gap, a relationship with the signified that can only be reclaimed in the context of an erotic event, what he calls "a process of signification." The dotted line between signifier[1] (S^1) and signified (*s*) is an erotic narrative that allows for the restoration of the sign.[9] If language is that which links a signifier (sound-image) and the signified (concept), then eroticism in language links the signified with the newly substituting signifier[1], which by another name is a metaphor. Interestingly, Sarduy labels that new link between signifier[1] and signified as hyperbolic and erotic wastefulness.

Moving along with proliferation, Sarduy proposes that

> Otro mecanismo de artificialización del barroco es el que consiste en obliterar el significante de un significado dado pero no reemplazándolo por otro, por distante que éste se encuentre del primero, sino por una cadena de significantes que regresa metonímicamente y que termina circunscribiendolo al significante ausente, trazando una órbita alrededor de él, órbita de cuya lectura—que podríamos llamar radial—podemos inferirlo.[10]

> [Another mechanism of Baroque artificialization consists in the obliteration of the signifier of a given signified, but rather than replacing it for another, however distant this one might be from the first,

it involves replacing the signifier with a chain of signifiers that move metonymically and end circumscribing the absent signifier, tracing an orbit around it; we can infer the absent signifier by reading this orbit—a radial reading—, if you like.]

He represents this operation as follows:

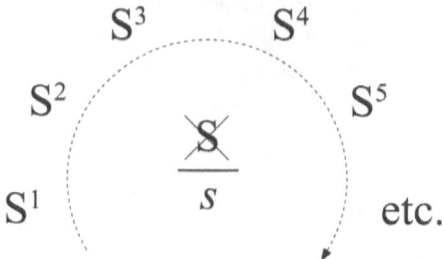

Sarduy is in fact suggesting that the veneer of the absent signifier gets traced by a proliferation of a chain of signifiers, whose sole purpose is alluding, approximating, or hinting toward that absence. The effect of proliferation is the figuration of the negative of a signifier, it is about marking the emptiness caused by the evacuation of the signifier, thus alluding to the Baroque *horror vacui*, horror to the emptiness in representation. The Baroque paradox of the "empty object" forces a prolific articulation. In proliferation, Sarduy finds within the operation of metonymy "the best definition for all metaphor ... displacement, movement, and trope."[11] Furthermore, he reveals in his own definition a particular performance of what he means by *proliferation*:

> La proliferación, recorrido previsto, órbita de similitudes abreviadas, exige, para ser adivinable lo que oblitera, para rozar con su perífrasis el significante excluido, expulsado, y dibujar la ausencia que señala, esa traslación, ese recorrido alrededor de lo que falta y cuya falta lo constituye: lectura radial que connota, como ninguna otra, una presencia, la que en su elipsis señala la marca de significante ausente, ese a que la lectura, sin nombrarla, en cada uno de sus virajes hace referencia, el expulsado, el que ostenta las huellas del exilio.[12]

> [Proliferation, its sweep foreseen, orbit of abbreviated similitudes, demands to make knowable what it obliterates, to caress with its

periphrastic articulation what is excluded, the expelled signifier, and to draw (out) the absence which it signifies, that trans-latio, that traveling around what is lost and whose very loss is what constitutes it: radial reading that connotes, like none other, a presence, whose ellipsis signals the mark of an absent signifier, which the act of reading, without naming it, makes reference to its absence in each of its [readerly] twirls, the expelled, the one who flaunts the scars of exile.]

I pay special attention to this particular instance in Sarduy complex writing because it allows us to appreciate both a style and an autobiographical moment. Let me advance that proliferation allows Sarduy to enact and construct a particular Imaginary constellation of the exiled body and a tacitly queer self. Elsewhere I have argued that the force of Sarduy's self-narratives as an exiled Cuban in Paris have obfuscated and displaced his queer identity.[13] His particular queer identity formation is revealed uneasily through leaks, elliptically, though periphrastic approximations. Importantly, his notion of "radial reading" marks an opening through which we may peek into Sarduy's queer self. Radial reading, that is reading through circumlocution, may in fact be understood *as a counterpoint* to homographesis, an inscription of the homosexual in textuality. Radial reading would suggest a special relation wherein the reader may only locate the queer subject in a roundabout way, always elusive and on the move; also, the reader may find her- or himself trapped as a queer subject within the text through the act identification that happens as an act of radial reading.

Finally, Sarduy explains condensation, his last cataloged form of the Baroque, as "analogous to the oneiric process."

$$S^1 \rightleftarrows \frac{S^3}{S} \rightleftarrows S^2$$

He sees this process as a complicated melding of two or more signifiers (S^1 and S^2, a "synchronic condensation" in the example of cinematography) that creates a hybrid signifier form (designated above as S^3), and which relates to the signified. Sarduy stresses that this condensation of signifiers is not just simple juxtaposition, but a "tension" or a dialectic.

To summarize, Sarduy notes that

Si en la sustitución el significante es escamoteado y remplazado por otro y en la proliferación una cadena de significantes circunscribe al significante primero ausente, en la condensación asistimos a la "puesta en escena" y la unificación de dos significantes que vienen a reunirse en el espacio exterior de la pantalla, del cuadro, o en el interior de la memoria.[14]

[If through substitution the signifier is exchanged by a sleight of hand and replaced by another, and through proliferation a chain of signifiers circumscribed the absent, first or "original" signifier, then in substitution, we are witnesses of a *mise-en-scène* and to the unification of two signifiers that come together in the exterior space of a screen, a frame, or in the interior of memory.]

Now these operations that promote the Baroque as a process of creating the artificial—substitution, proliferation, condensation—are just a preface to Sarduy's larger theoretical insights. In fact he argues that these mechanisms are central to the Spanish and other European Baroques, monumentalized in the works of Góngora, Velásquez, Cervantes, Rabelais, Shakespeare, and other masters.

I have hinted—and will now argue outright—that these Baroque formulations might be useful to understand queer subjectivity in Latin American and Latino cultures. Like *modernismo*, they offer alternatives to understanding the narratives of sexuality that Latino American authors and subject may use for self-figuration. To summarize, the Baroque formulations that Sarduy gives us are the following: first, *substitution* with its erotic excess and "wastefulness" contains a tacit language that must be drawn out; second, proliferation in its roundabout way signifies the absent subject; and third, condensation is a capacious packing on of multiple signifiers intended to create a dialectic that is meant to con-fuse (etymologically, to fuse together) other intersectional identitites. Each of these Baroque descriptions and mechanisms are part of a history of Baroque representation—and become further exaggerated and complicated in the context of Latin America and the Neo-Baroque.

Sarduy will go on to propose that in Latin America, a specific and significant spin signifies on the European expression of the Baroque. He observes that "[e]n la medida en que una obra del barroco latinoamericano sea la desfiguración de una obra anterior que haya que leer en filigrana para gustar totalmente de ella, ésta pertenecerá a un género mayor..."[15] ["only to the degree that a work of the Latin American Baroque is the disfiguration of a previous work that must be read in detail *(leer en filigrana)*, will it then be enjoyed it fully, and in so doing the Latin American work becomes a major work"]. Again Sarduy is suggesting that the Latin American Baroque (first as *barroco de Indias*, and then as Neo-Baroque) inaugurates a particular relation with the Spanish Baroque, a relation that involves a complex act of reading and rewriting, through which the Master narratives of Spanish or European texts must be accounted for *in the very textuality* of the work (he proposes the term *leer en filigrana* [literally "reading in filigree"], which suggests a special attention to texture and details), understanding the Spanish Baroque as a watermark that *anamorphically* haunts the Latin American text. While Sarduy links this particular relation to Bakhtin's notion of parody and literary history, I am interested in this metaphor of reading for its philosophical, its postcolonial theoretical import, as well as its centrality in informing Latin American subject formation. By imagining the Spanish Baroque as a watermark that ever-presently inhabits and hovers around the text, we must understand it not simply as a textual but also as a material presence—the watermark of Spain is visible from and to a degree; it disrupts, it casts a shadow over the text of Latin American. Also, by reimagining the Latin American Baroque as a particular relation to the Spanish Baroque, it opens up a series of questions about how the Latin American subject relates him- or herself to European mastery. How does a Latin American subject enjoy a full sense of identity with and against the presence of a European other that continuously provides the aesthetic materials and social rules for self-figuration? How do Latin American subjects imagine themselves in their own terms? It is essential here to acknowledge that these questions have framed much of that dialectical relation between Latin America and its histories of colonialisms.

I return to Sarduy's exposition, which focuses more on the formal questions of the Baroque as a literary event. In his essay he proposes a semiology of the Latin American Baroque—in brief, he looks principally at citationality, reminiscence, and wordplay (or puns) as strategies for deconstructing master narratives. In explaining these specific mechanisms peculiar to Latin American Baroque representation, he proposes particular qualities persistent in the Baroque.

First, Sarduy underscores the notions of excess and waste that define Baroque space. He suggests that Baroque language thrives in its search for a partial object; specifically he wants to claim that the real object to be found is what Lacan identifies as *l'objet petit* a. He continues then by looking at the place of eroticism alongside the Baroque: "Juego, pérdida, desperdicio y placer, es decir, erotismo en tanto que actividad que es siempre puramente lúdica, que no es más que una parodia de la función de reproducción, una transgresión de lo útil, del diálogo 'natural' de los cuerpos."[16] ["Game, loss, waste, and pleasure, that is eroticism insofar it is a purely ludic activity, that it is not more than a parody of reproduction, a transgression of what is useful, of the 'natural' dialogue of bodies."] It is surprising to see Sarduy's heteronormative framing that explains eroticism as a parody of reproduction. Instead, I would stress that the queerness of sexuality—that sense of strangeness in naming an identity *through* the sexual act—might be the basis of comparison between the erotic and the Baroque. Sarduy is right to propose later on that "[e]n el erotismo, la artificialidad, lo cultural, se manifiesta en el juego con el objeto perdido, juego cuya finalidad está en sí mismo y cuyo propósito no es la conducción de un mensaje [. . .], sino su desperdicio en función del placer."[17] ["in eroticism, artificiality—the cultural element—manifests itself in the play with the lost object; this play has itself as an object, and it not a means of conveying a message (. . .), rather it is about wastefulness in function of pleasure."] What I find striking in this passage is that culture gets read as the expression of the artificial element within eroticism; in other words, Sarduy seems to be suggesting that *artificiality or cultural difference provides the rules of how eroticism*—here I would open it up to all sexuality—*speaks*. Sarduy often depoliticizes eroticism; by insisting on sexuality inasmuch as it operates as a discourse of power, in the broadest sense, I want to stress sexual politics. For Sarduy, eroticism gets expressed through cultural difference. I also think that sexuality gets articulated through cultural difference, that is, through the specific signifiers that circumscribe nations and cultures otherwise; sexuality may only be known through a certain cultural register that is necessarily artificial—and temporally and historically knowable. The play of sexuality has itself as an end;

it is a play whose very erasure gets teleologically referenced as pure pleasure. Again, it is important to stress that Sarduy and his critics have too often ignored sexuality as a political discourse. I want to be very cautious not to get so enthralled with this idea that sexuality's erasure or expendability might be a desirable thing. Politically, I am still convinced of the need of knowing the ways in which sexual expressions get marked, not to eschew them away, but rather to appreciate the mechanisms of cultural power that permit access to the realm of the social and political. In much of Latin America, certain forms of sexual practices and identities still remain in the space of silence, so speaking about how sexuality might be known—rather than actively unknown—is indeed necessary.

Second, Sarduy pays attention to Baroque structure as a mirror. The spectacularity of the Baroque reflects a cultural desire and image. Although this image is necessarily distorted because of the technological insufficiencies of different representational vehicles, Sarduy argues that the European Baroque or the early Baroque of colonial Latin America "may potentially contain [what it is trying to represent], or at least *point to* representation as a potentiality."[18] Baroque as such relies on the harmony or faith in mirroring, on the potentiality of symmetry. However, Sarduy notes, "el barroco actual, el neobarroco, refleja estructuralmente la inarmonía, la ruptura de la homogeneidad, del logos en tanto que absoluto, la carencia que constituye nuestro fundamento epistémico."[19] ["the contemporary Baroque, the Neo-Baroque, structurally reflects discord, rupture with homogeneity, with the *logos* as an absolute; it is this lack that constitutes its epistemological foundation."] The context of Latin America makes Neo-Baroque possible. Therefore, the Neo-Baroque is about understanding the asymmetry among the object, its representations, and its modes of articulation; more importantly, it is about appreciating how that asymmetrical distance gets framed socially, culturally, economically, and politically.

Homo-Baroque Correctives

Now, I would like to go back, recapitulate, and rethink of some of Sarduy's genealogical project; in particular I am interested in the ways in which I may render visible some of the queer sutures that make this text coherent. First, I want to take up the mechanism of substitution, specifically how the process of signification links the signified to the new signifier. The signifier[1] is in fact the same as and different from the "original" signifier for which it has been swapped. Working back to restore some linkage, however distant, between the signifier[1] and the signified involves a process of signification, to which Sarduy attributes a dimension of eroticism. Moreover, the critical narrative that links the signifier1 and the signified must necessarily be erotic, despite it being wasteful. I want to hold on to this particular conceptualization, rethinking not so much about waste, but rather about its potentiality in recycling. I propose that the critical narrative that binds the signifier1 and the signified in the mechanism of substitution is sexually inflected, and in this manner necessarily productive of new sexual narratives and identities.

Second, on the question of proliferation, I want to expand on the concept of "radial reading" and reframe it alongside Freud's idea of identification. If proliferation is an mechanism that permits articulation of what is not there, the expelled or absent signifier, then it is necessary to remember that "speaking around he or she who is not there" might be repurposed as a very productive figure of speech that reveals the silhouette of a queer body. I locate this critical practice in Latin American letters back to Sor Juana—from there it would be possible to draw an important genealogy of queer representation that concentrates on the challenges and possibilities of speaking with and about an absent body. It is ironic that it is only through excess that absence may be reconfigured, if only as a negative of what is sought.

Freud has suggested that the process of identification is always a partial and limited relation. After the subject partially identifies with an object or a performance, and incorporates or introjects it, this partial adaptation and relation grows—if you like, it proliferates—into a new narrative of the self that takes form to constitute subjectivity. I would like to suggest that the practices of identification as efforts to approximate or approach an object or performance are parallel to the metonymic proliferations enacted to recover the lost signifier. If we consider radial reading as a particular reworking and rewriting of subjectivity, similar to the work of identification, we might begin to imagine rich and prolific strategies for queer subject formation. I want to be emphatic that I am not proposing the imposition of queer identity into a text indiscriminately: rather I begin with the trope of the "expelled signifier" that motivates the act of proliferation, and as a queer subject identify with that absence, a figure or moment of loss, as a site that beckons to be claimed or inhabited.

Last, I want to look at the act of close reading, what Sarduy denotes as *leer en filigrana*, "reading in filigree." This is a call to read between the lines, to read the fine threads and grains of filigree that compose a work of art, more generally, to understand the structuration of a text. Moreover, *leer en filigrana* also refers to the presence of a watermark in the background of a page; as I suggested, a watermark that tacitly lies as the presence of the absent Master that regulates the formation and interpretation of the Latin American text. This relation of lordship and bondage assigns the project of Latin American subject-formation essentially to one of resistance and decolonization. If in fact the Latin American text is both under the influence of a "prior" European text (more recently, under the shadow of the United States) as well as a radical rewriting of it, then this relationship of bondage signifies on the question of colonialism. I am proposing that this bondage relation is not necessarily unidirectional, but rather a tension, a dialectic, that centrifugally represents complex and spectacular subjectivities. What are the implications, we might ask, of such a bondage relationship in the formation of queer subjectivities? It would thus behoove the queer subject to engage in this project, to act affirmatively in writing Latin America. Earlier I asked: How does a Latin American subject enjoy a full sense of identity with and against the presence of a European (or United States) other that continuously provides the aesthetic materials for self-figuration? A queer echo of this question might sound like this: How does a queer Latin American subject overcome the particular limitations of a queer European (or United States) cultural aesthetic—and imagine her- or himself differently? This question has very concrete implications when we recall that Sarduy is writing about Latin American literature from Paris as a participant of the *Tel Quel* group, friends with Roland Barthes, Philippe Sollers, François Wahl, and others, as well as attending Lacan's *Séminaires*.

The correctives above that highlight the potentially queer dimension of Sarduy's genealogy of the Baroque is what I call the Homo-Baroque. I would like to stress that this neologism is not meant for mere play, a Mexican *albur*, or a game of one-upmanship, but rather a critical act that is attentive to the enactment of queer identities in Latin America. This critical practice is not meant to be exhaustive, but rather complementary to the many other strategies of queer self-figuration that come out of a culture of silence, excess, and distortion. In that small measure, the Homo-Baroque is yet another echo that manages to escape the chamber of sexual silence, and whispers in the ear other possible ways of being, of speaking, of knowing.

Taking up the body

If Sarduy's investment in structuralist and poststructuralist French theory offers us a scaffold to conceive of subjectivity, as well as to approach the complex relation between Latin American writing, and Europe and the United States, then his novelistic writing might offer us a practical deployment of his theories. In the rest of this chapter, I am particularly interested in the ways in which bodies circulate in his literary text.

I have been wondering: after theories of performativity staked a claim to how we universally read gender and sexuality, is there any room left to talk about bodies themselves or has the notion of the body withered away? Butler's gender performativity has been already too well and enthusiastically registered in our intellectual script: gender is performative—gender as well as sexual identities become constituted at the moment they are iterated, and so forth. Thus genders and sexualities become culturally constructed through the repetition of stylized acts in time. Moreover, in their repetition, these stylized bodily acts establish the appearance of an essential, ontological "core." But where or when does that body emerge into the critical scene? we might ask. The temporal status of the body as a purveyor of some truth becomes quite fragile when we become aware that it might be falling apart at tremendous speed under the duress of HIV and its medical treatment.

Severo Sarduy died June 8, 1993, from AIDS-related complications. His last novel, *Pájaros de la playa*, was published posthumously in September of that year.[20] I would like to examine the narrative forms in which Sarduy relates his understanding of subjectivity and its uneven relation to the body in this oeuvre.

Latin American and Caribbean subjectivities hinge on a complex recognition and relationship to the body. The body appears in culture and narrative in rather imposing ways. I would argue that the making of a gendered identity happens through bodily writing; the mechanics of this identity construction can be simple: the Self recognizes a body as one's own and then it is transformed, rewritten, and recycled. The simplicity of this practice may appear to verge on essentialism; however, the body is always placing some kind of constraint on the supposed freedom or fluidity of performance and performativity. It is a cultural practice that manifests itself over and over again in Latin American letters—and Sarduy is no exception. In fact, while on the surface, his work resists fixing any sense of identity to the body, on another level, his writing operates as a negative dialectic to such a practice.

The opening line of Sarduy's *Pájaros de la playa* gives us an image: "En la arena rojiza dejaban un momento sus huellas los pies fuertes de los corredores"[21] ["On the reddish sand, the runners' strong feet left their prints for a moment."] Right away, we remember Sarduy's discussion of proliferation: the footprints of the runners is what is left to signify the body. I want to think about those footprints (or traces) as emblematic of the difference and challenges that Sarduy as an important voice in Latin American writing bears on queer theory (especially as articulated in the United States). Indeed, Sarduy's theorization of transvestism—both in his critical writings of *Escrito sobre un cuerpo* and *La simulación*, as well as in his novels, *De donde son los cantantes* and *Cobra*, for instance—anticipates and exceeds a conceptualization of drag as a critique of gender performativity.

Sarduy's theory of gender subjectivity begins with his idea of simulation, which he links to the project and practice of transvestism: Gender, for the Cuban critic and author, is a process of an endless approximation of a highly idealized, yet elusive, referent. The transvestite dramatizes this process of simulation par excellence; Sarduy remarks, "La mujer no es el límite donde se detiene la simulación. [Los travestís] son hipertélicos: van más allá de su fin, hacia el absoluto de una imagen abstracta, religiosa incluso, icónica en todo caso, mortal. Las mujeres—vengan a verlo al *Carrousel* de París—los imitan."[22] ["Woman is not the limit where [transvestitic] simulation ends. [Transvestites] are hypertelic: they go beyond their end, toward the absolute of an abstract image, inclusively religious, iconic in every case, mortal. Women—come see it at the *Carrousel* in Paris—imitate them."] I would like to unpack his notion of a hyper-*telos*—a Sarduyan oxymoron, if there ever was one. This idea of going beyond a finality (*telos*), of pushing and breaking the limits explains how Sarduy understands gender articulations. Consider that a *telos* is a "desired limit"—History, knowledge, society—then any extension on such a teleological concept would necessarily represent a rupture by and from desire. Thus, for Sarduy, gender is presented as a desire for a *telos*, a tension or dialectic that cannot be stable because it is always, already being taken elsewhere. For Sarduy, gender and sexuality are a struggle to go beyond the object of desire and to break with desire.

I would like to sketch out my critique of Sarduy's concept of simulation. For example, he resists any direct relationship between transvestism's simulation and effeminacy or homosexuality:

> Relacionar el *trabajo corporal* de los travestís a la simple manía cosmética, al afeminamiento o a la homosexualidad es simplemente ingenuo: esas no son más que las fronteras aparentes de una metamorfosis sin límites, su pantalla "natural."[23]

> [Relating the *corporeal work* of the transvestite to the simple cosmetic mania, to effeminacy or to homosexuality is simply naïve: those are nothing more than the apparent borders (*fronteras aparentes*) of a metamorphosis without limits, their 'natural' screen.]

Sarduy's commentary sounds *avant la lettre* surprisingly like Butler's criticism of the collapse between homosexuality and drag performance.[24] Clearly, simulation is a metamorphosis and performance without limits, and Sarduy is interested in pushing his theoretical intervention beyond any possible limits—a practice in and of theory that I accept. However, by placing "cosmetics," "effeminacy," and "homosexuality" on the same relative plane, he is ignoring that these "apparent borders" (read: physical bodies) might also be sites of cultural contestation and political struggle, thereby he commits an ingenuous act of political violence on the queer body, an act which is more difficult to accept altogether. Along similar lines, Sedgwick makes a powerful critique of the use of the trope of "cross-dressing" in the "virtual erasure of the connection between transvestism and ... homosexuality": "Critics" she argues, "may well feel that the rubric 'cross-dressing' gives them ... a way of tapping into this shared knowingness [the idea that 'everyone already knows' that transvestism generally alludes to homosexuality] without having to name its subject; without incurring many of the punitive risks of openly gay enunciation in a homophobic culture. ..."[25] In other words, what Sedgwick points out is that often "transvestism" is an easy way out to "discuss" homosexuality or, at least, to "assimilate" it into the cultural imaginary, thereby stabilizing and naturalizing a gender binary. In other words, by linking homosexuality as drag, there is an effort to keep being "gay" and "normatively masculine" as separate categories that cannot coexist at the same time. This social practice serves heteronormative subjects who do not want to "contaminate" masculinity with gayness—indeed, it is a manifestation of homosexual panic.[26]

Sarduy's critique is that connecting homosexuality to transvestism places a limit on simulation (or corporeal work) and restricts its voracious and greedy economy. I propose that Sarduy's theorization of simulation has greatly to do with his refusal to become satisfied with or ossified by an identity that is frozen and permanently—or even temporarily—knowable. Notwithstanding, what happens in his approach is that the status of those "apparent borders" or bodies in his work remains highly problematic. His engagement with the body is always uneasy: On the one hand, he is representative of a Latin American tradition of inscribing the body in writing; on the other, he almost seems to neglect the body and defines gender/sexual difference exclusively as an operation of desire.

Whereas, in his earlier novels, *De donde son los cantantes* and *Cobra*, the body is portrayed as a site of pleasure to be acted on, mutilated, painted, or transformed: the body is submitted and rendered plastic to the acrobatics of simulation, in *Pájaros de la playa*, we see a discursive shift that oscillates between bodily preservation (Siempreviva's discourse) and disavowal (articulated by the Cosmologist). In what follows, I shall discuss the text's characters' bodily attachments and narrative maneuvers.

Pájaros de la playa takes us to a colonial, pentagonal mansion-hospice on an island where men afflicted by "el mal" ["illness and evil"] retire to die: "eran jóvenes prematuramente marchitados por la falta de fuerza, golpeados de repente por el mal."²⁷ ["they were young men prematurely crest-fallen by the lack of strength, suddenly struck by illness or evil."] Though the disease is never named directly, its symptoms and treatment reminds readers of HIV/AIDS. To this place comes Siempreviva, an old woman who would rather live among infected young men than to live alone and lonely. Her collection of *Harper's Bazaar*s and costumes suggest that she might be a transgendered subject, but that is neither confirmed nor denied. Her only desire is to be young again.

Likewise, the overwhelming feeling among the "jóvenes viejos" ["the old youths"] is to regain their strength and vitality by any method available, even just sitting in the sun contemplating the birds go by. One nameless patient notes that: "—La luz cura, pero no a mí. Mi espíritu ya no habita mi cuerpo; ya me he ido. Lo que ahora come, duerme, habla y excreta en medio de los otros es una pura simulación. El sol anima, es verdad, pero algo en la piel tiene que captarlo, y es eso precisamente lo que desaparece con el mal. [...] ya todo es póstumo. Me escapé del sufrimiento físico."²⁸ ["Light cures, but not me. My spirit no longer inhabits my body; I've already left. What he now eats, sleeps, speaks and excretes among others is pure simulation. The sun revives, it's true, but something in the skin must capture it, and that's precisely what disappears with the sickness/evil (*el mal*) (...) everything is already posthumous. I escaped physical suffering."] There are four separate ideas formulated in the passage: spirit, body, simulation, and agency. What is the relation among the four critical terms? It appears that the spirit has left the body, leaving behind a series of behaviors or everyday performances that get marked as simulation. The empty body itself is defective since it lacks the thing needed to capture the sun's energy. So, the sense of agency escapes physical suffering. There is too much going on here, too many contradictions to go unnoticed. Several critical positionings seem to pull in different directions, thereby making the event of illness difficult to read and to grasp. This critical messiness can be conceived as a primal scene, one which others may use to identify a particular politic(s) of AIDS. Although the young men's ultimate wish is not only to keep their bodies from falling apart but to make themselves perfect again, their poor health, which only accelerates their bodily changes, dramatizes their failure to arrest time and to move it back. Strikingly, we notice that the body places limits on the flows and circuits of desire.

The traditional body/spirit split (in the above passage) seems to give way to a performance of the everyday. The spirit is gone and the body gets marked as sick: this body is then displaced by the force of simulation. The classic trope of the sun's curative powers becomes complicated in this brief soliloquy: for the sun to perform its function, there must be a willing receptor, a "something in the skin," to transform the sun's energies. This something is missing: the skin affected by "el mal" suggests the insufficiency of the "apparent borders." So rather than debunk the common myth of sun as health inducement, what gets rewritten is the skin and body itself as faulty and incomplete. The body becomes useless and must be abandoned to transcend physical pain. These anonymous narratives of spiritual flight and uninhabiting the body maintain Sarduy's resolve regarding the priority of simulation: the dying men's everyday actions are registered as "pure simulation."

This prioritizing of simulation over the actual body itself becomes further complicated by the narrator and other anonymous voices in the following scene:[29]

> También los viejos eran pájaros de la playa. [. . .]
> Hoy, aquejados por el mal, incapaces por levantar el vuelo, rememoran a lo largo del día las hazañas pasadas. Algo, sin embargo, les queda del cuerpo en majestad de ayer: la agudeza de la mirada, vultúrido al acecho, tornada hacia lo alto de la cúpula, como en espera de un signo celeste y diurno.
> —La vida volverá.
> —La vida volverá.
> —Sí, ¿Pero cuál?
> —La otra. La muerte es como un cambio de ropa. He sentido el movimiento de mi cuerpo ahogado tratando de nacer, de respirar aire claro. Intuyo incluso el lugar: en otra isla.[30]

> [Even the old men were birds on the beach. (. . .)
> Now, grieved by the sickness or evil, incapable of taking to flight, all day long they rush through their memories past adventures. Something, however, is left of their bodies' majesty of yesterday: the sharpness of the gaze, vulture-like to the hunt, turned toward the highest point of the cupula, waiting for a celestial and daytime sign.

"Life will return."
"Life will return."
"Yes, but which?"
"The other. Death is like a change of clothing. I have felt the movement of my body drowning trying to be born, to breath clear air. I even have an intuition of the place: in another island."]

Although something had been lost earlier, here some things remain, in fact, become heightened: a memory of a former physical majesty and the acuity of a gaze, which wanders in search of future signs. In other words, the old youth are positioned between a past and a future, always uninhabiting their bodily presence and the present; that is to say, the old youth disengage from space and time. Moreover, memory and gaze are disembodied elements of subjectivity: memory exiles and recasts the now body into another more glorious-looking one; the gaze seeks the possibility of escape. A chorus of disembodied voices—"Life will return"—is met with a challenge. Another anonymous voice speculates that the life that returns is the figure of the other, death. If we follow Freud's negative definition of pleasure as the absence of pain, then the ultimate pleasure is also the ultimate absence of pain, death, which becomes an encounter with the other. What is powerful about the understanding of the role of death in this scene is that it suggests that it is nothing more than a "change of clothing"; thus, the body ranks on the order of textile and fabric, the raw material of simulation for Sarduy's transvestite subject. The real body can be replaced by another, an imaginary one that outlasts sickness. This desire to continue resisting the perversions of sickness and evil (*el mal*) is best articulated yet by someone else: "Que otros acepten [el mal] con resignación; yo no."[31] ["Let others accept sickness/evil with resignation, but I will not."] I want to contrast the word *resignation* here with another, more accurate interpretation of what these old youths are doing, resignification. *Resignation* suggests a humble acceptance of the status quo; *resignification* looks for strategies of self-figuration as acts of resistance. Resignation is an act of passivity; whereas resignification is an active attempt, almost desperate at times, to give new meaning to a body (of knowledge). In this sense, my conceptualization of resignification moves and operates very much like Sarduy's voracious push for simulation.

What the anonymous voices of these old youths seem to present is a hysterical struggle to come to terms with a new identity created by "*el mal*, illness and evil. The multiple and, at times, contradictory positions offered by this chorus of anonymity seeks to perform subjectivity *without a body*, an impulse of simulation. Therefore, I am proposing two separate strategies: simulation as a general practice of surpassing a telos, or of going beyond the body. The weakened bodies of Sarduy's aged youth need to be transcended, forgotten, and left behind altogether. Their presence—or rather, awareness of their presence—restricts the operations of the body. Resignification, otherwise, takes account of the bodies, its limitations and creative potential.

It is here where Siempreviva enters the scene. The old woman at first becomes disillusioned by any cosmetic or medical efforts to recuperate her fabulousness; she too found that "poco sentido tenían ya los días y los nombres."[32] ["days and names had little meaning."] In other words, she too has become as detached as the other men in the mansion. This all changes the day that Caballo arrived. The new male nurse— "el hombre que parecía caballo" ["the man who looked like a horse"] alluding to Rafael Arévalo Martínez's 1914 homoerotic short story—Caballo, and Siempreviva begin a torrid love affair that did not shy away from the physical..

> Nuestros alientos se mezclaron, como los de dos animales fétidos; nuestros cuerpos se eslabonaron, se trabaron: un enredijo de ropas arrugadas y de miembros. La piel no fue límite, ni la consciencia: todo se anudó en un garabato, incomprehensible y furioso como un ideograma, sin otra voluntad que el placer, sin más que el goce en su borrosa immediatez.[33]

> [Our breaths became one, like that of two fetid animals; our bodies became linked and stuck together: a knot of wrinkled clothes and members. The skin was not a limit, nor was consciousness: everything was knotted into an incomprehensible scribble like an ideogram, without any other goal than pleasure, with no end but the *jouissance* in its blurry immediacy.]

What is represented here is a primal scene in the classic sense, where pleasure reigns supreme. Their bodies together remind us in many ways of the scene when La Manuela is being beaten by Pancho and Octavio in Donoso's novel, also Sergio and la Regine's torrid love affair in Lemebel's chronicle. However, for this scene to be effective, Siempreviva tells us that neither she nor Caballo dared look at each other. The violence and pleasure of the event can only happen when neither party acknowledged the other's body and presence. The narrator or Siempreviva reminds us that "Mas los cuerpos que se aman jamás son los cuerpos reales, sino otros que suscita y proyecta la imaginación de los amantes." ["Yet the bodies that are loved are never the real bodies, but other bodies that the lovers' imagination awakens and projects."] I want to propose that the beloved's body is not Real, only Imaginary, therefore and by extension, Sarduy's conceptualization of other's body is but a projection of the self, the very trope of narcissism. This insight also affirms Lacan's axiom that "il n'y a pas de rapport sexuel" ["there's no such a thing as a sexual relationship"]. Siempreviva imagines that "Así, me vi desnuda, bajando de un tren muy antiguo, un ramo de flores moradas en la mano. El que yo ahora le ofrecía a Caballo era ese cuerpo imaginario, sin pesadez, astral casi, y no este amasijo de tendones vencidos, de nervios inútilmente alertas, de flacidez y hastío."[34] ["Thus, I saw myself nude, getting off a very old train, with a bouquet of purple flowers in my hand. The body I was offering Caballo was that imaginary one, without heaviness, heavenly almost, and not this bunch of defeated muscles, of uselessly alert nerves, of flaccidity and laziness."] Again, the realness of the body must be transcended, and another more perfect idealization must be offered in its place. The real body is an inconvenience for Siempreviva; yet the real body is a *trace* and excess of the other body, which she is always conjuring up to bring into being in the present. This other and Imaginary body becomes highly stylized and fictionalized as the "apparent border" where simulation might rest politically. But what kind of politics does it represent? Certainly, the case of Siempreviva, who is always looking backward, presents a romanticized view of the "good old days" when she was more beautiful; this backward glance posits an incredibly conservative understanding of the body politic. Yet, does a forward glance necessarily signify a more "progressive" outlook? In other words, how does simulation get marked politically? That is, what kind of work gets done through simulation?

Even though taking simulation to the extreme produces a

theoretical impasse and the inability or unwillingness to make a "tragic choice," simulation might be valued for its deconstructive power to recast political choices—and that might be a politic to privilege. This discussion leads me to reconsider a more complicated question than the one I started with; namely, that what is at stake is not a question of performance or simulation versus real body (as the regulating metaphor that defines subjectivity), but rather that how simulation gets marked politically cannot be answered outside of a particular context, which defines the politics of the investment or disinvestment in the body.

Siempreviva becomes obsessed that her body is not good enough for Caballo. She even asks him boldly: "Te has aburrido . . . singando con una vieja?" ["Have you become bored . . . fucking with an old woman?"] She then decides to begin a rejuvenation treatment with Caimán, the phytotherapist, who is always making new concoctions to alleviate the pain of the patients in the hospital. This process, of course, fails—and moreover leads to Caballo abandoning her for good because he thought she was betraying him with Caimán. After some initial success, where Siempreviva's feet becomes smooth and youthful, so they decide to "[a]ccelerate the treatment."[35] The treatment works wonders, and Siempreviva is youthful again, well almost . . .]. Caimán convinces Siempreviva that he should use the procedure to give her perkier breasts. So while he massages her body, they begin to have what looks like sex. It is at this moment that Caballo walks in and kicks the "quasi-fornicators."[36] Later, Caballo and Caimán get up and are given orange juice with some hallucinogen. After chasing after some visions, they disappear. For her part, Siempreviva retains her youth (*estiramiento*) however, when she looks at herself in the mirror the next day, she sees nothing but "an old woman crucified with wrinkles."[37] In other words, cosmetics do not work. So, she is back where she started.

* * *

I would like to go back to the opening scene of *Pájaros de la playa*: "In the reddish sand, the runners' strong feet left their prints (or traces) for a moment." The runners remind me of another intertext, which I think relates very closely to Sarduy's novel: I am referring to Luchino Visconti's brilliant film adaptation of *Death in Venice*. The final scene when Gustav von Aschenbach tries to get up to rescue the beautiful youth Tadzio is comparable to the desire for youth in *Pájaros de la playa*. Gustav seeks to find beauty outside and wants to possess it; Siempreviva seeks beauty within and desires to animate. I would argue that Sarduy's novel is a rewriting of the *Death in Venice*—both Thomas Mann's text and Visconti visual interpretation.

The runners at the beginning are a fleeting image of healthy bodies; they are the object of desire which gets conjured up incessantly throughout the text. I am interested in the foot traces because they signal the presence of the other, like the scene in Daniel Defoe's *Robinson Crusoe* when the castaway discovers the footprint and becomes alarmed that he is not alone. After the initial horror, the mark of the other anticipates the possibility of self-figuration. In *Pájaros de la playa*, the footprints are a figure of Siempreviva's—and, why not, Sarduy's—incredibly uneasy relation to the body. The footprints document a history of the body's presence, which becomes aestheticized and performed nonstop. The image of feet in the sand appears again at the end of the novel, this time, Siempreviva, desperate to find Caballo and Caimán, leaves the hospital mansion: "Arena húmeda. Quedaban un momento las huellas de los pies; el aire fresco de la mañana iba borrándolas."[38] ["Wet sand. For a moment the foot marks remained; the fresh air of the morning progressively erased them."]

The ephemeral trace of the once-present body is left and slowly vanishes; this trace contains a history of the Real, which is always inaccessible, just out of reach, but which regulates powerfully how the Self sees and narrates its objects of desire. However, the Real body always punctures a hole through the Imaginary narrative of Self. The hole is the inverse of the island (where the hospital mansion is located; for Sarduy, the island is always a direct reference to Cuba), also the hole is the inverse of the "I," which in health or in the face of illness is always being sought to be made complete and perfect.

part 4

Queer Latina/o Narratives

9

Queer *Latinidad*

Thomas's *Down These Mean Streets* and Díaz's *Drown*

> They may be contingent inverts. In that case, under certain external conditions—of which inaccessibility of any normal sexual object and imitation are the chief—they are capable of taking as their sexual object someone of their own sex and of deriving satisfaction from sexual intercourse with him.
> —Sigmund Freud, *Three Essays on the Theory of Sexuality*

Narratives

As a young man, I remember that the process of political awareness began with my understanding of racialization. An immigrant from an ever-shrinking middle-class Mexican family, I discovered literally overnight that I was no longer of a privileged class, but rather, on arrival to the United States, I became a minority. Certainly, this struggle to articulate my sense of identity came at the right moment, my freshman year in college. This complex set of negotiations led me to appreciate the weight that context carries in identity formation—at times, I even used to long to return to Mexico to feel the comfort of a certain class position. This longing would be seen as a break from always inhabiting the sense of racial and ethnic difference that I experienced in the United States, especially at a place like Yale. However, I got over that feeling of desire to return rather quickly.[1] It was there, after all, that I became politicized around questions of race, and also there that I "discovered" that I sort of preferred boys.

Arriving at my place at the queer table as a Latino would mean that my conversation with queer identification and politics was not necessarily a collaborative act, but rather one of "catching up." I might suggest *grosso modo* that, generally, for queer folks of color there is a genealogy of their coming to terms with their identities—first and often foremost comes the language of racial formation and identity, *then* the vocabulary of queerness is integrated. What might it mean for queers of color that "race" comes first, and then "queerness"?[2] How does this epistemological unfolding narrate queer *Latinidad* differently than, say, plain old queer subjectivities (implicitly raced white)? This sequence of identity formation—although seemingly elementary—might just be the strongest critique of intersectionality,[3] wherein measures of identity are often imagined as a symmetrical coming together. I would argue, in fact, that racial and queer identities do not always meet on equal footing or even at a same stage of "development"; rather, one form of identification always impinges on the other. Consider that if the tendency is for queers of color is to assume race first and then queerness, it might be interesting to figure that white queers might do it the other way around—queerness first, race (whiteness) second. This ordering of identity brings up a question of storytelling and politics—and challenges us to consider what the impact of narrative structures have on identity formation. There is always a priority of how a story gets told, the deconstructive swerve is not to posit which story form is necessarily "better" or more authoritative than the other, but rather to appreciate how the sequencing of identifications—qua order of things—allows for certain forms of cultural hegemony.

This chapter is about looking at alternative forms of identification with respect to queer Latino American subjects.[4] I will briefly discuss four texts by Latino American authors—Reinaldo Arenas, Piri Thomas, Junot Diaz, and Puig again. Along the way, I hope to give insights on the difficult theoretical questions that each work raises; also, how reading these works alongside each other, we might discern other forms of queer narrative. As I have been doing so far, I ask how different conceptualizations of the homosexual in the United States—from the homophile movement to gay liberation and lesbian feminism, as well as gay/lesbian studies to queer theory—been appropriated or transformed in the context of Latino sexual identities? If so, how?

More importantly, in this and the next chapter, I examine how have male-male, female-female, and other nonnormalized affective and sexual configurations been narrated within the context of a Latino American critical arena. Particularly, if the "coming out" narrative has been "homonormativized" in the U.S. scene as the regulating trope to achieve a gay, lesbian, or queer identity, which would be the tropes and narratives that have enabled a queer Latino American subjectivity?

Language

As I promised in the "Introduction," I wanted to think about "coming-out-of-closet" narratives. Throughout this book, I have shown that open articulation of one's sexual identity is not necessarily the predominant practice to claim or express one's homosexuality. Rather, we find over and again that silence, insinuation, ellipsis, and other strategies result as more effective narratives and tropes to capture and represent Latino American queer identities. Earlier, I also suggested that the closet might be a historically and culturally specific phenomenon, whose universalization might be deemed a cultural imposition. Also, from my cultural and historical vantage point, the closet is a *supplément*—in the Derridean sense, of excess and of alternative.

Now, in the spirit of finding more narratives of queer existence, I would like to turn to one form of naming of queer *Latinidad*, that is, *locura*. In a well-known and often cited chapter from his autobiography/extended suicide note, *Before Night Falls*, Reinaldo Arenas enumerates his taxonomy of *locas*.[5] For reasons that will become clear, I will refrain from translating *locas* and *locura*. He begins that after "[n]oticing such great difference between these and those homosexuals, [he] established some categories among them."[6] These different forms of *locas* or queer subjects are as follows: first, the dog-collar *loca*, who is so scandalous that the police just places a collar on him to make the job of arrest easier; then comes the common *loca*, who is politically engaged; afterward, Arenas talks about the covered-up *loca*, whom nobody knows is a homosexual because he condemns other homosexuals; and finally the royal loca, who has "the privilege of being a *loca* publicly."[7] I know that Arenas is being ironic here by making up his own set of categories; however, for a moment, let us take his conceptualization at face value, and see what happens.

Arenas links these four categories; however, if we try to trace some kind of relation among them, it is difficult to discern what is exactly being measured. For instance, if we take the question of homosexual openness as a measurement—going from most "open" to least "open"—such a system does not work because, in the end, the royal *loca* is in fact the most "open" in terms of his standing and privilege. If we go from most scandalous to least, we are met with a similar predicament. The only possible trajectory that we can distinguish is that each category is defined on how close it is to the Castro regime. What regulates Arenas's categorization is not sexual or cultural in nature, but rather political attachment. Following Arenas's categories, being a *loca* is a function of how close the homosexual is to the regime. This is a rather different conceptualization of how gays or lesbian are categorized in the United States or other parts of the continent, for that matter.

Another important issue that Arenas defines is how each *loca* behaves. I would like to point out two details. First, with respect to the common *loca*, he writes, "la loca común es ese tipo de homosexual que en Cuba tiene su compromiso, que va a la Cinemateca, que escribe de vez en cuando algún poema, que nunca corre un gran riesgo y se dedica a tomar el té en casa de sus amigos. [...] Las relaciones de estas locas comunes, generalmente son, con otras locas y nunca llegan a conocer a un hombre verdadero"[8] If we look at the published English translation, I would like to point out some discrepancies, important ones. "This is the type of homosexual who has his commitments." Something is lost here: "Es ese tipo de homosexual que en Cuba tiene su compromiso." First, the location—"in Cuba"—is not noted in the translation; thus, the common *loca* is rendered as the "common gay"—he is universalized in the English translation of Arenas's autobiography. Also, "tener su compromiso" means more than just "to have a commitment," which sounds more like "having a date" in the English version; "tener su compromiso" means to be *politically* engaged or committed. So in fact the English translation depoliticizes the representation of the common *loca*. The cultural specificity as well as the political work of the *loca* is rendered as generic and unexceptional.

Also, Arenas suggests that common *locas* "nunca llegan a conocer a un hombre verdadero," that is, "they never come to know a real man." In other words, common *locas* do not partake in sexual encounters with self-defined heterosexual men, a particular sign of risk and prestige among *locas*. This particular relation between a *loca* and a "real man" signifies on the *feminized* position that the *loca* occupies in the social imaginary of Cuba, the Caribbean, and in parts of Americas. For a *loca* is not exactly a "gay" man, as we understand the category in the United States. A *loca* is not just a man who has sex with other men, but rather one who assumes membership in a particular subculture, one of whose traits is effeminate (even slightly effeminate) role-playing and gender enactment. Moreover, what Arenas might be doing here when he says that *locas* have sex with other *locas*, he may be parodying a version of U.S. gay male culture that seeks comfort in "secure" (nonthreatening) relations between men who look and act like themselves.[9]

Another detail that I would like to point out has to do with the translation of *loca tapada* as "closet gay." If we consider that "gay" delineates a subject produced out of relational attachment between men, and one who has his own political history, then *loca* just does not match up. Each category signifies a different identity *and* politic. Also, the "closet" represents more than a site, but an act; whereas just being veiled (*tapada*) describes a condition of being hidden from plain sight, without the relational complexities of knowingness and unknowingness through which gay male identities are produced. I do not want to discard that there are overlaps between the idea of being in the closet and being "*tapada/o*," let me just suggest that the concept of being *tapado/a* has to do with what I have noted elsewhere—that emphasizes queer identity to bodily presence, rather than performativity.

The point I really want to make here is that *loca* cannot be translated as gay, or even as queer; instead, let me suggest that the categories that we use to label sexual identities in Cuba or the Caribbean or elsewhere must be framed to locate queerness—one cannot translate *locura*, rather one locates queerness, meaning that when we speak across cultures about sexual identifications, we can only approximate those identifications and understand that what we have come across is an ideological template that resonates as something similar, but never the same. Not taking into account the ways in which those templates are unable to represent the other represents an act of cultural imposition that reduces the richness of how other cultures see themselves and how they negotiate differences. Here I would also add that the history of racial formations in Cuba transforms this taxonomy of *locura* even further.

Importantly, one next needs to ask how the concepts of *locura* and *loca* subjectivities translate; in other words, what happens when *locas* cross borders and inhabit new spaces?[10] I would like to look at two scenes from works by Piri Thomas and Junot Diaz to consider such movements.

Practices

In Piri Thomas's 1967 masterwork, *Down These Mean Streets*, we come across a particularly queer scene.[11] Piri and his Puerto Rican friends are hanging out, when all of a sudden, "[t]he talk turned way out, on faggots and their asses which, swinging from side to side, could make a girl look ridiculous, like she wasn't moving. There were some improbable stories of exploits with faggots. Then one stud, Alfredo said, 'Say, man, let's make it up to the faggots' pad and cop some bread.'"[12] What we notice here is how the normal homosocial bantering goes "way out," and the young men begin speculating about those "faggots": their wily ways, their huge dick size, how disgusting they really are, and so forth. Despite all this, as narrator asks, "so why were we making it up to the *maricones*' pad?" Alfredo knocks . . .

> "*Quién es?*" said a woman's voice
> "It's me, Antonia—open up"
> "Who ees eet, Antonia?" said another woman's voice from behind the closed door.
> "Eet is Alfredo," said the first voice.
> "*Bueno*, let heem in," the voice said.
> The door opened and I saw that the women's voices belong to men.[13]

Opening the door and seeing effeminate men, really *locas*, not women, invites Piri to reconsider his present situation. Interestingly, the voice alone fools the narrator to believe that he will meet some girls. Moreover, the voice is accentuated—"Who ees eet?"—and marks the speaker on the other side of the door as foreign. As Barbara Johnson reminds us, "The surprise of otherness is that moment when a new form of ignorance is suddenly activated as an imperative."[14] Piri must then proceed to make sense of that foreignness. He resorts to smoking pot, and in a drug-induced high he wonders: "*Hey world, do you know these mean streets is like a clip machine. It takes, an' keeps on taking, till it makes a cat feel like every day is something that's gotta be forgotten.*"[15] It would seem that if he is going to proceed and inhabit this new world, the everyday or quotidian must be forgotten; his present condition in the mean streets must be actively forgotten—and all there is left is what he has in front of him. He must confront that unknown. After he awakens from his high:

> I awoke because somebody was touching me where only me or a girl should touch. I came back, but my body was still relaxed. I felt my pant zipper being pulled open and cold fingers take my pee-pee out and begin to pull it up and down. I opened my eyes to a shadowy scene of smoke and haze and looked at the owner of the cold fingers. It was Concha.[16]

Again, Piri opens his eyes, or awakens to a new reality. The narrator never fully assumes agency of what is happening to him. All around he notices that Alfredo is fucking another *loca*, La Vieja, while his friends Waneko and Indio are getting a blow job from Antonia. To return to Piri:

> I looked down in time to see my pee-pee disappear into Concha's mouth. I felt the roughness of his tongue as it both scared and pleased me. *I like broads, I like muchachas, I like girls*, I chanted inside me. I felt funny, like getting dizzy and weak and lazy. I felt myself lurching and straining. I felt like I wanted to yell. Then I heard slurping sounds and it was over.[17]

He is now witnessing his manhood being swallowed up by Concha—ironically, the name "Concha" is short for Concepción, it also means "shell" and sometimes it is a derogatory word for "vagina." Hence, this represents a kind of castration. What is interesting to note in this scene is Piri's internal chant—*I like broads*, and so on—this internal dialogue is reflective of his masculinist subjectivity that counteracts the threat of castration and emasculation. Moreover, beyond the negotiation of masculinity, the internal chant responds both to the fear and pleasure that this queer encounter with otherness causes the narrator to experience. Significantly, this scene returns to normal when Alfredo discovers shit on this penis, the stain of the Real, and he beats La Vieja. The homophobic violence normalizes in the men's minds what had just elapsed. Piri leaves the room, smokes more pot, and concludes, "damn, that whole scene was a blip." The present scene is simply forgotten—in other words, that experience of otherness is never acknowledged—it is diminished as something insignificant, a blip, and eventually becomes repressed. And in Thomas's text it has to be displaced because as we know throughout the novel he is coming to terms with his national and racial identities. His national identification (as a Puerto Rican and Cuban) and his blackness coexist in a rather uneven and uneasy way—and while his sexuality intervenes in very strategic ways, the author certainly prioritizes national and racial identity before the sexual (which is necessarily heterosexual).[18]

Very briefly, the young men participated in the kind of scenario where their masculinity was really never compromised: they are after all *bugarrones*,[19] men who engage in sexual acts with other men, but at no moment see themselves as implicated in homosexuality. The slightest possibility of being marked—like some shit on their penis, for instance—requires a homophobic response to restore a sense of the heteronormal. It is important to remember that Alfredo has been here before—this was not his first visit. Hence, his violent beating of La Vieja might just be a performance for the other men to witness just how manly he really is, shit on schlong notwithstanding. What this performance of *bugarrón* masculinity does signal is that homosexual panic is never far behind and is always linked with homosexual fascination; *bugarrón* masculinity would be best described by Piri when he says that "I felt like I wanted to yell." It is unclear what that desire to yell signifies—it is a response that expresses both fear and pleasure alongside the *loca*'s body. This very conjunction of homosexual fear *and* pleasure not only describes *loca/bugarrón* Latino sexual practices, but also informs a variant of queer *Latinidad*.

Silences.

The final text that I would like to discuss is the chapter titled "Drown" from Junot Diaz's eponymous novel.[20] Here Yunior, the narrator, discovers that his best friend Beto is back home—and he does everything to avoid him. Yunior's mother tries to figure out what is wrong, but he does not say a word; he is trapped in silence. The narrative progresses about the mundane life of an underemployed Dominican youth in Perth Amboy, New Jersey, then the narrative breaks and we are told: "Twice. That's it."[21] The silence is broken. The narrator does not reveal right away what "it" is: "The first time was at the end of that summer. We had just come back from the pool and were watching a porn video at his parents' apartment."[22] It is at this moment that Beto reaches in Yunior shorts, and masturbates him: "[Yunior] came right away, smearing the plastic sofa covers."[23] Before we analyze this encounter. I would like to discuss the setting, the young men are watching porn: "His [Beto's] father was a nut for these tapes, ordering them from California and Grand Rapids. Beto used to tell me how his pop would watch them in the middle of the day, not caring a lick about his moms, who spent the time in the kitchen, taking hours to cook a pot of rice and gandules."[24] This moment reveals a rather odd family romance. Beto's father's sexual life is permeated by porn fantasies; his mother is physically relegated to the kitchen, taking hours to cook food that requires little messing with. The videos come from "California and Grand Rapids": it makes sense that they come from California, namely the Porn Valley, but why Grand Rapids? I can only suspect that these are amateur (or generally speaking, "nonmainstream") videos. In fact, the movie the boys are watching is "some vaina that looked like it had been filmed in the apartment next door."[25] Again, porn representation is described as something less-stylized and quite quotidian, literally found "next door."

Beto's father makes a space for himself, a masculinist space where he can watch porn, and leave his wife outside. On occasion, Beto joins his father: "Beto would sit down with his pop and neither would say a word, except to laugh when somebody caught it in the eye or the face."[26] Obviously, the father thinks that he is socializing his son to be a man. First, the father is *tacitly* instructing his son that a woman's place is in the kitchen, period, and that a man can do whatever he wants without having to account for the feelings of his wife or any woman. He instills a conventional understanding of heterosexuality, in which women are either subservient to men's pleasure—and therefore almost superfluous. They both watch the movie "without saying a word." This silence can be read in two different ways, and its meaning gets revealed in the laughter following the cum-shot-in-the-eye scenes, a veritable trompe l'oeil if there ever was one. First, we might consider that for the father, the cum-shot-in-the-eye represents the abjection of women; second, for Beto, it might just be comic relief or a form of embarrassment. But more importantly to all of this, one has to ask, what are each, father and son, doing and seeing? With whom are they identifying in the sexual scene? More explicitly, are they *having* (possessing) the woman or *being* the woman in the scene? I would argue that the father identifies himself in the role of the fucker, the one who shoots in the woman's face—the semen defaces her identity; whereas Beto might be identifying as the receiver, like the woman,[27] abjected. The negative Oedipal configuration is thus, Beto needs to *be* "like a woman," in order to *have* and possess the father. It is as if Beto were to receive the father's lesson, like the cum shot, slapped on his face, and resigns himself to accept the abject role. It is this sense of abjection that might explain his strong desire to leave the neighborhood, which he hated so much. It may also be the weight of abjection and passivity next to the father that he needs to overcome, and this pushes him to make the first move with Yunior. The boys were watching that

> vaina that looked like it had been filmed in the apartment next door, when he reached into my [Yunior's] shorts. What the fuck are you doing? I asked, but he didn't stop. His hand was dry. I kept my eyes on the television, too scared to watch. I came right away [. . .] My legs started shaking and suddenly I wanted out. He didn't say anything to me as I left, just sat there watching the screen.[28]

Again, the sexual encounter is surrounded by silence. The rhetorical question, "What the fuck are you doing?" contains its own response smack in the middle: fucking. After this initial protest, Yunior keeps his eyes on the television. I suggest that Yunior continues watching the porn movie to create for himself an "excuse" that his hard-on and orgasm were the result of the heterosexual porn movie—and not of being fondled by another man.[29] Homosexual contact is normalized through the triangulation with a heterosexual porn flick. Symmetrically, at the end of the scene when Yunior leaves, Beto too is left behind "watching the screen." The porn movie "screens" queer desire.

Over the next day, Yunior goes into a tailspin: "Mostly I stayed in the basement, terrified that I would end up abnormal, a fucking pato, but he was my best friend and back then that mattered to me more than me. This alone got me out of the apartment and over to the pool [where Beto was] that night."[30] The fear of contagion is overcome by friendship. Their years of friendship move Yunior to resume his relationship with Beto.

After their swim, the boys end up in Beto's apartment again:

> Since his [Beto's] parents worked nights we pretty much owned the place until six the next morning. We sat in front of his television, in our towels, his hands bracing against my abdomen and thighs. I'll stop if you want, he said and I didn't respond. After I was done, he laid his head in my lap.[31]

This second time going at "it" happens without much of a build up. Just as they sit, Beto hold on to Yunior's abdomen and thighs, perhaps giving him oral sex. Beto speaks, and Yunior remains silent. We can read in the lack of details that this sexual event just "happens"—it does not require an elaborate language or explanation. It just *is*.

Thereafter, Yunior falls into a fantasy world, remembering his life in high school and considering whether or not he will make it in life. We notice here that, for both Piri and Yunior, same-sex encounters are surrounded by scenes of fantasy and daydreaming. Later,

> I had my eyes closed and the television was on and when the hallway door crashed open, he jumped up and I nearly cut my dick off struggling with my shorts. It's just the neighbor, he said, laughing. He was laughing, but I was saying, Fuck this, and getting my clothes on.[32]

The first time that the boys did "it" may have been "accidental," but Yunior's second time, in the name of friendship, reveals a paradigm. Yunior's repeat experience happens to completion without him saying a word. This seems to suggest that homosexual encounters can happen as long as they are not discussed. Yunior's return is a tacit acknowledgment that something other may exist between him and Beto, yet it cannot be named outright. This silence is not passive, but rather an active affirmation of silence. Furthermore, no one must know about these rendezvous. This is confirmed when the possible presence of the other, a noisy neighbor, threatens the veil of silence and privacy that both friends share.

Silencing practices, silencing identities

In both Thomas's and Díaz's texts we can be read how silence surrounds sexual desires, practices, and identities. I want to be emphatic that what is being silenced does not operate equally around each element of the sexual persona. In other words, silencing one's desire is not exactly the same as not acknowledging a particular identity, or not giving language to the practices through which desire might get expressed. The linkage among desire, practice, and identity is always uneven—and indeed quite complicated. I proposed the term *epistemerotics* as a way to bring awareness of the close-knit or loosely related links among these three facets of a sexual persona.

If we begin to mark the site where silence intervenes around certain sexual practices, we might read Yunior's and Piri's sexual adventures as simply being on the "down low." They would not be considered self-hating homosexuals exactly. Rather their desire (Piri's repetition "I like girls" and Yunior's staring at the "straight" porn flick) works against the sexual practices themselves (getting a blow job from a transvestite or a *pato*), and together these do not jive exactly with their "heterosexual" identity. Epistemerotics is the recognition of these different nodes that eventuate in a sexual persona for which there might not be a name yet.

I would like to close this chapter by going back to a Latin American text, a sex scene from Puig's *Kiss of the Spider Woman*. In the following dark scene, we learn rather elliptically that the gay Molina and his cellmate Valentín are having sex:

> —Valentín... si querés, podés hacerme lo que quieras... porque yo si quiero.
> —...
> —Si no te doy asco.
> —No digas esas cosas. Callado es major.
> —Me corro un poco contra la pared.
> —...
> —No se ve nada, nada... en esta oscuridad.
> —...

—Despacio.

—...

—No, así me duele mucho.

—...

—Esperá, no, así es mejor, dejame que levanté las piernas.

—...

—Despacito, por favor, Valentín.

—...

—Así.

—...[33]

["Valentín, if you like, you can do whatever you want ... because I do want it."

"..."

"If I don't gross you out."

"Don't say those things. Being quiet is better."

"Let me move up against the wall."

"..."

"One can't see anything, nothing ... in this darkness."

"..."

"Slow."

"..."

"No, not that way, it hurts too much."

"..."

"Wait, no, this way is better, let me lift my legs."

"..."

"Slowly, please, Valentín."

"..."

"Like that."

"..."]

In this penetration scene, we have two different approaches to the sexual event. First, Molina who is openly homosexual is upfront that he wants to get fucked or whatever the other man wants. So Molina is completely open about his desire for another man, his identity as a homosexual, and how he wishes to give of himself sexually (getting fucked) to link his desire with his identity. Desire, practice, and identity flow seamlessly one into another, and produce a certain epistemerotic coherence around the term *homosexual*.

The other man's sexual experience is quite different. Throughout the novel, his desire is for a woman who is given the pseudonym "Jane Randolph," in order to protect her identity from the police. Valentín always claims over and again a heterosexual identity. In this scene he is trying to console Molina who is depressed about being in prison, and in the process of taking care of him, he begins caressing Molina, and eventually has sex with him. Molina narrates the sex act: "Wait, no, this way is better, let me lift my legs," "Slowly, please, Valentín," and so forth. Throughout it all, Valentín remains silent. He only insists, "Being quiet is better." So as we read this sexual act from Valentín's perspective, we can see that his desire is shrouded in silence and when he is penetrating the other man he does not speak. Any desire and identity can only be surmised as an effect. Also, at that particular moment with Molina, his unspoken desire, the very sexual act in the darkness where nothing can be seen, and any resulting identity from this encounter are sealed and narrated with those ellipses ("...")—these do not just represent the absence of language, but as I have argued before, the affirmation of silence. Silence as a particular form of epistemerotics, a way of knowing or unknowing, of doing and undoing, one's sexual persona.

After that moment of pleasure, Valentín asks Molina if he is feeling better, and he concurs. Molina asks him the how he is feeling, and again Valentín is reluctant to express himself, "No sé ... no me preguntes ... porque no sé nada." ["I don't know ... don't ask me ... because I don't know anything."] Next he adds, "No hables ... por un ratito, Molinita."[34] ["Don't speak ... for a little while, Molinita."] I would like to argue that, when Valentín is saying that he does not know anything and that he does not want to be asked anything, we are hearing echoes of another kind conversation, perhaps an interrogation of his political life. His place in the world, his political *Umwelt*, is a something that he will not explain to anybody, especially the police; likewise his private life, the *Innenwelt* of sexuality, also must remain silent. Silence has a way of conceptualizing his outer and inner worlds.

* * *

The sexual inner and outer worlds of Piri and Yunior, like the ones that Arenas proposes in his *loca* taxonomy or Puig shows between

Molina and Valentín, always reveal an incongruence or a gap between them. This gap gets filled by fantastic narratives of heroic masculinity and seduction, militant homosexuality, some sexual parody, or simply remains empty.

I opened this chapter citing from the first essay of Freud's *Three Essays on the Theory of Sexuality*. There he describes the "behaviors" of sexual inverts, namely, exclusive, amphigenic (or bisexual), and contingent. As with much of queer theory, this study too has been interested in "contingent" sexualities, those that are accidental and by happenstance, rather than deliberate or deliberative. Extending Freud's definition of invert behaviors, contingent "inverts" (and sexualities) are those who seem to come about from a lack of an available object choice, that is, sexual behavior and possibly identity through a *faute-de-mieux*. Additionally, contingency is not simply a question of a lack of sexual object, but also the particularity of the spaces, wherein which "contingent" queers might find themselves—for example, the boarding school, the prison, the gang, the homosocial spaces of certain cultures. Abel Sierra Madero has proposed that in Cuba, for instance, one must speak of an *ambiente homoerótico habanero* [a Havana homoerotic context], rather than a gay community to understand how same-sex relations then get framed as sexual identities. He explains,

> En Cuba no debe hablarse de una comunidad homosexual, sino de un ambiente homoerótico habanero. [...] Por ambiente homoérotico entiendo aquí, una dimensión espacio temporal en la que se reúnen o interactúan individuos identificados no sólo con la homosexualidad, sino que son espacios de diversidad cultural, no excluyentes por razones de orientaciones o identidades sexuales—aunque esas exclusiones también existen—, donde tienen lugar procesos culturales y se comparten códigos lingüísticos, estéticos y se establecen redes de amigos. Hablo de prácticas homoeróticas como las referidas a las relaciones sexuales o encuentros eróticos entre personas de un mismo sexo, sin suponer el fundamento de una identidad social...[35]

> [In Cuba, one must not speak of a homosexual community, but rather of a Havana homoerotic context (*ambiente*). [...] What I mean here by homoerotic context is a spatial-temporal dimension where individuals, not just those who identify with homosexuality, meet or interact;

homoerotic contexts are spaces of cultural diversity that do not exclude on the basis of sexual orientations or identities—although those exclusions happen—also, [they are spaces] where cultural processes take place and where linguistic codes, aesthetics are shared, as well as networks of friends are formed. I speak of homoerotic practices as those which refer to sexual relations or erotic encounter between people of the same sex, but that do not presuppose a foundation of a sexual identity . . .]

Sierra Madero's conceptualization of this homoerotic space might serve as one basis and another perspective to theorize about how contingent (homo)sexualities might be formed and narrated among Latino American subjects. Indeed, for Piri, the house of Antonia and the other *locas* is that kind of place; for Yunior, it is Beto's family's empty apartment. I appreciate Sierra Madero's work here, however, my work is still very invested in subject formation, and I do not want to credit completely the idea of context as the predominant and exclusive regulating dimension of how queer subjects come into being. I still want to retain the question of the body and the many practices of agency that exist in Latino American queer subject formation.

As we read gay, lesbian, queer, male-male relations in Latino American cultural contexts, we begin to see a complex and its unfolding. How does queer Latino subject formation happen as a differential of desires, practices, identities, and also contexts? These many facets contribute to queer Latino subject-formation intersectionally, yet asymmetrically. Furthermore, how we begin to unpack those sexual identities, and how we write a "thick" description of them signifies on a new political story of queer *Latinidad*.

10

Traveling North, Translating Queerness
Rivera-Valdés and the Trouble with Discipline

> [T]heory has to be grasped in the place and the time out of which it emerges as a part of that time, working in and for it, responding to it; then, consequently, that place can be measured against subsequent places where the theory turns up for use. The critical consciousness is awareness of the differences between situations, awareness too of the fact that that no system or theory exhausts the situation out of which it emerges or to which it is transported.
>
> —Edward Said[1]

Queer Translations

What happens to a person or a theory when it travels across time or space? That question structures Edward Said's important essay "Traveling Theory." He proposes a theoretical framework to examine this question by first looking at the theory's (or the person) point of origin, second, the spatial and temporal distance traversed, third, the conditions that confront the transplanted (how the new context transforms the theory or person), and finally the new uses of that the theory or person once settled in its new space (how the theory or person transform the new context).[2] He differentiates between the reification of theory with its universalist tendencies and critical consciousness as that moment of reflection of the particularities that mark the "original" conceptualizations of theory and its afterlives.

The crisis in theory is that moment when we discover that theory's universalism is nothing more than a conceit, as no theory is able to explain or exhaust an event in its totality.

I am interested in this Saidian formulation because it relates to my critical approach to queer theory. One of the distinctive features of queer theory has been its capaciousness, its ability to capture subjectivities, events, movements, and so forth that exceed or do not quite coincide with the identity politics of heteronormativity or homonormativity. In describing new queer subjects and in reading queer theory as it travels elsewhere, we encounter those moments of noncorrespondence and resistance. These moments of crisis, which according to Said, "concretely represent the essence of reification"[3]— that is, crisis renders visible the ways in which theory cannot capture the totality of the new context, as well as how the new context impinges on theory itself. We are then left to ask, how do we read queer theory transnationally?

Said asks that we consider "the place and the time out of which [theory] emerges." If we consider, queer performativity as a particular articulation of queer theory, we are able to situate it in a historical context—for example, one narrative might begin with the "coming out" imperative of the late 1960s. And although theorists resist historically grounding a particular theory, nevertheless, the historical moment and crisis of, say, Stonewall emerges as a kind of watermark in the very textuality of theorizing queer performativity. Is such a specific history possible to avoid? Is such a history universal to queer identification and performativity elsewhere?

In the context of Latino American cultures, queer performativity might be useful—but how? It also may have limitations—and which? More importantly, I have been arguing throughout this book that queer Latino American cultures have had different historical groundings, as well as literary traditions, critical vocabularies, epistemologies, indeed theoretical watermarks, that have shaped and transformed gay, lesbian, and queer desires and identities otherwise. In describing this taxonomy of queer desires, circuits and identities, I align my work with scholarship in queer of color critique (as well as Black and Latino and Asian American and Native American queer theorizations), which have challenged, contested, and reframed the discussion of a "queer theory."[4]

José Quiroga has proposed the idea of "intervention" as a gesture of critical consciousness that resists social and cultural impositions of other (and foreign) queer subject formations. In his *Tropics of Desire*, Quiroga seeks to conceptualize modes of intervention, what he describes as "visibilities within forms of social praxis in the Latino American contexts . . . that allow different publics to participate in the social sphere."⁵ Quiroga's concept of "intervention" functions similarly to Said's idea of "critical conscious." To the English-speaking ear, "intervention" sounds like an aggressive imposition of (military) force; however, in Spanish "hacer una intervención" is mostly about making a contribution to and presenting alternative perspectives in an extended dialogue. In "translating" this term, which is a false cognate, Quiroga is making his own "intervention" into queer studies: on the one hand, presenting alternative views on a subject, while on the other, strongly insisting on the queer differences that might emerge from the South as a modes of critical consciousness or resistance.

Discipline

In this concluding chapter, I would like to examine the movement of queer identities and theories in Sonia Rivera-Valdés's masterful *The Forbidden Stories of Marta Veneranda*.⁶ I am particularly interested in the crises of queer identification that happen through what might be called the transnational flows and operations of queer *Latinidad*. All along we have been seeing how a similar set of sexual desires and practices get cast as identities differently. Rivera-Valdés's text does an exemplary job of demonstrating how the different pressures of definition, the epistemologies, shift how sexual identities appear and circulate in Latino American cultures.

The text is organized as a collection of nine stories, each in a confessional mode, with an "Explanatory Note" that contextualizes their assembly. Each of the narratives tells a sexy story by different characters (some who know and make reference to each other). The "author" Marta Veneranda has collected them as part of her research in anthropology. In classic form, she begins, "The stories collected in this volume are true. The names have been changed to protect the identity of the narrators."⁷ These forbidden stories were sought out to reveal "the disparity between what human beings commonly consider shameful to tell about lives and the ignominy of the deed itself."[8] The difference between personal shame and public disgrace (ignominy) becomes the regulating determinants that hover underneath each story. What becomes forbidden is marked by this gap between private and public shames, and it is quite important here because it defines sexual identity. It is not shame itself, but rather the willingness to go public with that shame, that inaugurates the sexual subject in the text. Lawrence LaFountain-Stokes has shown brilliantly that in Latino American cultures, *sinvergüencería*—shamelessness—is a cultural strategy that initiates Latinos into a process of queer identification.[9] To embrace being a *sinvergüenza* (shameless), getting rid of any sense of culpability about one's desire or breaking free from social and cultural discipline, means a rejection of authority and pressures, and allows for the emergence of a queer identity.

Marta Veneranda is the collector of desires, and organizes them. Her name is quite significant in this endeavor of managing desire. The etymology of Marta is "lady" or "mistress." In Italian, *veneranda* means "venerable"—also, *veneranda* is a related to the Latin *veneris* and *venus*, meaning love, beauty, or having sex. From this game of etymologies we see that the author Marta Veneranda is literally a venerable mistress—or perhaps with a dominatrix tone to her name "Venerable Mistress." She has been placed in the role of *sujet supposé savoir* [subject supposed to know], whereby she has the advantage of piecing together the forbidden stories, and making them anew, by the sheer power of her position and privilege as author.

Marta Veneranda tells us that she proposed this idea of collecting stories as a doctoral project in anthropology, drew up the necessary questionnaires, and began data collection. It is important to underline here that the collection began as an ethnographic project. Marta is confident in her abilities as ethnographer: "As soon as I had interviewed my first subjects, I knew that to understand the complexity of their secrets, I would have to hear about part of their lives that went far beyond what was covered in the questionnaire."[10] Interestingly, here she reveals an important fact, that secrets cannot be found in and of themselves, but rather, secrets are part of a complex. The secret message is always already packaged with other stories, stories that exceed the efficiency of a questionnaire. Indeed, the methodology of gathering secrets and information was lacking something. Her professor "advised that [she] was missing the concrete details needed to computerize the data." Indeed her teacher (and master) was insisting on obtaining information that could be rendered as digital and binary, however, Marta had "devoted attention to other details that would not allow [her] to draw any scientifically valid conclusions."[11] In other words, there was too much information, too much "complexity" covering up the kernel of the secrets that she sought. This would suggest that the secrets of sexuality are always already wrapped up in other narratives that hide or deflect any sense of unadulterated truth. It also means that some forms of "secret" knowledge do not lend themselves to be gathered and understood under the microscope of scientifically valid methodologies.

This inability to organize and "computerize" her information becomes quite frustrating for Marta. Her adviser insisted as scientific rigor, but Marta discovers something different: "what the transcription consistently offered me was not a set of quantifiable data but a new story too fascinating to resist."[12] Thus,

> The situation grew more distressing and unbearable until the day a revelation hit me: The solution was not to change my research method but to change my discipline. Though it didn't seem so at first sight, this decision reflected, to a large extent, my devotion to the truth.[13]

This is a moment of tremendous insight for Marta Veneranda. The subject supposed to know acknowledges the limitations of her primary discipline, and trades them in for another. The scientific method gets replaced by literature, empiricism by discourse analysis. The "new story" offered by the data collected deconstructs the theoretical conceits of Marta's original research methods. Therefore, this disciplinary change reminds us of Said's warnings that traveling theories cannot fully grasp the totality of the event.

In what follows, I would like to look at two stories by Rivera-Valdés, "Five Windows on the Same Side" and then "Lunacy." I hope to explore in greater detail the ways theories, like immigrants, travel and get framed.

Points of Reference

"Five Windows on the Same Side" is the first story of the collection, and we are introduced to Mayté Perdono Lavalle. She is a Cuban American journalist living in a New York apartment with her husband Alberto. Mayté immediately prefaces her story by noting that "[s]o many lurid things take place in New York every day that hardly anything seems forbidden. But *forbidden* is a relative term. Any event that is embarrassing enough for someone to keep it a secret is that person's forbidden story."[14] We notice right away that she contextualizes the notion of forbidden to a place, New York, and that somehow in that context few things would be considered forbidden. The public arena diminishes the sense of what is forbidden; rather, in Mayté's case, what is forbidden is deeply personal. Thus, she continues,

> You'll judge my story according to your own criteria, but for me this whole matter is very disturbing. Not just that I had a sexual relationship with a woman, but the series of circumstances that surrounded the episode and the impact it had on me. It changed my life.[15]

Immediately one notices the structure of address—Mayté addresses herself to "you"—both Marta as well as the reader. This deflects Mayté's complete authority to comprehend the forbidden story. This deflection makes the notion of forbidden all the more "relative." Then, we are told that Mayté has had a relationship with a woman, but again it's the "series of circumstances" around the relationship make for this a forbidden story. Like we saw earlier, it is not the supposed secret— here a lesbian affair with a distant cousin—that makes Mayté's story forbidden, but rather it is those things that surround and go beyond the story.

We begin to see an interesting series of concentric circles emerging here. At the center is a lesbian affair—not a problem; then we have the circumstances surrounding the affair—here is the problem; finally there is the larger circle, New York as context—again, not a problem. Again, Mayté had already stressed that "*forbidden* is a relative term." So, to locate the forbidden story, it means that we must look for a specific point of reference, rather than a general abstraction. What is forbidden—or in different terms, the site of crisis—may move and circulate according to different actors, authors, contexts, and temporalities. Therefore, historical specificity and grounding—and as we shall see cultural specificity—become necessary parameters or contexts to make sense and to define of that crisis.

Mayté makes it clear that she wants to address this situation, and reveal the "truth" to her husband Alberto:

Yes, I told him. We have always been very frank with each other and I couldn't keep quiet. As soon as he got back from Chicago, the whole story popped out. Minus the details of course. It all happened so quickly that my concern might seem silly, but I've spent whole weekends unable to focus on anything by my obsession about whether I may have been a lesbian my whole life and not realized it until now.[16]

Mayté's storytelling comes in the form of a logorrhea. There is an urgency in her words, wanting to express something that she feels she has done wrong. Her "confession" finally arrives to discuss the affair itself: "I've been talking for half an hour now and I still haven't started to tell you my story with Laura. I think that your being Cuban makes me remember things I'd thought were forgotten."[17] Mayté identifies with Marta Veneranda—that is, Marta's Cubanness brings back memories. Their common national background provides a context where certain stories may be told and acknowledged.

In classic analyst-analysand form, Mayté declares: "Just this second, I realized something so obvious over the episode with Laura, to the point of blaming it for having changed my life, when in reality my confusion began before she appeared. Am I blind for now having seen that?"[18] She goes on to say that the problems began when Alberto announced that his company was moving to Chicago—this news affected her physically. It was once before that she had had such a feeling: the night after her family had received authorization to leave Cuba for the United States, she heard her name being whispered. This was a chilling event, similar to the one she felt when Alberto made the announcement of the move. Her reaction to the move was a long reproach: How could she leave her New York apartment, her home? Here we find one of Mayté's forbidden stories—the story of departure. As a child she could not respond—as an adult the very suggestion of leaving a home unleashed a strong protest. This story of departure only gets told in the context of another secret, her affair with Laura.

How does the loss of home relate to the potentiality of a queer identity? I would suggest that the loss of home—in both cases, leaving Cuba and moving out of New York—is motivated by a patriarchal desire to find a better life elsewhere. Mayté's protest to Alberto may in fact be echoing another protest that had remained unspoken until now, that is, a protest against her father's own desire to move the family out of Cuba or blaming Castro (as a national *pater familias*) for provoking their exile. Alberto gets the brunt of her anger against these fathers. The affair with Laura may be understood as another form of protest against compulsory heterosexuality. I do not want to suggest here that Mayté only "became a lesbian" in order to "get back" at her husband—that simply would be wrong. Rather, I am trying to link two secrets or forbidden stories—one speaking about loss of home and the other of queer potentiality—and in both cases propose that what they have in common is a form of protest against certain practices that patriarchy has over the lives of women. These two forbidden stories have become intertwined—each covering and highlighting parts of the other. The narrative imbrication or palimpsest of these two forbidden stories make for addressing the question of referentiality much more difficult to discern. Thus, it is only accidentally or inadvertently that Mayté is able to recall a singular story or to account for the full breadth and implications of her forbidden stories.

I would like to turn now to the affair itself—and, most importantly, how each woman conceives of their encounter. For how each woman understands what has happens reveals another forbidden story.

The Place from Where She Speaks...

A month after Alberto's fateful announcement, he travels for a two-week trip to Chicago. Mayté learns that her second-cousin Laura is visiting her Aunt Rosario in Miami—she sends her the money and invites Laura to meet her in New York. When they meet at the airport, both women find themselves crying:

> ...our meeting meant that standing before me was more than just one relative I was seeing for the first time, but someone with my blood in her veins whose eyes had watched the sun rise and set every day over Caibarién [Mayté's hometown]. Someone who had heard the Cuban birds singing when she woke up, who had stepped on Cuban grass when she went out into the yard. I looked at her, unable to think of anything else, and I cried.[19]

This scene of mirroring is told from Mayté's perspective, and again we can appreciate that she identifies with Laura's Cubanness, in particular with a very romanticized version of Cuban. Identification always involves a partial object (in this case, the same blood, the sunset, the grass, the birds singing) and this object gets blown out of proportion. These lost objects get conjured up and narrated again in a narcissistic story of a lost past. The immigrant always looks back at the country of origin through this romanticized lens. In other words, Mayté does not really recognize Laura; rather, she recognizes what she has lost. Moreover, Mayté is not encountering Laura in the present, but rather she is projecting onto Laura's figure and body a version of herself in the past: it is a figure with whom she is inevitably destined to (fall in) love. Once more, we see the slippage between falling in love with another woman—or simply remembering a version of oneself which one had forgotten how to love. That is, the difference between homosexuality and narcissism.

Nevertheless, the women enjoy each other's company, talking for hours about family and events. They relaxed listening to boleros by Marta Valdés, and then Lucesita Benítez—and then they began to dance. And then they made love. For the next two weeks the women stayed together; most of the time they "spent in bed and dancing boleros in the living room."[20] Then after this long romance, they have a conversation about what is going on:

> I was aghast at my own behavior, but Laura seemed at ease. She admitted that this wasn't the first time this had happened, although with me it was something special. I didn't believe the second part. I asked if her husband knew.
> "Are you nuts? How would he know?" she responded, looking at me as if I were kidding.
> "I'm going to tell Alberto," I said. "Otherwise, I couldn't live in peace with myself."
> Her eyes widened. She was flabbergasted.
> "You are crazy in the head," she said, shaking her own from side to side. "Look, my first husband was with the Ukrainian woman for years before I found out. She even bore him a pair of twins behind my back. César, my current man, is very good, but do you think I don't know that he sleeps with any woman that comes along as soon as he has the chance? I'm not going to pass up a good time myself when it appears. I have no interests in affairs with men. I look to women for that. What can you do? To each her own, and besides, there's no risk of getting pregnant.[21]

This exchange reveals two worldviews on sexuality and desire. It cannot be reduced to a debate of faithfulness and unfaithfulness. Instead, this discussion speaks to different epistemologies and politics of desire. We remember that Mayté conceives of her same-sex experience as an initiation into lesbianism—or perhaps a confirmation of a latent homosexuality. I would like to argue that within the United States context, Mayté has a very restricted understanding of female-female sexual relations as lesbianism proper. After several conversations, Mayté acknowledges that

> [w]e were speaking different languages, whenever we spoke on the matter. In the final analysis [. . .] I think this was the most astonishing part of the experience—*the different weight we gave to things*. Laura didn't understand how I, with the worldliness she attributed to me because of my education, the trips I've taken, the exposure I've had to different cultures, my living in such a cosmopolitan city, could think that not to tell Alberto what had happened would be an act of betrayal.[22] (Emphasis mine.)

As Mayté observes, the women spoke different languages on the matter. Whereas Mayté sees the conversation with Alberto as an act of honesty about her sexuality, Laura suggests that their affair might come across as a betrayal in the context of marriage. Now, as I suggested above, Mayté's idea would make sense in the context of the United States, where same-sex relations (defined predominately through an object choice) might be considered "lesbian" or "homosexual." In this sense, Mayté has adopted the particular understanding that one's sexual identity is defined by the object. We notice that she does not even consider bisexuality as a possible option—she only thinks of herself as a lesbian. And most importantly, she must tell someone, her husband. Again, the United States culture of coming out weighs heavily on Mayté's decisions—otherwise this part of her life becomes something forbidden.

Laura sees things differently. She does not see the episode as an act that "inverts" her heterosexuality; instead, it is an expansion of heterosexual desire. Laura equates those encounters he has had with other women on par with the affairs that her first husband and now her "current man" had or might be having. Laura is thinking of sexual desire as something that can be experienced for a woman's own pleasure with the added benefit that "there's no risk of getting pregnant." Laura is using an entirely different language or epistemology to imagine her affair with Mayté. For her, having an extramarital encounter with either a man or a woman is considered a betrayal, and she is surprised that Mayté does not appreciate it the same way, especially given her cosmopolitism. In Laura's eyes, Mayté is a woman of the world, and thus she should possess a sensibility of wanting and having a mistress. We remember one small detail that confirms Laura's donjuanesque attitude—not only has she been with other women, but she states that with Mayté "it was something special." Thus, Laura performs and owns a particular version of Latino masculinity, which is different from identifying as a lesbian. She inserts herself in a heterosexist narrative of seduction, and thus expands what it means to be a heterosexual, what it means *not* to be marked by the object choice.

In the end, Mayté finds herself at an impasse: "We parted without my understanding her need to live a secret life nor her understanding my need to live an open one."[23] In either case, each woman does not understand the codes by which the other lives—their episodes get read differently depending on the place from where she speaks. "Five Windows on the Same Side" contrasts beautifully with what I have been arguing about: how cultural difference shapes queer identities in provocatively new ways. Moreover, if we go back to Said's understanding of traveling theory, this short story demonstrates the idea that traveling bodies, like traveling epistemologies, sometimes do not capture the complexities of the new context, neither are they understood correctly either. Traveling theories, queer theories, always contain a gap, a crisis, that might just seem overwhelming. How we go about narrating that gap or resolving that crisis requires a critical understanding and the sensibility to allow otherness to educate us.

At the end of the story, Mayté stays in her apartment in New York and buys a huge collection of bolero records. Most interestingly, even with her insistence on her newfound sexual persona, she has doubts:

> To be honest, what disturbs me at this point, after having this conversation with you, during which I've clarified several things for myself—the magical power of language—is not knowing, despite the explanations I gave Alberto, whether I didn't go to Chicago because of the problem with Laura, or whether the problem with Laura was caused by my desire to find a reason not to go to Chicago.[24]

In other words, Mayté considers whether she did not go to Chicago because she "became a lesbian" (presented here as "the problem with Laura")—or whether she "became a lesbian" as an excuse to avoid going to Chicago. Or, stated in a radically different way, did Mayté not leave her home to become a lesbian, or did Mayté become a lesbian to avoid leaving her home? Does it matter?[25] Indeed, in either case, Mayté ends her forbidden story by reclaiming a queer domesticity. In her twisted way, through "the magical power of language," Mayté reveals what might just be truly forbidden: linking queer identity (as a potential for a certain openness) and domesticity (a form of closure, a kind of antithesis to queerness)—and then figuring out what the politics of this dialectic might just be.

Disciplining Queerness

The next story I would like to discuss, "Lunacy," introduces us to an anonymous narrator. Unlike Mayté, whose free association with language takes her to uncover new secrets of her life, he is quite methodical and even brings an outline to talk with Marta Veneranda. His professional discipline accounts for how he structures his narrative:

> As a good mathematician, I'm precise and I don't like to digress.
> Let me say that it's been more than 20 years since I've slept with a woman. It's always men, and black ones. Or at least men of color, by the standards of this country. Whites don't appeal to me sexually. I know where this comes from. What I don't know about is the other thing that I'll talk about later.[26]

This self-presentation brings us back to our initial discussion of disciplinary approach in the text. The narrator is invested in a scientific formulation of his story—these component parts are enumerated along his story as origins, upbringing, leaving home, and his first homosexual experience, and the "dark side" of his story. He is a child from the provinces, with a certain amount of class privilege, with a father as the town doctor and his mother as the pharmacist. He is also a sickly child with asthma and therefore is overprotected by all the women in his family. In my discussion of his story, I would like to explore his homosexual desire and that "dark side" in his erotic life.

The narrator is quite sure of how he wishes to be seen as a homosexual with a particular attraction for black men or "men of color." He explains to Marta: "there's no way I could be speaking with you so openly if I hadn't been in therapy since I got to this country. Conclusively accepting that I'm a homosexual and coming out of the closet the way I've done has not been so easy."[27] We could argue that, similarly to Mayté's queer socialization or perhaps more aggressively so, he has been "normalized" to accept the "standards of this country" as a measure of his sexual identity. Homonormativity operates here as an imposition delivered through therapy. His sexual desires are limited.

There are plenty of clichés in the narrator's story that contribute to making him a homosexual—he is a sickly and fragile child with an overprotective mother; he can't eat certain foods, especially fish; he is shy and a hermit; and so forth. The narrator contrasts his closed life with the cook's son, Genaro, who is fearless and possess a level of personal freedom that the narrator envies. Genaro's nickname is Sandokan, after the nineteenth-century orientalist character from Emilio Salgari's adventure novels. The narrator wants to be like Sandokan—and the two boys are set up as opposites in the story.

When the narrator starts high school in Havana, he tells us that he goes from "an overprotected childhood to an almost completely independent adolescence." While in college, he meets Armando, his first love, who reminded him of Sandokan:

> There was no physical resemblance, nor did their personalities match. Besides, their upbringings were quite the opposite. One night as we drank coffee, after dinner, we began to flirt in a subtle way, and that's when I realized that it was the brown tone of his skin that made me associate him with Sandokan. Since that time that's been the color of love for me. We became lovers. It wasn't a problem for me to discover I was attracted by my own sex.[28]

Here the narrator reveals where his desire for men of color comes from: his attraction for the young boy's life is so overwhelming that it makes him want to have his skin—he wants literally to be in his skin. The dark skin represents a synecdochal relation whereby the narrator wants all the physical freedoms that this dark skin affords. Here we are reminded of another similar scene in Richard Rodríguez's *Hunger*

226 *The Avowal of Difference*

of Memory, where the college-aged Richard looks at the men in the fields and gardeners, and he desires their lives:

> And though I feared looking like them, it was with silent envy that I regarded them still. I envied their physical lives, their freedom to violate the taboo of the sun. Closer to home I would notice the shirtless construction workers, the roofers, the sweating men tarring the street in front of the house. And I'd see the Mexican gardeners. I was unwilling to admit the attraction of their lives. I tried to deny it by looking away. But what was denied became strongly desired.[29]

In this scene, Richard conflates a particular pastoral desire for the life of the laborers with a sexual desire that he cannot articulate yet.[30] A similar conflation happens in the mind of the narrator of "Lunacy." Despite the abjection that Rodriguez feels for having dark skin (at one point he tries to shave off the darkness), he nonetheless fetishizes it. If we understand a fetish to be a process of valuation through which a fetishist gives an object an esteemed value, then both the narrator and Rodriguez are writing on the body of others their forbidden stories. For the narrator of "Lunacy," in particular, his desire for men of color is really a desire for a different kind of upbringing, liberated from all those fears imposed by his mother and his class status. Social freedom becomes expressed later on as sexual freedom; moreover, sexual freedom and expression get compacted in the desire to have (and be) in the skin of darker man. The metaphor "I want to be a darker man" is taken up literally as "I want to have a darker man."[31] And as the narrator announced from the very start, he knew where his desire for black men came from—however, what he did not know may have been the significance of this desire. He narrates social freedoms through race, and sex with men of color become his way of achieving those freedoms that he longed for since he was a child. But this is not the end of his story—nor does it really constitute his "forbidden" or secret text.

We know from the narrator himself that he was never been overly sexual. Also, how he met Matthew, his beau of six years, is in keeping with his character. He placed a personal ad in a paper to search, evaluate, and interview the perfect partner: "Many people find it strange that someone with my social position and seriousness would resort to that means of finding a partner, but the explanation is simple."[32] He has been dating men whom he considers friends; however, after they break up, he loses both the lover and the friend. So a more professional or methodical approach of questionnaires and interviews seems to the narrator the safer option. He receives fifty-four responses in a week, and he selects Matthew.

The narrator explains that Matthew's and his personalities are the most compatible; the only difference between them is that Matthew has a "fiery temperament" versus his more calm sexual drive. From the beginning the men try different methods to increase the narrator's desire—they were all failures to the point that the relationship became threatened. Yet,

> One afternoon Matthew came home from work with a bag full of pornographic films of all different subjects and styles for me to choose the ones that excited me. [...] I devoted long hours over the next few days to my selection. It was a desperate measure after a series of situations too humiliating and intimate for me to describe. I'd never been too enthusiastic about gay erotic films, but to my astonishment and Matthew's satisfaction, I've suddenly become an excellent lover.[33]

The porn films supplement the narrator's desire, and prompt him to perform sexually. Yet this is only the first part of the story, because as the narrator continues:

> I keep watching Matthew's films so that he won't discover the truth, which is that those aren't the ones that do it for me. It's the others, which I buy in secret and watch alone before he comes home. The scenes from these films throb in my memory while we're in bed and give me strength. I hide them in the basement among some old science books. They're all heterosexual—that's my secret.[34]

First, what is the significance of having to watch straight porn to get turned on and perform gay sex? Indeed, I had suggested this before in the sex scenes with Piri and Yunior in the previous chapter. Heterosexuality lies as a template to frame and enable male-male sexual interactions. That is, in order to make male-male sex happen, the narrator has to hold on to a heterosexual script (throbbing in his memory) to trigger some kind of passion for the other man. I would also suggest that racial difference contributes to this sexual queering. That is, the narrator's object choice of *men of color* signifies a particular belief often held by some men that the partner of the lesser social or racial status is less of a man—from here these men fantasize that they occupy a higher or more "masculine" status next to their "feminized" male companion, thereby reinscribing a heterosexist "man on top / woman on the bottom" model on their queer encounters.[35]

Second, if indeed the narrator's "erotic object is a vagina that lives in [his] head,"[36] why not just leave the other man, and begin a normative heterosexual life? This of course would imply that the narrator is a sexual "top"; however, his desire for black men or men of color would *stereotypically* suggest that he is searching for a penis to penetrate him. The distribution of desires appears conflicting—and queer. But let us pause and isolate this idea that the narrator's erotic object is a pussy on his mind, and ask, what motivates his seemingly straight interest and identity?

Going back to his childhood, we learned that the narrator had a nursemaid into adolescence. Teresita was responsible for bathing him until he was eight years old. After each bath, she would carry him to bed and cuddled with him there:

> Neither the towel nor the girl may have been as immense as I remember, but that's how they lodged in my imagination. She would put me to bed and there I'd stay for a while, naked, wrapped in the softness of the terry cloth until I was "normalized," a mysterious expression used by my grandmother on my mother's side. Teresita accompanied me under the towel in the process, her body warm and broad, and me like a little lizard folded into her breast and thighs.[37]

I quote from the original Spanish and offer a more literal translation: "Teresita me acompañaba en el proceso [de hacer *reacción*] bajo la toalla, su cuerpo tibio y amplio calentando el mío de lagartija encajada en su pecho y en sus muslos."[38] ["Teresita joined me in the process under the towel, her warm and broad body heated my lizard body, which was embedded in her breasts and thighs."] The process of "normalization" [in Spanish, literally "to make or provoke a reaction"] is one of the grandmothers' popular home remedies to help the narrator. At another moment, the narrator refers to his mother and grandmothers' concern that a drizzle might provoke a "whistling in the chest,"[39] thereby exacerbating his asthma. Indeed, despite being the son of a doctor and pharmacist, the narrator grows up in a domestic sphere that gives him notions of his body and health that we might associate with a small-town ideology. The narrator describes his own body as that of a lizard, meaning that it is cold-blooded, and he needs to have his temperature brought up to normal. Of course, the reptile reference suggests a phallic representation. "Provoking a reaction" appears to be the warming up of the body—and in some strange way, the provocation of an erection. The narrator would sleep "embedded" or "fitted" (*encajado*) in the nursemaid's breasts and thighs; this without doubt suggests a sexual initiation that would be inspected by the mother or grandmothers: "their shadowy beatific faces smiling at this placid scene."[40] Of course, this daily practice ends once the family discovers that Teresita is pregnant, and she gets fired:

> They thought I was too innocent to know why she was being fired, but I knew better, because Teresita had often spoken to me about her boyfriend, and I was precocious enough to guess what she didn't say. From the time they fired her, I refuse to "normalize," which made them all cry. I didn't care. Without Teresita's warmth it wasn't any fun.[41]

Indeed, the "normalization" naps with Teresita are more than just about warming up the body after a bath—they are signified as kind of sexual initiation between narrator and nanny—all this under that watchful (and up to a point, approving) eye of the family matriarchs. Firing the nanny immediately raises questions about the paternity of the child. This scene suggests, moreover, that perhaps the narrator was socialized as heterosexual, and that his later homosexual or, really, queer encounters represent nothing more than his refusal to normalize, another kind of "reaction" provoked against the matriarchal world. When the narrator takes up watching straight porn videos to get "warmed up" for his meetings with Matthew, we might be witnessing a return of the repressed. That is, his desire for "normalization" is awakened and what he is left with is the imprimatur of the vagina on the mind.

Finally, I would like to reread this image of the "vagina on the mind" as a memory of a lost heterosexuality; from there it would seem that the narrator's homosexuality is really a case of a *heterosexuality in disguise*. It is easier for him to deal with his lost heterosexuality by just putting the straight porn movies in the basement, underground, rather than deal with the full implications of his childhood desire. He has indeed been "homonormalized." Essentially both his public homosexual and his private heterosexual desire collude to provoke a reaction in a sexual identity and persona that is thoroughly queer.

Another way of understanding the figure of the "vagina in the mind," at the present moment in the narrator's life, would be to consider it particular reflection and understanding of hysteria. One outrageous (and wrongheaded, pun intended) explanation for hysteria has been that a woman had a floating uterus that ends up wrapping around a woman's brain[42]—this sexist explanation for hysteria circulated and, surprisingly, still has some traction among some. The figure of the "vagina in the mind" helps explain the hysterical narrator, always on the verge of losing his sense of identity; also, that figure helps explain the title of the story, "Lunacy." The Spanish title is "Desvaríos" ["Deliriums"]—I find "Desvaríos" to be quite a provocative title because it compacts the undoing (*des-*) of difference (*varíos*) that this story tries to negotiate. Also, "desvaríos" hints at the impossibility of capturing a totality in singularity in a label, a theory, or a person.

* * *

With its rich and complex understanding of sexual difference, *The Forbidden Stories of Marta Veneranda* captures queer identities, but most importantly these stories reveal that more than individual psychic desires, cultural contexts powerfully inform the figuration of those sexual personas. Paying attention to this dimension of where we come from fleshes out a narrative of who we are. Accounting for that elusive concept of culture allows for a momentary and fleeting conceptualization of identities, sexual and otherwise. It is my contention that the avowal of (cultural) difference delivers us a more nuanced understanding of queer Latino subjects—their forbidden desires and pleasures.

Notes

Introduction

1. Octavio Paz, "Máscaras mexicanas," in *El laberinto de la soledad*, ed. Enrico Marío Santí (Madrid: Cátedra, 1993), 170. Given my emphasis in close reading and analysis, all translations of Paz's essays are mine, unless specified.
2. B. Sifuentes-Jáuregui, "National Fantasies: Peeking into the Latin American Closet," in *Queer Representations: Reading Lives, Reading Cultures*, ed. Martin B. Duberman (New York: New York University Press, 1997), 293.
3. Here we can think of José Muñoz's *Disidentifications: Queers of Color and the Performance of Politics* (Minneapolis: University of Minnesota Press, 1999); his work on disidentifications as survival strategies that sexual minorities deploy to navigate a public sphere that disciplines or avoids them for not behaving within the terms of normative citizenship. Throughout this study, I analyze the concept of identification, relying mainly on Freud's conceptualization, and link it to primal scenes.
4. Another example of this anxiety to the universality of a "general" queer existence was heard at a preconference meeting of the Sexualities section of the Latin American Studies Association Meeting in San Juan, Puerto Rico, in March 2006. There, many participants criticized the "sopa de letras"—the alphabet soup—to designate LGBTQQTSI identities. Many rejected all these all-encompassing identifications; some claiming that the "alphabet soup" dispersed any coalition-building potential of identity politics.
5. Annamarie Jagose, *Queer Theory, An Introduction* (New York: New York University Press, 1996).
6. Here I am underscoring the subtitle of Altman's classic work, *The Homosexualization of America: The Americanization of the Homosexual* (New York: St. Martin's Press, 1982).
7. José Quiroga, *Tropics of Desire: Interventions for Queer Latino America* (New York: New York University Press, 2000), 4.
8. Carlos U. Decena, *Tacit Subjects: Belonging and Same-Sex Desire Among Dominican Immigrant Men* (Durham: Duke University Press, 2011). Decena's concept of a "tacit subject" pertains to a particular complicity that gay male subjects and those around them may have about those subjects' sense and understanding of homosexuality. My study looks at the question of silence not only as an unspoken knowledge, but more aggressively as the *affirmative refusal* to know and identify

232 Notes

gay, lesbian, or queer identities. In addition, I am thinking of Nicholas de Villiers's term "opacity" (vis-à-vis the closet) to designate a certain blurring of sexual difference, also as an expression and strategy to retain a certain level of privacy, all the while calling into question the overdetermined sense of "truth" of being "out." See his *Opacity and the Closet: Queer Tactics in Foucault, Barthes, and Warhol* (Minneapolis: University of Minnesota Press, 2012). In very different contexts, both Decena and de Villiers offer productive alternatives to the inside/outside binarism of the closet.

9. Thomas Mann, *Death in Venice* (A Norton Critical Edition), ed. and trans. Clayton Koelb (New York: W. W. Norton & Co., 1994), 34.

10. It may strike so readers as queer that I use Thomas Mann's novel as an example of the kind of elusive silences that I want to discuss in the Latin American and Latino contexts. However, I have deliberately used the Mann example because I find it interesting how critics have often commented on Mann's style—particularly, some going as far as suggesting that it owed to his mother being brought up in Brazil.

11. "Máscaras mexicanas," 164.

12. Ibid., 165.

13. Ibid.

14. Here I am thinking of Norma Alarcón's critique of Paz's sexist formulations in her now classic "Traddutora, Traditora: A Paradigmatic Figure of Chicana Feminism," in *Cultural Critique* 13, no. 3 (Fall 1989): 57–87. See also Jean Franco's *Plotting Women: Gender and Representation in Mexico* (New York: Columbia University Press, 1989), especially chapter 6, "On the Impossibility of Antigone and the Inevitability of La Malinche: Rewriting the National Allegory" (129–146).

15. "Máscaras mexicanas," 165.

16. On the one hand, we have Luce Irigaray's critique of the wound as a displacement of female genealogies. On the other hand, we remember Gloria Anzaldúa's characterization of the borderland as an "open wound."

17. "Máscaras mexicanas," 171.

18. Gayle Rubin, "The Traffic in Women: Toward a 'Political Economy' of Sex," in *Towards an Anthropology of Women*, ed. Rayna Reiter (New York: Monthly Review Press, 1975), 157–210.

19. "Máscaras mexicanas," 171.

20. Ibid., 174.

21. Indeed, Paz seems to argue that women's feminine and erotogenic masochisms become a model for masculinity.

22. Sedgwick, *Between Men: English Literature and Homosocial Desire* (New York: Columbia University Press, 1985).

23. "Máscaras mexicanas," 170.

24. Judith Butler, *Gender Trouble: Feminism and the Subversion of Identity* (New York, Routledge, 1990).

25. Judith Butler, *Bodies that Matter: On the Discursive Limits of "Sex"* (New York, Routledge, 1993), 15.

26. Certainly, trans studies radically calls into question this assumption.

27. I am very indebted to José Quiroga's work in *Tropics of Desire*; in particular, I appreciate his conceptualization of "Latino American" to frame the transnational dimensions of sexuality and other subject identities through a South-North dialectic. Bringing together theories from Latin American and Latino studies, Latino American makes it possible to imagine how spaces and theories from the South impact the North, and vice-versa. I use this interdisciplinary category throughout the book in an effort to encourage a dialogue of the ways in which queer

theories are read elsewhere, namely to call into question the conceit of universality of "queer," while providing new epistemologies out of other particularities.

Understandably the term *Latin America* is an equally complex geopolitical designation. I am fully aware of the ways it conflates Spanish America, Brazil, and the Caribbean, and how it might erase the very specificities that I often wish to highlight. Sometimes in my analyses, I draw theoretical readings and insights that come from very specific national and cultural contexts, and extend them to the larger context of "Latin America." In making such a gesture, I am in no way imposing the universality of theory; rather, it is my hope to offer each reading as alternative theoretical templates about queer sexuality, and thereby imagine and suggest a more capacious theoretical apparatus to read across the many versions of Latin America. Obviously, some of these suggestions will meet with the specificities of other regions and cultures, thereby delimiting the borders and margins of each theorization. It is at these limits where my conversation with other scholars begins.

28. Up to now, I have traced a single critical route, and have argued to give more stress to the body as a site from which gender(ed)/knowledge comes into being. It is important to consider other similar debates in Latino, African American, and Ethnic Studies; for example, I am thinking about the processes of racialization. For a historical overview of this process, see Robert Miles and Malcolm Brown's *Racism* (1989); another useful discussion of racialization is Jorge Duany's definition in *The Oxford Encyclopedia of Latinos and Latinas in the United States*, 535–544. This work importantly restores the place of the body as central to the process of identity formation.

29. José Martí, "Nuestra América," in *Ensayos y crónicas*, ed. José Olivio Jiménez (Madrid: Cátedra, 2004), 161.

30. Ibid.

31. Ibid., 164.

32. Ibid.

33. I am fully aware that I have relied on very traditional and canonical authors (Paz, Martí, Butler, and Sedgwick) to open up my argument on queer Latino American sexualities and identities. I should remark at this point that I shall bring in broader perspectives and critiques throughout this study. I just find it very useful to create a critical genealogy based on canonical works, to deconstruct them, and find alternative readings behind many of their assumptions.

34. Sylvia Molloy, *En breve cárcel* (Barcelona: Seix Barral, 1981), 37.

35. Ibid., 38.

36. *Tropics of Desire*, 1.

37. Ibid., 5.

38. Carlos Monsiváis, "Un mundo soslayado," Prologue to Salvador Novo's *La estatua de sal*. (Mexico, DF: Consejo Nacional para la Cultura y las Artes, 1998), 28.

39. Ibid., 29.

40. Ibid., 30.

41. Here we can compare Novo's uses and projection of his queer body and language in the same way that Oscar Wilde used "excess" to signify on others. See Sylvia Molloy's "Too Wilde for Comfort: Desire and Ideology in *Fin-de-Siècle* Spanish America," in *Social Text* 31/32 (1992): 187–201. I return to Molloy's analysis in chapter 6.

42. "Máscaras mexicanas," 167.

43. Ibid., 175.

44. Ibid.

45. There is an extensive bibliography that details this paradigm. See works by Joseph Carrier (1995) on Mexican homosexuality; and Tomás Almaguer on Chicano

gay men (1991). Robert M. Irwin offers a succinct analysis and critique of the penetration paradigm in his *Mexican Masculinities* (2003)

46. Here I am committed to avoiding the *application* of psychoanalytic theory to the literary work, and instead understanding the *implications* of literature for psychoanalysis. See Shoshana Felman, "To Open the Question," in *Yale French Studies* 55/56 (1977): 5–10.

Chapter 1

1. We might echo that oft-cited and famous dictum of his "Palabras liminares" of *Prosas profanas*: "Yo no tengo literatura 'mía'—como lo ha manifestado una magistral autoridad—, para marcar el rumbo de los demás: *mi literatura es mía en mí*; quien siga servilmente mis huellas perderá su tesoro personal..." (545). ["I do not have a literature that is 'mine'—as a magisterial authority has proclaimed—to mark the route for others to follow: *my literature is mine in me*; whoever follows my steps slavishly will lose his personal treasure..." (italics mine).] So, in fact, we could argue that if Darío is attentive to his own words, he is not following someone else either: indeed, he is resisting any poetic influence that comes from elsewhere. This position would put him at odds with the more traditional reading of Darío and the *modernista*'s emphasis on the mediated object. Here he is a believer in his own originality (a literature that is "mine in me"). Thus, his love for the "Greece of France" might be in fact for a Greece that is from elsewhere, exiled—a love for the radical decontextualization and rewriting that this newly represented object contains. Such a decontextualization necessarily would call for a new language.

2. Gerard Aching, *The Politics of Spanish American Modernismo: By Exquisite Design* (Cambridge and New York: Cambridge University Press, 1997), 5.

3. Ibid.

4. I take a lead here from Cathy L. Jrade's discussion on the *modernistas*' use of language: "The search for a language that can reflect the needs and wants of the writers and thinkers struggling against the narrow, rigid percepts of the ruling establishment [namely positivism] becomes the foundation of *modernista* goals. The mission is to create a spontaneous, natural, fluid, intuitive language that is truer, more authentic, more representative of the native spirit than that which is imported from Spain, imposed by neoclassical rules, or the external realities of the positive sciences but would turn to the subtle realities of the soul—the national essence and the individual being" (*Modernismo, Modernity, and the Development of Spanish American literature* [Austin: University of Texas Press, 1998], 33).

I want to stress that we do not want to confuse *modernismo* with the English cognate *modernism*, or variant *modernity*. Although both *modernismo* and modernism overlap as turn-of-the-last-century movements interested in rethinking about a crisis of subjective presence (and the present). I am highlighting here the narrative and thematic characteristics of *modernismo* that will be useful in writing of a sexually queer subject.

5. Max Henríquez Ureña's *Breve historia del modernismo* (Mexico: Fondo de Cultura Económica, 1954), outlines a rich compendium of the literary trends and tendencies of *modernismo*.

6. For an astute reading of the permutations that the trope of the *reino interior* has among *modernista* writers, see Aching's chapter 2, "The *reino interior*" (27–54). He details how this imaginary *locus amoenus* becomes an existential site of the imaginary, a place of literary production, as well as subject formation, to transform

itself, at times, as a place of resistance and political consciousness. To this end, I am interested in this site, in particular, in its structuration of interiority and how it may relate to queer subject formation.

7. Amado Nervo (1870–1919) is best remembered as a *modernista* poet, although he was quite prolific as an essayist and novelist. *El bachiller* was his first novel, and some critics have considered it autobiographical, given that like the protagonist his own father died when Nervo was very young. Nervo went to Mexico City in 1894, and began publishing his work in *Revista Azul* (directed by Manuel Gutiérrez Najera); in 1898, Nervo helped found *Revista Moderna*. In 1900, Nervo went on assignment to Paris for the important liberal newspaper *El imparcial*; he lived there for two years, before returning to take on a series of positions in teaching, journalism, and as a diplomat.

8. Amado Nervo, *El bachiller* in *Obras completas, volume 1, Prosas*, ed. Francisco González Guerrero and Alfonso Méndez Plancarte (Madrid: Aguilar, 1954), 185. This work has never been translated into English, thus all translations of this story are mine.

9. At this point I bracket off any discussion of affect theory.

10. *El bachiller*, 185.

11. Gwen Kirkpatrick, *The Dissonant Legacy of Modernismo: Lugones, Herrera y Reissig, and the Voices of Modern Spanish American Poetry* (Berkeley: University of California Press, 1989), 9.

12. Not surprisingly, we have an echo here of Darío's own *ensimismamiento* (literally, into-himself-ness), when he characterizes his literature as his in him.

13. Graciela Montaldo, *La sensibilidad amenazada. Fin de siglo y modernismo* (Rosario, Argentina: Beatriz Viterbo Editora, 1994).

14. I do not want to flatten this structure as a simple body-spirit one. As we shall see the priority of the interiority—a primal interiority—is always left open for analysis and debate.

15. *El bachiller*, 187.

16. Ibid., 185.

17. Ibid., 188.

18. Ibid.

19. Felipe's desire for self-control is so overwhelming, almost equivalent to Fichte's idea of the subject as all-emcompassing, overwhelming, able to produce everything from his own resources.

20. By relationality, I am alluding to Michel Foucault's understanding of how subject formation and power get produced in the relational structures of society, rather than being self-contained and preformed.

21. Frank Browning, *The Culture of Desire: Paradox and Perversity in Gay Lives Today* (New York: Crown, 1993), 210.

22. Ibid.

23. I am echoing here Jacques Derrida's appreciation of the figure of the mise en abyme as a radical reflexivity: it is a structuration by means of which a text does what it says, displays its own making, and reflects its own process.

24. Ironically, Felipe seems to want to arrest the inner workings of the aesthetic of circumlocution by insisting on a fixed object/subject. However, the more he tries to restrict the *modernista* economy of circumlocution, the more he fails: his language is necessarily full of slips and leaks, of unintended significations.

25. *El bachiller*, 189.

26. Another possible version of the *Miserere* would be Gregorio Allegri's *magnus opus* of moral renewal and a call for purity. The complete title of Allegri's work is "Miserere mei, Deus" ("Have Mercy on Me, God"). Indeed that background music would function as a particular kind speech act, as if Felipe were saying "don't let

evil forces tarnish me—keep me clean," and singing the chant places him in a submissive position before God, all the while he insists on becoming his own man.

27. *El bachiller*, 191.
28. Ibid.
29. Ibid., 190.
30. Sigmund Freud, "The Economic Problem of Masochism" (1924), in *The Standard Edition of the Complete Psychological Works of Sigmund Freud*, Volume XIX, *The Ego and the Id and Other Works*, ed. James Strachey (London: Hogarth Press and the Institute of Psycho-Analysis, 1953), 159.
31. Ibid., 161.
32. The best analysis of the relationship (really, the *non*relationship) between sadism and masochism as separate practices and structures that each lead to subject formation is Gilles Deleuze's essay "Coldness and Cruelty," which serves as an extended introduction to Leopold Sacher-Masoch's *Venus in Furs*: Deleuze, Gilles and Leopold Sacher-Masoch, *Masochism* (New York: Zone Books, 1989).
33. Ibid., 163.
34. Ibid.
35. Ibid., 163–164.
36. Ibid., 164.
37. Ibid.
38. Kaja Silverman, *Male Subjectivity at the Margins* (New York: Routledge, 1992), 197. Indeed, chapter 5, "Masochism and Male Subjectivity," of Silverman's text offers us a useful expansion of Freud's model. She extrapolates the idea of Christian masochism from her reading of Reik's *Masochism in Sex and Society*; she pins down Reik's examples of moral (he calls "social") masochism to illustrate certain Christian figurations that impinge on masculinity (195–201).
39. *El bachiller*, 192.
40. Ibid.
41. Ibid.
42. Jacques Lacan, *The Seminar of Jacques Lacan, Book XX: Encore, On Feminine Sexuality, the Limits of Love and Knowledge*, ed. Jacques-Alain Miller (New York: Norton, 1998), 7.
43. *El bachiller*, 192.
44. Ibid.
45. Ibid., 192–193.
46. *The Metamorphoses of Ovid*, trans. Allen Mandelbaum (San Diego: Harcourt Brace and Co., 1995), 92–93.
47. We can trope off this pun: Felipe has a desire for Asunción, meaning he has a desire for the girl, for spiritual levitation, as well as a physical levitation, a hard-on. The pun captures the complexity of naming a singular object of desire—the pun is messy and captures more than just a spiritual need, but also a physical one. This messiness could only be eliminated by the surgical removal of signifieds.
48. Importantly, I should remark on Asunción's being represented as blonde. It is tempting (and appropriate) to comment on how the idealization of woman gets filtered through race: the ideal woman is always white. In this and other *modernista* cases, I suspect that her blondness and whiteness corresponds to a European ideal of woman as object of desire; lest we forget Alfonsina Storni's response to the modernistas and vanguard poets, "Tú me quieres blanca" (1918), we should underscore that *modernista* obsession with the alabaster and translucent skin of virginal maidens to be more a marker of a moribund woman than necessarily a racially white one. Thus, Asunción's whiteness can be read into two ways: one, the idealized femininity as white only heightens that femininity, and by contrast the longing author becomes, if you like, more masculine within the heteronormative

dyad that he has imagined; and two, as a marker of whiteness and Europeanness. In my reading of *El bachiller*, I will emphasize the former and not the latter. Given that I will argue that Felipe will eventually reveal a certain anxiety over his own masculinity, the desire for a blonde woman as a marker of hyperfemininity gets deployed, thereby to raise his own masculinity. In later chapters, I pay more attention to the way in which queer subject formation gets narrated through racial formations—or how queer subjects deploy race in their self-figuration.

49. *El bachiller*, 195.
50. Ibid.
51. Ibid., 198.
52. Ibid., 199.
53. Ibid., 198.
54. Ibid., 199.
55. Ibid., 197.
56. Ibid., 199.
57. Ibid.
58. Lacan, *Encore*, 9.
59. Harold Bloom, "The Breaking of Form," in *Deconstruction and Criticism* (New York: Seabury Press, 1979), 1.
60. Again the end of the novella takes us back to the beginning. The text ends with a textual gap (a series of periods [. . . . .] sections off the final sentence): "Allá, lejos, en un piélago de oro, se extinguían blandamente la tarde" (199). ["Over there, far away, in a high sea of gold, the afternoon was fading softly."] Back in the opening paragraph of the text, we learned that Felipe desired "fundirse en el piélago escarlata del ocaso" (185) ["becoming one in the sea of the scarlet sunset"]. The scarlet sunset of the opening becomes the blood mark of castration, only to conclude metonymically as a golden sea.

Chapter 2

1. Sigmund Freud, "Instincts and their Vicissitudes" (1915), in *The Standard Edition of the Complete Psychological Works of Sigmund Freud, Volume XIV, On the History of the Psycho-analytic Movement; Papers on Metapsychology and Other Works*, ed. James Strachey (London: Hogarth Press and the Institute of Psycho-Analysis,1953), 133.

2. Miguel Barbachano Ponce is better known for his work as screenwriter, filmmaker, and producer. *El diario de José Toledo* was his first novel, followed by *Los desterrados del Limbo*. He is author of numerous plays and screenplays, as well as collections of essays on cinematography and film history. For more information on Barbachano Ponce and his views and contextualization of his novel, see Clary Loisel, "Interview with Miguel Barbachano Ponce," in *Harrington Gay Men's Fiction Quarterly* 3, no. 2 (2001): 17–25. The novel has been translated with a general introduction by Clary Loisel, *The Diary of José Toledo: A Translation and Critical Edition* (New Orleans: University Press of the South, 2001); Loisel offers useful contextual information about the author and novel in his introduction to the novel (vii–xix). All translations of citations of the text in this chapter are mine.

Finally, the bibliography on *El diario de José Toledo* is quite limited. David William Foster briefly comments on the novel: he argues generally that the multiple textualities that form the text (newspaper, diary, second-person narrative) reflect the very complexity of the narrator's identity (*Gay and Lesbian Themes in Latin American Writing* [Austin: University of Texas Press, 1991], 56–58.) In *Danger*

Zones: Homosexuality, National Identity, and Mexican Culture (Tucson: University of Arizona, 1996), Claudia Schaefer offers a useful contextualization and analysis of the novel, focusing on the shift from a "traditional" 1950s to a "modern" 1960s Mexico, and seeing how the protagonist's sense of identity is shaped by the cultural and social values and changes of these decades (15–36). For useful discussion of the novel and gay space in Mexican literature, see Marina Pérez de Mendiola, *Gender and Identity Formation in Contemporary Mexican Literature* (New York: Garland Publishing, 1998). Chapters 4 on José Joaquín Blanco, 5 on Barbachano Ponce, and 6 on Rosamaría Roffiel are quite helpful to contextualize gay and lesbian writing in Mexico from the 1960s to the turn of the century.

3. Miguel Barbachano Ponce, *El diario de José Toledo* (Mexico, DF: Premiá, 1988), 10.
4. *El diario*, 8.
5. Ibid., 126.
6. Ibid, 8.
7. Ibid., 9.
8. Ibid.
9. Ibid., 10.
10. Ibid.
11. Ibid., 13.
12. Ibid., 61.
13. Ibid., 33.
14. Trauma injures the very ability to retell the event. See Shoshana Felman and Dori Laub, *Testimony: Crises of Witnessing in Literature, Psychoanalysis, and History* (New York: Routledge, 1992), in particular Felman's essays, chapters 4, 5, 6, and 7. Also, on trauma and the problem of sequence within historical and narrative emplotment, see chapter 5, "Traumatic Awakenings: Freud, Lacan and the Ethics of Memory," in Cathy Caruth, *Unclaimed Experience: Trauma, Narrative and History* (Johns Hopkins University Press, 1996), 91–112.
15. *El diario*, 42.
16. Ibid., 52.
17. Ibid., 68.
18. Ibid., 79.
19. Ibid., 93.
20. Sigmund Freud, "Mourning and Melancholia" (1915), in *The Standard Edition of the Complete Psychological Works of Sigmund Freud, Volume XIV, On the History of the Psycho-analytic Movement; Papers on Metapsychology and Other Works*, ed. James Strachey (London: Hogarth Press and the Institute of Psycho-Analysis, 1957), 245.
21. *El diario*, 43.
22. Ibid., 106.
23. Ibid., 123.
24. Ibid., 15.
25. Ibid.
26. Ibid.
27. Ibid.
28. In my *Transvestism, Masculinity, and Latin American Literature*, I have argued that across different historical moments in Latin American cultures, transvestism has served as a means to attain of homosexual identity. In conservative contexts, the gender spectrum becomes rather dichotomized, either masculine or feminine, and one of the few means of homo*sexual* self-figuration happens through the literalization of the gender trope "to act like a woman"; hence, in this context, *male homosexuality as a sexual identity gets scripted through a gender performance*.
29. *El diario*, 99.

30. For a general overview of the Teachers' Movement and their struggle to unionize, see Carlos Monsiváis's tribute to one of the movement's leaders, Othón Salazar: http://www.eluniversal.com.mx/editoriales/46082.html (last accessed October 9, 2012).
31. *El diario*, 100.
32. Kath Weston, "Get Thee to a Big City: Sexual Imaginary and the Great Gay Migration" *GLQ* 2 (1995): 253–277.
33. *El diario*, 117–118.
34. The new Buenavista station, just 500 meters north of the original station, was inaugurated March 8, 1959. The site of the both stations was just steps from the Monumento a la Revolución, and just beyond that, you can find the Monument to Columbus on Avenida de la Reforma.
35. *El diario*, 13.
36. Ibid., 15.
37. Ibid., 80.
38. Ibid., 121.
39. Here I am making a clear allusion to Lacan's famous dictum.
40. *El diario*, 125.
41. Ibid.
42. See Edward W. Said, "Introduction: Secular Criticism," in *The World, the Texts, and the Critic* (Cambridge: Harvard University Press, 1983), 1–30. *Filiative* refers to the context of the family (romance) in shaping the subject; *affiliative* becomes at a different stage when the subject chooses institutions (church, government, profession, and so forth) against which to define him- or herself. It might be said that the "real" father is replaced by the "metaphoric" father of the nation. *Filiative* and *affiliative* thus refer to the contexts that (in)form how subject formation develops.
43. I take up the question of the place of silence and queer Latino American identities in further detail in chapter 3.
44. John D'Emilio, "Capitalism and Gay Identity," in *The Gay and Lesbian Studies Reader*, ed. Henry Abelove, Michele Aina Barale, and David Halperin (New York: Routledge, 1993), 467–476.
45. Ibid., 468.
46. Ibid., 470.
47. Ibid., 471.
48. For a discussion on the imperative of having to leave the domestic sphere as a "sexile" in order to claim a queer identity, see Yolanda Martínez-San Miguel, "Female Sexiles? Towards an Archeology of Displacement of Sexual Minorities in the Caribbean," in *Signs* 36.4 (Summer 2011), 813–836.

Chapter 3

1. Luis Zapata, *Las aventuras, desventuras y sueños de Adonis García, el vampiro de la Colonia* Roma (Mexico, DF: Grijalbo, 1979). *El vampiro* won the prestigious Grijalbo prize. The novel has been translated into English: Luis Zapata, *Adonis García: A Picaresque Novel*, trans. E. A. Lacey (San Francisco: Gay Sunshine Press, 1981). All citations are from the Spanish original, and translations are mine.
2. It has become commonplace in Latin-American letters to understand literature as a reading of history—and vice-versa. I am not talking about a cheap quid pro quo substitution, but rather a complex of narrative and historiography that signify on each other. González Echevarría (1990) suggests that the narratives of

Latin-America have been inscribed with the authorial paradigms of the legal acts (or *relaciones*) and chronicles of the Conquest in the sixteenth and seventeenth centuries; of travelogues of nineteenth-century scientists, and of anthropology in the early twentieth century. Furthermore, I would add that it is important to underscore that the status of Latin American literature exceeds the literary thing, and enters readily into the realm of the social and political. This is a particular phenomenon of which readers must be aware, especially since literature has often been seen as a "safe space" where authors and critics are able to declare other perspectives. This is especially true for homosexual identifications and narratives. In some sense Claudia Schaefer presents her reading of *El vampiro* as a postmodern utopia that opens up new spaces for Mexican gay men in the late 1970s and the1980s (see chapter 2 of her *Danger Zones*, 37–58).

3. I began thinking about how bodily inscriptions and disfigurations relate to the act of writing in an essay on the *Lazarillo de Tormes* (Sifuentes-Jáuregui 1998). In that work, I looked at the legible markings as signs of a queer sexuality on Lazarillo's body and text. I was concerned with how the bodily gets written, with the relationship between sexual and textual bodies. Here and in the previous chapters, I have begun exploring how masochism as a strategy of subject formation relates to Latin American narratives.

4. I want to conceive of the "postcolonial" in the widest sense possible. Here I mean that postcolonial is that process with which (colonized) subjects react and respond to varying degrees of social and cultural imposition from outside. More commonly, colonialism comes across as racial and ethnic forms and protocols, I would add that all colonial imposition also has sexual and gender expression. In the case of Latino American sexuality, subjects are always being bombarded by a host of sexual meanings—that is, Latin American and Latino subjects are always being pressed to be sexually different. Moving beyond (hence the "post") this limiting and reductive situation means that Latino American subjects must consider how to expand and reclaim a realm of sexuality that they might call their own.

5. Ben. Sifuentes-Jáuregui, "National Fantasies: Peeking into the Latin American Closet," in *Transforming the Categories: A CLAGS Reader*, ed. Martin B. Duberman (New York: New York University Press, 1997), 293–294.

6. Likewise, in the previous two chapters, I have tried to show such cultural inflections—how the discursive contributes to subject formation. In this chapter, with *El vampiro*, a text that is so unapologetically gay, I hope to articulate much more explicitly the way silence as discourse becomes a signature form of queer Latino American representation.

7. Lee Edelman has written about the inscription of gay identity in his book *Homographesis: Essays in Gay Literary and Cultural Theory* (New York: Routledge, 1994). Following his discussion of homosexuality as a marked sexual identity within the space of textuality, I want to look at those unmarked or blank textual spaces in the re-creation of Mexican (I hazard the generalization, Latin American) homosexuality. In other words, I want to read homosexuality both as *excessive presence* and as *absence*. It is my contention that homosexuality is not always either an overly graphic inscription or "unmarked"; rather, homosexuality is defined as the oscillation between these fundamental dichotomies, thereby creating an (il) logic of signification.

8. Judith Butler, *The Psychic Life of Power: Theories in Subjection. The Psychic Life of Power* (Stanford: Stanford University Press, 1997).

9. Ibid., 2.

10. I want to stress that as a Latin Americanist (and I deliberately claim this identification as a highly strategic positioning), I always want to maintain

certain level of tension (another word for *dialectic*) between my work and those critics with whose ideas I engage. As a Latin Americanist, the history and weight of colonialism is much too present to repeat it again in the *application* (often reflected as *imposition*) of certain theoretical approaches into my work. Too often this gesture of imposing (U.S.-produced) theory onto other national texts seems the status quo, where theory is the privileged language needed to explain other ways of knowledge. My research projects have always been driven by the question of what Latin American texts provide to understand U.S. theory, and not simply finding in theory illuminating ways to reformulate Latin American texts.

Also, I want to clarify that I am very aware that the present reading of Butler hinges on a summary. However, I hope this reading shows *performatively* certain resistances to the totalizing tendencies of some of her philosophical work.

11. Octavio Paz, "Máscaras mexicanas," in *El laberinto de la soledad* (Madrid: Cátedra, 1993), 164–181.

12. An *albur* refers to a sexual wordplay between two opponents, where one tries to make a turn of phrase of the other's speech, thus topping him off by eventually questioning his sexual prowess. The homoerotics of this kind of wordplay are common and always expected.

13. "Máscaras mexicanas," 175.

14. A body of anthropological work on Mexican gay life always brings up those categorizations: *activo* (as unmarked), *pasivo* ("true" homosexual), and *internacional*. This last group has struck at least one scholar as funny: "*Internacionales* (internationales) are those who take on both [active and passive] roles. This humorous term indicates that males who do not take just one sex role are a 'bit foreign,' not like Mexicans" (see Taylor, 119). What is interesting to note here is the repetition and insistence of a cultural inscrutability that is privileged in the claim of a Mexican identity.

15. For an important reading of Mexican masculinities, especially as a sociohistorical context for the penetration paradigm, see Robert McKee Irwin, *Mexican Masculinities* (Minneapolis: University of Minnesota Press, 2003). For a deconstructive reading of this paradigm as it relates to Chicano identities, see Tomás Almaguer, "Chicano Men: A Cartography of Homosexual Identity and Behavior," in Henry Abelove, et al., eds. *The Lesbian and Gay Studies Reader* (New York: Routledge, 1993), 255–273.

16. This was Freud's point in his *Three Essays on the Theory of Sexuality*. Sexual identity cannot only be defined as a function of sexual object choice, but it must necessarily include an understanding of the ways sexual aim completes the sexual persona. Paz's penetration model of male homosexuality hinges almost completely on how sexual aims are socially organized and narrated.

17. Roland Barthes, "At the Palace Tonight . . .," in *Incidents* trans. Richard Howard. (Berkeley: University of California Press 1992), 45.

18. Of the limited bibliography on Zapata or *El vampiro de la colonia Roma*, see Bladimir Ruiz, "Prostitución y homosexualidad: interpelaciones desde el margen en *El vampiro de la colonia Roma* de Luis Zapata," in *Revista iberoamericana* 65, no. 187 (1999): 327–339; Alicia Covarrubias, "*El vampiro de la colonia Roma* de Luis Zapata: La nueva picaresca y el reportaje ficticio," in *Revista de crítica literaria latinoamericana* (1994): 183–197; Alejandro Herrero Olaizola, "Homosexuales en escena: Identidad y performance en la narrativa de Luis Zapata," in *Antipodas* 11–12 (1999–2000): 249–62; as well as Paul Vek Lewis, "La noche delincuente: La representatión del prostituto en *El vampiro de la colonia Roma, Las púberes canéforas* y *La Virgen de los Sicarios*," in *Journal of Iberian and Latin American Research* 9, no. 1 (2003): 73–94.

19. For a good history of the Colonia Roma in the twentieth century, see José

Joaquin Blanco's "Introduction" to the English translation of the novel. It should be noted, however, that in recent years Roma (along with Colonia Condesa) has become an exclusive neighborhood in Mexico City.

20. A similar space of decadence could be seen in Tomás Gutiérrez Alea and Juan Carlos Tabío's *Fresa y Chocolate* (1993, Cuba). The gay hero Diego traffics around a city that is falling apart, and up in an attic apartment constructs a space for himself by recycling fragments of other eras in Cuban culture. Benno Thoma captures photographically the space of a decaying La Habana in his *Somos Cubanos*; for an analysis of Thoma's photography, see Quiroga's *Tropics of Desire*, 9–11.

21. *El vampiro*, 8.

22. I should add that in more recent printings of the novel in Spanish, this note has been suppressed altogether.

23. I am in agreement with E. Patrick Johnson's analysis of ethnography *as* a particular kind of fiction that gets mobilized to produce a critical agency. Following Clifford Geertz's idea that ethnography is a dialogic product by both researcher and the researched that might be called a "fragile fiction," Johnson adds that "[t]o construe ethnographic practice as, in general, a 'fiction' and, more specifically, as practice that is 'acted out' or performed, is to liberate it from the assumption that the informant is a fixed object and therefore inferior to the ethnographer. Instead the informant is recognized as a thinking, theorizing, and culture-processing human being" (*Appropriating Blackness: Performance and the Politics of Authenticity*, Durham: Duke University Press, 2003, 10). In this sense, Adonis's narrative can be seen as a critical and theoretical performance about gay life and culture in Mexico at a particular moment. More importantly, the hustler provides a whole series of vocabularies, codes, and protocols on how to perform as a gay man. How he arranges his story offers us a conceptualization of gayness that also doubles as a different model of queerness and as a critical epistemology.

On a separate matter, I am using the term *testimonio* in the broadest sense possible, in particularly paying attention to the mediated quality of the autobiographical narrative. Though *El vampiro* is not an autobiography per se, it functions as such; additionally since the story is so highly framed by the presence of another, this gives the story its *testimonio* features. See Beverley's *Testimonio: On the Politics of Truth* for his discussion on the problematics of defining *testimonio*, as well as on the political uses and deployments of the genre.

24. In "The Politics of Translation" (*Outside the Teaching Machine* [New York: Routledge, 1993]), Gayatri Spivak suggests that "[l]ogic allows us to jump from word to word by means of clearly indicated connections. Rhetoric must work in the silence between and around words in order to see what works and how much" (181). Her insight allows us to understand the rhetorical force of silence.

25. Shoshana Felman and Dori Laub, *Testimony: Crises of Witnessing in Literature, Psychoanalysis and History* (New York: Routledge, 1992), 183.

26. We cannot ignore here Sor Juana's *Respuesta a Sor Filotea*, which can be read as a radical conceptualization of silence as a privileged epistemology for subject formation. For a reading of the ways in which silence operates in the *Respuesta*, see Ludmer; further elaboration of silence and ways of knowing can be found in Martínez-San Miguel (1999: 69–103). Furthermore, I would propose that the tradition that Sor Juana inaugurates in Mexican letters—that is, silence as a strategy of self-figuration and of speaking from the place of the subaltern—gets rewritten and universalized in Octavio Paz's oeuvre as a national symbol of *lo mexicano* in his *El laberinto de la soledad*, and many other essays.

27. I make reference to the Plaza de las Tres Culturas at the heart of the Tlatelolco neighborhood; the plaza serves an important site that collects three architectures—the remains of an Aztec temple, next to the Santiago de Tlatelolco

Church (in Spanish colonial style) and modern architecture (of the former offices) of the Secretaría de Relaciones Exteriores (Foreign Ministry). The three cultures are the pre-Columbian, the Spanish colonial moment, and the resulting modern *mestizo* nation. The Plaza de las Tres Culturas symbolizes the complexity of the Mexican nation and its racial formation—the history of a remote and yet-to-be-fully known indigenous roots, Spanish intervention, and *mestizaje*.

28. Throughout the novel, Adonis will make references to other *chichifos* [male hustlers], *locas*, *putos* ["faggots"], as well as *bugas* ["straights"], and *mayates* ["straight" men who have sex with other men]. The taxonomy is particular to urban Mexico city of the 1970s.

29. "Those things don't happen here" [*Esas cosas no pasan aquí*] was heard quite loudly from the highest levels of government in Mexico after the publication of the episode where Adonis and some friends are stopped by the police and the entire group of men ends up having sex (85–88). I thank Carlos Monsiváis for sharing with me this incident of censorship.

30. We should not ignore here the importance of the literary history of the picaresque in the framing of contemporary Latin American writing. (Refer to note 3 above.)

31. *El vampiro*, 9.

32. Jaén, Didier T., "La neopicaresca en México: Elena Poniatowska y Luis Zapata," in *Tinta* 1, no. 5 (1987): 25.

33. The importance of the picaresque in Zapata's novel cannot be underestimated. As a trained Medievalist, the author knew very well the use of plot and character development in the picaresque. For a good structuralist reading of the picaresque in *El Vampiro*, see Covarrubias (1994). For a queer reading of the Lazarillo, see my "The Swishing of Gender: Homographetic Marks in the *Lazarillo de Tormes*."

34. In his *Segunda parte*, Juan de Luna appropriates the voice of the "original" Lazarillo. In other words, he usurps the voice and identity of Lazarillo, who in his anonymous text had usurped many identities to protect himself from prosecution in ménage-a-trois scandal.

35. *El vampiro*, 17.

36. Ibid., 15.

37. Roberto González Echevarría, *Relecturas: Estudios de literatura cubana* (Caracas: Monte Avila, 1976), 21.

38. *El vampiro*, 72.

39. Ibid., 223.

Chapter 4

1. Christ, Ronald, "A Last Interview with Manuel Puig," in *World Literature Today* 65, no. 4 (1991): 574. (Hereafter denoted as "Last Interview.")

2. Sigmund Freud, "From the History of an Infantile Neurosis" (1918), in *The Standard Edition of the Complete Psychological Works of Sigmund Freud, Volume XVII, An Infantile Neurosis and Other Works*, ed. James Strachey (London: Hogarth Press and the Institute of Psycho-Analysis, 1953), 1–122. Hereafter cited as *Wolf Man*.

3. Ibid., 34.

4. Manuel Puig, *The Buenos Aires Affair* (Barcelona: Seix Barral, 1986); hereafter referred to as *BAA*. The novel was translated into English by Suzanne Jill Levine (Champaign, IL: Dalkey Archive Press, 2010). The first edition of the novel contained the subtitle "Novela policial" ["detective novel"]. Indeed much criticism has relied on this tidbit of information to frame the reading of the text: see Lucille

Kerr's chapter on *BAA* in her *Suspended Fictions: Reading Novels by Manuel Puig* (Urbana: University of Illinois Press, 1987), 131–183. Kerr's reading shows how Puig parodies the formal conventions of the detective novel to deconstruct the structuration of knowledge and truth. Also, for an excellent reading of the novel's use of genre(s) to effect masculinity, see Rebecca Biron's chapter on *BAA* in her *Murder and Masculinity: Violent Fictions of 20th-Century Latin America* (Nashville, Tennessee: Vanderbilt University Press, 2000), 90–119.

5. *BAA*, 24–52.
6. Ibid., 79–102.
7. Ibid., 53–69.
8. Ibid., 38.
9. Ibid., 38–39.

10. Hesse's novel tells the story of Emil, who trusts in *Scheinwelt* (world of seemingness or illlusion) as a way to feel protected from the outside threats and anguishes. Gladys too creates her *Scheinwelt* throughout her life story. Inhabiting the *Scheinwelt*, this world of deception as "reality," points to Gladys's psychotic tendencies and other mental health concerns.

11. *BAA*, 30.
12. Ibid., 39.

13. Jean Laplanche, and Jean-Bertrand Pontalis, "Fantasy and the Origins of Sexuality" in *The International Journal of Psychoanalysis* 49, no. 1 (1968): 17.

14. Sometimes Gladys would paint her closed eye as a hummingbird—the eye becomes a site for artistic production, and not for negative imagery. On the one hand, we could argue that she has lost her sight, and her perspective; however, this loss enables a different arrangement of her art collages as well as her way to narrate her life history, hence her sense of agency. See David T. Mitchell and Sharon L. Snyder's *Narrative Prosthesis: Disability and the Dependencies of Discourse* (Ann Arbor: University of Michigan Press, 2000) for a discussion of the ways in which the self-naming, indeed a revision by "disabled" subjects, detracts from his or her dismissal by the condescending terms of a "normal" bodied culture. Rather than consider disability as something that needs to be healed, the authors ask us to consider the ways in which the disabled body presents new logics to conceive the world.

15. *BAA*, 46.
16. Ibid., 46–47.

17. Here I am thinking of another example of a woman needing many men to define her: the protagonist of Spike Lee's *She's Gotta Have It* (1986), Nola Darling, is wooed by three different men. Each promises her something different, however, she places her independence and pleasure above the men's words.

18. White masculinity, Latino masculinity, black masculinity, working-class masculinity, youthful masculinity, and so forth ... each variation of "masculinity" triggers different conceptualizations of the masculine. Masculinity is defined *through* something else—always aggressively adding or taking away a sense of force. The gender category (masculinity, but also male) is the noun—the racial or class category (Latino, black, working class, and so on) only is an adjective. This difference between which categories can achieve noun versus adjective status suggest an asymmetry. Importantly, the noun and the adjective together become intersectional, *but not symmetrical.* How Gladys's own femininity identifies alongside or against these varying forms of the masculine show a wide dynamic self-figuration. In other words, how she sees her whiteness and femininity depend on whom she is with.

19. *BAA*, 56.
20. Ibid., 58.

21. Ibid., 59.
22. Ibid., 60.
23. Ibid., 61.
24. Ibid., 62.
25. Ibid., 63.
26. Ibid., 64.
27. Ibid., 65.
28. Ibid., 66.
29. Ibid., 67.
30. Ibid., 68.

31. In *Gay Hegemony/Latino Homosexualities* (New York: Routledge, 2006), Manolo Guzmán looks at how white male fetishistic gazes shape the lives of gay Puerto Rican men. He astutely looks at how homoraciality links with the figure of the Latin lover, and he explores strategies to comprehend the representation of ethnic, Latino subjectivities, and their relationship with queer identity. Specifically, the author "identif[ies] the sexual aftermath of a social organization of homoerotic desire that is shaped by the history of race, and how that history . . . is itself shaped through technologies of gay selfhood" (3). Although his focus is on gay Puerto Rican men, I find his intersectional reading quite useful to illustrate in general how race, nationhood, gender, and sexuality are put into motion in a series of identity formations. We can speculate that when Gladys looks at Frank, she may not be seeing his racial and sexual complexity, the depth of intersectionality; rather, she only sees one part of him—his race, his nationality, his marital status—one dimension, not his all.

32. *BAA*, 66–67
33. Ibid., 67.
34. Ibid., 69.

35. In *Transvestism, Masculinity, and Latin American Literature*, see my analysis of the footnotes on homosexuality in Puig's *Kiss of the Spiderwoman*. I argue that the "scientific" discourse of Puig's footnotes serves as a counterpoint to the discussion of homosexuality that ensues in the main body of the text, which present homosexuality as affect rather than an "abnormality." In other words, for Puig, the footnote as *supplément* to the main text provokes a dialectic to approach the ways in which the homosexual gets defined in the novel. In this scene from *The Buenos Aires Affair*, Gladys's masturbatory fantasy is the main text, and the actual physical action noted in the footnotes are intricately linked as a dialectical process whereby the subject is always touching (and tampering with) herself, her memories, and ultimately her identity.

36. For an exploration of the discursive routes of masturbation, see Paula Bennett, and Vernon Rosario, eds., *Solitary Pleasures: The Historical, Literary, and Artistic Discourses of Autoeroticism* (New York: Routledge, 1995). For a fascinating medical and cultural history of masturbation, see Thomas W. Laqueur. *Solitary Sex: A Cultural History of Masturbation* (New York: Zone Books, 2003).

Eve K. Sedgwick notes that "As the historicization of sexuality, following the work of Michel Foucault, becomes increasingly involved with issues of representation, different varieties of sexual experience and identity are being discovered both to possess a diachronic history—a history of significant change—and *to be entangled in particularly indicative ways with aspects of epistemology and of literary creation and reception*" ("Jane Austen and the Masturbating Girl, in *Tendencies*," 110). From this perspective, masturbation cannot simply be regarded in isolation as a practice or an act, but rather it has a tradition in the realm of culture, and it connotes an epistemology, that is, a way of knowing (oneself), and feeling and imagining the world around the self.

37. *BAA*, 54.
38. Ibid.
39. Mary Louise Pratt, "Arts of the Contact Zone," in *Profession* (1991): 33–40.
40. Puig is not an author we would normally associate with "postcolonial" thinking, so I am asking my readers to take this leap of faith. I hope this detour might in fact show how even an author so canonically "white" as Puig can display the sensitivity to articulating modes of resistance to heteronormative sexuality. I am equating heteronormativity with colonial forms of domination, with colonial master narratives of sexuality that get imposed to frame subjects' gender (normative masculinity and femininity), as well as compulsory heterosexuality. Puig's oeuvre resists such overarching ideological templates. For example, he creates gender types like Juan Carlos in *Boquitas pintadas*, who is both overly endowed (one marker of masculinity), yet suffers tuberculosis (a historically gendered "feminine" malady), or Molina from *El beso de la mujer araña*, who performs lavishly as an effeminate homosexual, yet performs as a masculinized hero at the end. Not only in terms of gender roles, but also in terms of sexual performances, Puig resists the confines of heterosexual narratives—I am thinking about the ménage-à-trois that closes *Buenos Aires Affair* or Nené's unhappy marriage and her desire to be possessed by Juan Carlos in *Boquitas* or so many other sexual encounters and relations that defy and resist compulsory heterosexuality and imposed heteronormative framings. I read these gendered and sexual modes of resistance as analogous to "postcolonial" practices and critiques; these resistances are strategies of debunking master narratives of sexuality and gender.
41. *Wolf Man*, 37.
42. Ibid., 45.
43. Peter Brooks, "Freud's Masterplot," in *Reading for the Plot: Design and Intention in Narrative* (Cambridge: Harvard University Press, 1992), 276.
44. Ibid.
45. Fernando Ortíz, *Cuban Counterpoint: Tobacco and Sugar* (Durham: Duke University Press, 1995), 87.
46. "Contact Zones," 6.
47. Ibid.
48. Joseph Conrad, *Heart of Darkness, A Norton Critical Edition* ed. Robert Kimbrough (New York: Norton, 1988), 11
49. Michel Foucault, *Discipline and Punish*, trans. by Alan Sheridan (New York: Vintage, 1979); Homi Bhabha, *The Location of Culture* (New York: Routledge, 1994), especially his essay "Of Mimicry and Man: The Ambivalence of Colonial Discourse," 121–131.
50. I digress: it's quite impactful to see how the boy can put his finger "there," anywhere he wants; his male privilege allows him to name and control. Very differently, Gladys must act shamelessly to claim her identity (sexuality) and can only put her finger "there," under a veil of secrecy and at the risk of being caught.
51. *Heart of Darkness*, 11–12.
52. "Fantasy and the Origins of Sexuality," 11.
53. Here I am reminded of the ways in which works such as Ann Laura Stoler's *Carnal Knowledge and Imperial Power: Race and the Intimate in Colonial Rule* (Berkeley: University of California Press, 2002) approaches the archive to articulate an understanding of intimacy in power relations. Stoler focuses on how both the colonizers and colonized as they are defined through sexual control, moreover how "gender-specific sexual sanctions and prohibitions not only demarcated positions of power but also prescribed the personal and public boundaries of race" (42). This multiple layering of subjection that considers sexual, gender and race dimensions offers us a capacious understanding of the dynamics of how colonizer

and colonized identities are interdependent. I would say that my conceptualization of epistemerotics involves a similar effort to discern the layers (or forces) that shape a sexual (or a gendered) subject (or the interplay between gender and sexuality in arriving at some category); however, rather than focus on the *relational* story of colonizer-colonized interdependence, specifically rather than focus on the "Americanization of the homosexual" and how it imposes itself the Latino American queer narrative, I venture to imagine that within the spaces themselves of Latino America there have been—and there are—bold, autochthonous, and unique articulations of queer sexual identities. These articulations avoid or exceed the "Americanization of the homosexual"—they tend toward originality. Epistemerotics is that effort to reflect and ponder on the ways cultural difference and other cultural archives produce these queer crystallizations of subjectivity might just be an experiment—some insist that we are never outside the watchful surveillance of the Other—but I believe it is an experiment worth thinking about.

54. "Fantasy and the Origins of Sexuality," 17.
55. *BAA*, 80–102.
56. Ibid., 86.
57. Ibid., 87.
58. Ibid., 87–88.
59. Kerr notes that "Leo's and Glady's biographies in Chapters VI and II are organized around the details of their psychological and sexual development, and each comes to look like a 'classic case': Leo the sadist and Gladys the masochist are designed for each other . . ." (137). Alberto Giordano reads Gladys and Leo as "una pareja perversamente complementaria: son la víctima y el victimario unidos por los vínculos sádicos y masoquistas" (231), ["a perversely complementary couple: they are the victim and perpetuator united by sadist and masochist ties"]. Puig was not one for such simplistic equations as we can see above: Leo might be sadistic, but his sexual persona is one that requires being-looked-at-ness (to borrow Laura Mulvey's term), which displaces that sadism in a feminine position. This sexual complexity is precisely the Gordian knot that is signature of Puig's oeuvre. In other words, sadism and masochism are interlaced together in just one subject.
60. "Last Interview," 574
61. Briefly I make mention of the man's blond hair, again, as a marker of his whiteness. Different than Felipe in *El bachiller*, where his love for a blond virgin as a *modernista* unfolding of desire for a particular European subject, here in the 1974 Argentine novel, the blond hair signifies a race and class marker differently. Insofar as Argentina could be considered the whitest nation in the American hemisphere, the blond hair does not draw our attention as much as it would in other Latin American or Caribbean countries. For Leo, the blond man could be just another man. We contrast this encounter with Gladys's, in which the men's race and class positionalities did matter more as they impacted more directly on her sexual and gender persona.
62. *BAA*, 91.
63. Ibid.
64. Ibid.
65. In her translation of the novel, Suzanne Jill Levine uses "the person" instead of "the subject."
66. *BAA*, 91.
67. Ibid.
68. Ibid., 92.
69. Ibid.
70. This tension is elegantly captured by Sedgwick: "Because 'homosexuality' and 'homophobia' are, in any of their avatars, historical constructions, because

they are likely to concern themselves intensely with each other and to assume interlocking or mirroring shapes, because the theater of their struggle is likely to be intrapsychic or intra-institutional as well as public, it is not always easy (sometimes barely possible) to distinguish them from each other" (*Between Men*, 20).

71. *BAA*, 93–94.

72. For a discussion of how masculinity and violence relate through the trope of "aguantar(se)" in Puig's *Kiss of the Spider Woman*, see my *Transvestism, Masculinity and Latin American Literature*, pp. 155–159.

73. For a fascinating reading of censorship in *BAA*, see Vittoria Martinetto's "*The Buenos Aires Affair*: anatomía de una censura" in José Amícola and Graciela Speranza's *Encuentro Internacional Manuel Puig* (Rosario: Beatriz Viterbo Editora, 1998): 212–223. Martinetto traces the sections of the novel that were censored by the Argentine authorities; indeed one such censored passage is the rape-murder and the whispering into the dead man's ear, "tell me you like it." Martinetto concludes that "[s]i sobre el cuerpo y a través de la prohibiciones a ello relativas parece haber históricamente nacido la repression, es precisamente a partir de la sexualidad que tiene que empezar la revolución capaz de acabar con ella. Por eso la utilización del sexo en las novelas de Puig, empezando por *The Buenos Aires Affair*, no es pornográfica sino política" (222) ["if repression seems to have been historically borne on the body and through all prohibition related to the body, then it is precisely out of sexuality where the revolution to end with repression must begin. For that reason the uses of sexuality in Puig's novel, beginning with *BAA*, is not pornographic, but political instead"]. Her conclusions coincide with my research interest to show how Puig deploys sexuality in the realm of politics.

Chapter 5

1. José Donoso, *El lugar sin límites* (Barcelona: Seix Barral, 1979. The English translation of the novel, *Hell Has No Limits*, is collected in *Triple Cross*, trans. by Suzanne Jill Levine (New York: Dutton, 1972). All translations of citations from the novel are mine.

2. Ibid., 132.

3. See chapter 2, "Gender Without Limits: The Erotics of Masculinity in *El lugar sin límites*" in my *Transvestism, Masculinity and Latin American Literature: Genders Share Flesh*, pp. 87–118. My comments on this scene can be found on pp. 116–118. I summarize my argument above in the next sentences.

4. *Lugar sin límites*, 138.

5. From an interview with Pedro Lemebel by Walescka Pino-Ojeda: "Gay Proletarian Memory: The Chronicles of Pedro Lemebel," in *Continuum: Journal of Media & Cultural Studies* 20, no. 3 (September 2006): 398. This interview was carried out at two different times—the first in October 1999, the second in March 2003, and translated and published in English. I would like to thank Professor Pino-Ojeda for sharing with me the original Spanish text, from which I cite here. The English text is from the published interview.

6. Any effort to translate *loco afán* will necessarily be insufficient. More than a desire, *afán* is a tendency, a drive toward doing something, very much like a compulsion to repeat. *Loco* is indeed mad or crazy, but in Spanish, *loco* tropes off *loca* or *locura*, which is a particular brand of effeminate homosexuality. So *loco afán* might be best understood as a compulsive tendency practiced by a queer subject. Importantly, a *loco afán* signifies an inevitable failure—that is, one does not have

a *loco afán* and pretend to succeed ever fully. Therefore, we might argue that *loco afán* is a transitory process of becoming. Given that transvestite subjects are at the center of Lemebel's essay, it only makes sense that he would highlight this process as the title of this work.

7. Pedro Lemebel. *Loco afán: Crónicas de sidario* (Santiago de Chile: LOM Ediciones, 1996), 57–61. All translations are mine.

8. A trope is a literary figure that signals a turn or detour within language, thereby making language unable to link up with the most self-evident of things it's supposed to name or represent. That is, a trope is when language cannot name what is "proper" to itself—a trope refuses properness and propriety. Transvestism functions analogously as a trope—for example, a man might dress otherwise, refusing the clothes and names that supposedly affirm his sense of self, of properness, and propriety.

9. Sigmund Freud, "From the History of an Infantile Neurosis" (1918) in *The Standard Edition of the Complete Psychological Works of Sigmund Freud, Volume XVII, An Infantile Neurosis and Other Works*, ed. James Strachey (London: Hogarth Press and the Institute of Psycho-Analysis, 1953), 45.
I give a more detailed analysis of this scene in the previous chapter.

10. *Lugar sin límites*, 132–133.

11. It is important to stress here that masculinity is not seen as the opposite of femininity, but rather of transvestism. In other words, the heterosexual matrix as a grid of gender and sexual intelligibility is being displaced by a different matrix (the other primal scene), embodied by the transvestite.

12. Sigmund Freud. "Group Psychology and the Analysis of the Ego" (1921), in *The Standard Edition of the Complete Psychological Works of Sigmund Freud*, vol. XVIII (London: The Hogarth Press and the Institute of Psycho-Analysis, 1957), 105. For a clear explanation of how identification is partial, see chapter VII, "Identification." Moreover, for an rich discussion of the different forms and processes of identification, see Diana Fuss, *Identification Papers* (New York: Routledge, 1995).

13. "Group Psychology," 107.

14. Judith Butler "Phantasmatic Identification and the Assumption of Sex," in *Bodies that Matter: On the Discursive Limits of "Sex"* (New York: Routledge,), 100.

15. *Loco afán*, 57–58.

16. Harold Bloom, "The Breaking of Form,," in *Deconstruction and Criticism* (New York: Seabury Press, 1979), 1.

17. I discuss Sarduy's transvestite aesthetics and their relation to the neo-Baroque in the following chapter.

18. *Loco afán*, 58.

19. These dynamics of naming can be contrasted with another essay that appears later in the collection, "El proyecto nombres" ["The Names Project"] (91–95), where Lemebel discusses the Names Project in the United States. He focuses that essay on how the wearing out of the embroidery represents the emptying out of meaning of the names the Project seeks to recover and memorialize.

20. *Loco afán*, 58.

21. This illegitimacy is what I theorize later on in the book as the abject.

22. "Gay Proletarian Memory," 399.

23. It is important to note here that in his chronicles, Lemebel uses the term *locas* in the broadest sense possible, to refer to transvestites as well as homosexuals. This conflation is very important because it suggests a continuity between effeminacy and homosexuality, hence, it also delineates the borders of queerness.

24. That gay ideal also reminds us of the Chelsea boy or the gay clone, the gay

New York ideal of the 1980s and 1990s, and that still appears in circuit parties, Manhunt, and other websites. It is worth remembering, as Dennis Altman has suggested, that the U.S. urban gay male aesthetic and ideal becomes a model for all gay men across the globe. I am thinking in his phrase, "the Americanization of the homosexual," which inverts the title of his book, *The Homosexualization of America*.

25. Lisa Duggan, "The New Homonormativity," in *Materializing Democracy: Toward a Revitalized Cultural Politics*, ed. Russ Castronovo and Dana D. Nelson (Durham: Duke University Press, 2002), 179.

26. Jaime Bayly is a conservative Peruvian television personality and author of the roman-à-clef *No se lo digas a nadie* [Don't Tell Anyone]. As a member of the upper class, his sexual and political persona thoroughly embrace a neoliberal "I-can-do-anything-I-want" attitude—and it is precisely this arrogance that irks Lemebel.

27. Lemebel comments:

> Hay todo un arribismo que construye esta visión de mundo desde algunas escrituras homosexuales, localizadas sobre todo en Argentina y Cuba, donde está presente todo el barroco latinoamericano, pero como una suerte de *bijouterie* que tapa con su fulgor la palidez latinoamericana. Entonces están las cenas, las plumas, esa construcción literaria del barroco lezamiano; eso se hace mucho más barroso con Néstor Perlongher, como ya hablamos. Él—en cambio—arrastra la cola de tafetán por el lodo. En ese sentido, toda cierta literatura desde lo homosexual, como Osvaldo Lamborghini—otro argentine—que en todo este espectro de escrituras homosexuales plantea una homosexualidad hombre a hombre, muy tanguera, donde reproduce el atractivo tremendo de esa virilidad que quiere cogerse a sí misma . . . (Entrevista con Pino-Ojeda)

> [There is a whole ambience of pretence coming from certain homosexual writings, located especially in Argentina and Cuba, where all the Latin American baroque is present, like a sort of *bijouterie* that covers up a Latin American drabness with its shimmer. And so we have the dinners, the feathers, that literary construction of the Lezamian baroque, that becomes much more muddy in Perlongher, as we have already said. He, on the other hand, drags the taffeta train through the mud. Another Argentinean, Osvaldo Lamborghini, presents a man-to-man homosexuality, very tangoesque, where he reproduces the enormous attractiveness of that virility that wants to fuck himself . . . ("Gay Proletarian Memory," 399).]

Lemebel appreciates Nestor Perlongher's rescripting of the *barroco* to *barroso*, from Baroque to muddy or murky, from *preciosité* and overstylized to being off-kilter.

28. We see this subsuming of homosexuality under a class analysis in Diana Palaversich, "The Wounded Body of Proletarian Homosexuality in Pedro Lemebel's *Loco afán*," in *Latin American Perspectives* 29, no. 2 (2002): 99–118.

29. The author suggests that AIDS came from the United States.

30. *Loco afán*, 11.

31. In a *Time Magazine* article, we read that

> Yet as the do-little conference wound toward an official close last week, delegates from many developing nations considered extending it for some days. And why not? What UNCTAD lacked in substance it more than made up for in fun and games. The partying was so intense that UNCTAD's founding father, the noted Argentine economist Raul Prebisch, noticeably avoided the

meeting, and one Belgian delegate went on a hunger strike in protest. The Chilean government had laid on a cultural program of symphony and folk music, ballet and theater—but had to cancel it after one week because of low attendance.

Other nocturnal activities were more pressing. Many delegates boasted of attending three highly liquid receptions a night ("Those Hot Chile Nights," in *Time Magazine*, May 29, 1972. http://www.time.com/time/magazine/article/0,9171,903554,00.html [accessed August 1, 2009]).

32. *Loco afán*, 14.
33. Ibid.
34. Ibid., 15.
35. Ibid., 16.
36. Ibid.
37. Ibid.
38. In Chilean gay culture, a *conchazo* is a snide remark meant to exaggerate a defect in an opponent. It should remind us to some degree of other similar Latin American word puns and plays, like the *albur* in Mexico or the *choteo* in Cuban. In the United States, we can compare it to the idea of "reading" or "throwing shade" in queer African American and Latino cultures, performed in Jennie Livingston's *Paris Is Burning*.
39. *Loco afán*, 16.
40. Ibid.
41. Ibid.
42. Ibid., 18–19.
43. Ibid., 21.
44. Ibid., 21–22.
45. Ibid., 22.
46. Ibid., 27.
47. Ibid., 31.
48. Ibid., 30.
49. It is critical to understand that the military never questions what they are doing with the queers. On the strength of their political position, they do not have to worry about being "marked" for affiliating themselves with the queers. Their brutal military strength can erase whatever they are doing with the queers, and in turn offer an "official history" of the events.

Chapter 6

1. Sylvia Molloy discusses the powerful ways in which the schoolboy narrative shapes identification into a particular social and cultural class and historical moment; also, how the "*ubi sunt* motif" reminds characters and readers of tradition and lineage. See Molloy, *At Face Value: Autobiographical Writing in Latin America* (New York: Cambridge University Press, 1991), 98–99.

2. Of course, I am making reference to Doris Sommer's work on foundational fictions. Sommer argues that heterosexual erotic passion in the nineteenth-century Spanish American novels (Jorge Isaac's *María*, José Mármol's *Amalia*, and countless others) allegorize the nation. See Sommer, *Foundational Fictions: The National Romances of Latin America* (Berkeley, University of California Press, 1993).

However, it would be important to consider other (queer) texts that also produce a different kind of national allegory; for example, I am thinking about

Adolfo Caminha's *Bom Crioulo*. How does a homoeroticism transform the national allegory? Indeed, *Los cachorros* suggests another alternative.

3. Mario Vargas Llosa, *Los cachorros*, ed. Guadalupe Fernández Ariza (Madrid: Cátedra, 2010). The English translation is collected in *The Cubs and Other Stories*, trans. Gregory Kolovakos and Ronald Christ (New York: Harper & Row, 1979). As with other texts in this study, given the experimental narrative that the author is using, all translations are mine.

Immediately I should state that *Los cachorros* might be considered a "minor" work in Vargas Llosa's oeuvre. Undoubtedly he is better known for his masterpiece, *La ciudad y los perros*, *El hablador*, *Tía Julia y el escribidor* and of course *Conversación en la Catedral*. Useful introductions to his work are Sara Castro-Klaren's *Understanding Mario Vargas Llosa* (Columbia: University of South Carolina Press, 1990) and Efraín Kristal's *Temptation of the Word: The Novels of Mario Vargas Llosa* (Nashville: Vanderbilt University Press, 1998).

4. *Los cachorros*, 55.

5. Indeed this anatomy of the "we" perfectly describes the construction of the neoliberal Latin American subject, who feels entitled to speak for the nation. The arrogantly essentialist utterance "we, Mexicans (Cubans, Peruvians, Chileans, fill-in-the-blank . . .) are like that . . ." is nothing but an aspirational moment expressed by a subject confident that his values are communal and shared equally by everyone around him.

6. *Los cachorros*, 114.

7. André Gide, *L'immoraliste* in *Romans* (Paris: Gallimard [Bibliothéque de la Pléiade], 1958).

8. Jaime Torres Bodet, *Tiempo de Arena* in *Obras escogidas* (Mexico, DF, Fondo de Cultura Económica, 1961), 189–384.

9. Osorio Benítez changes his name again in 1922 to Porfirio Barba Jacob; he is best known under the latter name.

10. *Tiempo de arena*, 247.

11. Ibid., 248.

12. Sylvia Molloy, "Too Wilde for Comfort: Desire and Ideology in *Fin-de-Siècle* Spanish America" in *Social Text* 31/32 (1992): 187–201.

13. *Tiempo de arena*, 249.

14. Ibid.

15. Salvador A. Oropesa finds that, according to Salvador Novo, Jaime Torres Bodet leaks out his homosexuality by translating Gide's *Les limites de l'art*. See Oropesa, *The Contemporáneos Group: Rewriting Mexico in the Thirties and Forties* (Austin, University of Texas Press, 2003), 41.

16. *Los cachorros*, 62.

17. Ibid., 65.

18. Ibid., 68.

19. Ibid.

20. Ibid., 74.

21. Ibid., 80.

22. Ibid., 82.

23. Ibid., 86.

24. Ibid., 91.

25. Another name for the disavowal of castration is fetishism. Freud notes that the boy disavows the threat of castration anxiety by attributing to the mother a phallus in the form of an overvaluation of a body part (the foot) or a bodily attachment (the slip). We notice Freud's conceptualization of the fetish as a gendered practice, a return of the (masculine) phallus to the mother figure. We can overlap what Cuéllar's friends are doing to this structure of the fetish: they are

endowing Cuéllar with a new phallus in order to disavow his castration, that is his feminization, which is another way of considering him a homosexual.
26. *Los cachorros*, 104.
27. Ibid., 104–105.
28. Ibid., 105.
29. Ibid., 115.
30. Ibid., 118.
31. Ibid.
32. Ibid., 118–119.
33. Ibid., 121.
34. Mario Vargas Llosa, "Breve discurso sobre la cultura," in *Letras libres* 139 (June 2010): 48–55.
35. Ibid., 49.
36. Ibid., 50.
37. Ibid.
38. Ibid.
39. Ibid.
40. Ibid., 52.
41. Ibid., 53.

Chapter 7

1. Michel Foucault, "Preface to Transgression," in *Language, Counter-Memory, Practice* (Ithaca, NY: Cornell University Press, 1977), 30.
2. Emir Rodríguez Monegal, "Sobre el *Paradiso* de Lezama," in *Mundo Nuevo* 16 (1967): 90. Both Rodríguez's Monegal's and Vargas Llosa's commentaries are published in the same issue of *Mundo Nuevo*, with the same title; furthermore, they are not in sequential order. To avoid confusion, I will cite them using by author's name. Also, I am not citing the original Spanish, rather I am only offering my translation of the essays.
3. Mario Vargas Llosa, "Sobre el *Paradiso* de Lezama," in *Mundo Nuevo* 16 (1967): 89.
4. Vargas Llosa on *Paradiso*, 89.
5. Rodríguez Monegal on *Paradiso*, 91–92.
6. For an important discussion on the relation of gay and lesbian studies to the literary and historical canon, see Sedgwick's *Epistemology of the Closet*, 48–59; also Sifuentes-Jáuregui's "National Fantasies: Peeking into the Latin American Closet," 298–300.
7. Farraluque's racial identity is left uncertain, as we do not know whether his Havana mother is mixed race.
8. Citations are taken from Cintio Vitier's critical edition of *Paradiso* (Argentina: Colección Archivos, [1966]1988). For a good, not to mention valiant, translation, please refer to Gregory Rabassa's work: *Paradiso* (New York: Farrar, Straus and Giroux, 1974)

To facilitate referencing to both the original and Rabassa's translation, I will use the following convention to quote pages from the critical edition, followed by pages from the Rabassa's English translation, for example,, (*P*: xx; *P*(E): yy). Although I cite the pages of the English translation, I have modified the translation in almost every single citation.
9. *P*: 199–200; *P*(E): 197.
10. *P*: 200; *P*(E): 198.

11. *P*: 203; *P*(E): 201.
12. *P*: 204; *P*(E): 201.
13. *P*: 204; *P*(E): 202.
14. Ibid.
15. Ibid.
16. By heteronormative, I want to underscore the guarantee of normativity secured by compulsory heterosexuality.
17. I want to retain a critical awareness that, given biological difference between men's and women's bodies, anal eroticism may signify differently. On a phantasmatic level, I suspect that that the difference between the sexes may amount to a different register on a *plaisir/jouissance* spectrum. For instance, for a (gay) male, anal eroticism may represent a pleasure that is initially or predominantly biologically inflected; whereas for a woman, it may be a question of fantasy and *jouissance*. Following this, I am proposing that for *la españolita*, this anal eroticism hinges more on a fantasy than on a biological fact.
18. *P*: 206; *P*(E): 204.
19. *P*: 207; *P*(E): 204–205.
20. *P*: 207; *P*(E): 205.
21. Ibid.
22. *P*: 208; *P*(E): 205.
23. *P*: 208; *P*(E): 206.
24. On this question, Gustavo Pellón summarizes in *José Lezama Lima's Joyful Vision* (Austin: University of Texas Press, 1989) that "Lezama and Sarduy conceive of the erotic in sex and in language as *dépense*, as the cultivation of the superfluous, the goal-less, for which the waste of the seed—whether as semen or seme—is essential" (28–29).
25. What I mean here is that, for a man, *anal* eroticism as the *aim* of sexual practice and pleasure tends to signify on him the orientation of "bisexual," whereas the *genital* sexuality would do so as either homosexual or heterosexual.
26. Early in his "Three Essays on Sexuality" (*Standard Edition VII* [1905]), Freud states that "the most remarkable feature of this perversion [sadism/masochism] is that its active and passive forms are habitually found to occur together in the same individual" (159). Freud discusses masochism as a reversal of sadism in "Instincts and Their Vicissitudes" (*SE* XIV [1915]:127–129). He never commits to distinguishing a masochism, emerging independent from sadism. It is only after *Beyond the Pleasure Principle* (in 1920) where he begins to note the possibility of a "primary masochism" (*Standard Edition* XVIII [1920]: 55).
27. Sigmund Freud, "The Economic Problem of Masochism," in *The Standard Edition of the Complete Psychological Works of Sigmund Freud, Vol. XIX,* ed. James Strachey (London: Hogarth Press and The Institute of Psycho-Analysis, 1957), 157–170.

In this discussion, I make primary reference to the first and third forms; feminine masochism presents certain issues and questions of social, historical, and cultural attachment with which I do not engage in my reading of *Paradiso*.
28. The best discussion of the psychosexual dynamics in Freud's essays on masochism is John K. Noyes, *The Mastery of Submission: Inventions of Masochism* (Ithaca, NY: Cornell University Press, 1997); see especially chapter 5, 140–163.
29. "The Economic Problem of Masochism," 159.
30. See Foucault (1975), esp. Part Three, Discipline, section 2 "The Means of Correct Training" and 3 "Panopticism." For a helpful discussion on the paradox of *assujettissement*, see Butler (1997), chapter 3 on Freud and Foucault.
31. David M. Halperin, *Saint Foucault: Towards a Gay Hagiography* (New York: Oxford University Press, 1995), 85.

32. Ibid., 86.
33. *P*: 208-211; *P*(E): 206-209.
34. In the description of the scene that follows, I will focus primarily on masochism. Following Deleuze analysis of masochism, I want to break apart the conjunction between sadism *and* masochism as proposed by Freud. Each practice is not the opposite of the other, both have the same end to produce a subjectivity. I would deem more challenging the language of the structuration of the subject that emerges in and from masochism.
35. *P*: 208; *P*(E): 206.
36. *P*: 209; *P*(E): 207.
37. The figure of a masked man is quite important here, reminding us of Paz's "Mexican masks." The mask hides and enables the subject to inhabit new spaces and engage in the forbidden. It is essential to underline here the idea that all sexual practices are permitted although at times certain identities must be masked in order to participate fully in the total array of the sexual.
38. *P*: 209; *P*(E): 207.
39. One of the most lucid readings of Lezama is Irlemar Chiampi's "La proliferación barroca en *Paradiso*," in *José Lezama Lima: Textos críticos*, ed. Justo C. Ulloa (Miami: Ediciones Universales, 1979), 82-90. She performs a reading of Baroque proliferation in *Paradiso*; among the different forms she discusses, there are syntactic, semantic, verbal, and so on proliferations. I agree that Baroque proliferation is a central practice in Neo-Baroque writings and, indeed, that Lezama (also, Sarduy) puts into play a whole series of proliferations in his narrative context. I have gone in a different direction with Chiampi's particular example of verbal proliferation of the "sexual organ." She correctly lists the many metaphoric substitutions of Leregas's phallus (her example from chapter VIII, though it can be said about Farraluque as well), and adds that "on the one hand, this metaphoric constellation [constructed by the phallic proliferation] connotes laughter and derision; on the other, it installs the unfulfillment (*desrealización*) of the object, by hyperbolizing its dimensions" (86). As I have been arguing, the very proliferation of the object is the result of other subject's inability to grasp the object, hence, my Lacanian reading of encountering the Real. She concludes that "[i]n order to describe the referent, the narrator is forced to produce an aphasia, a stutter, to designate that which cannot be spoken (*lo indecible*)" (86). This aphasia provoked in the speaking subject, *lo indecible*, is another name for disarticulation by the Real. I would add that, in my reading, I am more concerned not so much with naming *what* is the object of desire (this being always already an impossibility), but rather with understanding *how* this unnamed and unknowable object *signifies on the other*.
40. After the catalog, Rodríguez Monegal argues that "[w]hat determines the central homosexual nature of a considerable part of the book (when I spoke of a fourth of the book, I may have underestimated the matter) is not just the abundance of direct references; it is the entire system of allusions and metaphors that constitute the linguistic plot of the text" (92). Although he makes this adjustment to his argument, the critic continues cataloging those "allusions and metaphors," thereby preserving a closed circularity or a hermetics of queerness, without fully engaging the more provocative homographetic implications of his insight. For a provocative discussion on the inscription of homosexuality in the literary, see Lee Edelman's *Homographesis*. On a related conceptualization of textual inscriptions, see Roberto González Echevarría, "Lo cubano en *Paradiso*," in *Coloquio Internacional sobre la obra de José Lezama Lima. Vol. II: Prosa*, ed. Cristina Vizcaino and Eugenio Suárez Galbán (Poitiers: Centro de Investigaciones Latinoamericanas, Université de Poitiers, 1984), 31-51, where he traces the ways in which the national (inflected as *lo cubano* in the novel) is laced throughout Lezama's textuality.

41. Julio Cortázar, "Para llegar a Lezama Lima," in *La vuelta al día en ochenta mundos*, vol. II, 6th ed. (Mexico: Siglo XXI Editores, S.A. [1967]1972), 61.

42. Michel Foucault, *Surveiller et punir. Naissance de la prison* (Paris: Éditions Gallimard, 1975), 204.

43. Ibid.

44. *P*: 206; *P*(E): 203.

45. *P*: 210; *P*(E): 207-208.

46. *P*: 210; *P*(E): 208.

47. Ibid.

48. For a fascinating rethinking of how literature and ethnography interplay in the articulation of Cuban and Brazilian nationhood and cultures; more importantly, how the "voice of the masters" assume their authority through a ventriloquism and appropriation of otherness, see Jossiana Arroyo, *Travestismos culturales: literatura y ethnografía en Cuba y Brasil* (Pittsburgh: Instituto Internacional de Literatura Iberoamericana, 2003). Particularly useful for this discussion are chapters 1 and 2, pp. 3-61.

49. I would be cautious not to reduce these coal markings as another racist example of blackface, rather, I would read the markings as stains that require the marked body (the masked body?) to account for them in his retelling of his identity construction and narrative.

50. *P*: 211; *P*(E): 209.

51. We remember that José Cemí was named after his father, José Eugenio Cemí. Enrico Mario Santí (in "Parridiso," in *José Lezama Lima: Textos críticos*, ed. Justo C. Ulloa [Miami: Ediciones Universales, 1979]) notes that "[t]odo el capítulo VI de la novela está repleto de escenas que subrayan esta relación incierta entre padre e hijo. Las diferencias los separan, muy a pesar de los deseos a lo contrario del Coronel" (95) ["the entire chapter VI of novel is full of scenes that underscore the uncertain relationship between father and son. Differences separate them, despite the Coronel's desire for the contrary]. And, later on, Santí emphasizes that the father-son differences are inscribed in their names, José and José Eugenio: "El hijo parece marcado por la ausencia del segundo nombre: Eugenio, *eugenes*, el bien nacido. El hijo no es, no puede ser, el 'bien nacido,' que sería el padre" (95) ["The son seems marked by the absence of the middle name: Eugenio, *eugenes*, the well born. The son is not, cannot be, the well born one, who would have to be the father."] Arnaldo Cruz Malavé (in "El destino del padre: *Künstlerroman* y falocentrismo en *Paradiso*," in *Revista Iberoamericana*, LVII, no. 154 [1991]) intelligently points out that "[e]l destino del hijo será 'intentar lo más difícil': aclarar el 'oscuro' creado por la muerte de su padre, José Eugenio Cemí, 'transfigurándose' en el 'testimonio'" (51) ["the son's destiny will 'to try the most difficult task': to (en)lighten the 'darkness' created by the death of the father, José Eugenio Cemí, 'transfiguring' himself into a testimony (bearing witness of the father's absence)"]. My position is closer to Cruz Malavé's. Following my reading of Farraluque's identity, I would see the absence of the middle name not as a *sujet-manqué* (as suggested by Santí), always wanting to be (like) the Father, but rather I tend to privilege that blank/white space in the name José [ ] Cemí, for it represents a certain totality (as privilege) and its impossibility. In fact, the whiteness is a visual sign of the semen, so, in effect, we read his name José [blank space = whiteness = semen = Cemí] Cemí. The son carries the father's name as the sign of the double; he is the figure of dissemination/de-Cemí-nation, the figuration of the *petit histoire* (the son) as the *grand récit* of the Nation (the father), "the Cemí Nation," Cuba.

52. *P*: 211; not in English edition.

Chapter 8

1. Severo Sarduy, *La simulación* (Caracas, Monte Avila, 1980), 11: "And now, among Darian pillows and drapings, with screens and waltzes in the background—among birds and chickens—only I reign, traversed by the simulation, magnetic by the reverberation of an appearance, emptied by the laughter's shake: annuled, absent" (translation mine).
2. Severo Sarduy, "El barroco y el neobarroco," in César Fernández Moreno, ed. *América Latina en su literatura* (Mexico: Siglo XXI Editores, 1972), 167–184. There is a translation of Fernández Moreno's book, *America in Its Literature*, edited by Iván Schulman and translated by Mary Berg (New York: Holmes & Meier, 1980). However, given this translation's poor grasp of Lacanian psychoanalytic terms as well as several misreadings of poststructuralist theory (Kristeva, Derrida, Barthes, and others), I translate all passages.
3. For a comprehensive collection of texts that explicate the (European) Baroque, see Heinrich Wölfflin's classic *Principles of Art History*, as well as José Antonio Maravall's classic *Culture of the Baroque: Analysis of a Historical Structure*. On the *barroco de Indias* (the Baroque expression in the New World), and the contemporary (post-1920s) Latin American Neo-Baroque, Parkinson Zamora and Kaup's edited collection, *Baroque New Worlds: Representation, Transculturation, Counterconquest*, offers a wide range of readings on the dissemination of the Baroque in the new world; also, Yolanda Martínez-San Miguel's essay, "(Neo) Barrocos de Indias: Sor Juana y los imaginarios coloniales de la crítica latinoamericana," in *Revista de Estudios Hispánicos* provides the most comprehensive survey and analysis of the many lives of the Latin American Baroque and Neo-Baroque.
4. Lacan's work is without a doubt one of Sarduy's most marked influences in his theories and novelistic oeuvre. Unfortunately, the difficulty of the French psychoanalyst's work has become a challenge for most readers, who often misunderstand what Sarduy is doing with Lacan. For the best analysis of how Sarduy rewrites French psychoanalytic theory, see Ruben Gallo's "Sarduy avec Lacan: The Portrayal of French Psychoanalysis in *Cobra* and *La simulación*." Also helpful is Gallo's "Severo Sarduy, Jacques Lacan y el psicoanálisis: entrevista con François Wahl."
5. "El barroco y el neobarroco," 169.
6. Ibid.
7. This chapter makes use of Lacanian algorithms, most commonly the terms signifier (S) and signified (s). Sarduy reinterprets these algorithms, and adds numerical superscripts to his schemas, which might add to the confusion.
8. "El barroco y el neobarroco," 170.
9. The relationship signifier over signified that Sarduy is citing alludes to the Lacanian revision of the Saussurean sign. Whereas Saussure gives priority to the signified over the signifier, Lacan inverts the order of the algorithm. In his seminar on "The Purloined Letter," Lacan insists on the priority of the signifier, especially to argue how meaning is accomplished through a chain of relations among signifiers.

In his graphs Sarduy capitalizes "Signifier" and "Signified," but does not do so in his explanations. To avoid confusion, I have standardized the notations to follow the practice of using uppercase roman S for signifier and lowercase, italic *s* for signified.
10. "El barroco y el neobarroco," 170.
11. Ibid., 172.

12. Ibid.
13. See chapter 4, "Transvestite and Homobaroque Twirls: Sarduy on the Verge of Reading Structuralism/Psychoanalysis/Deconstruction," in my *Transvestism, Masculinity and Latin American Literature* (New York: Palgrave, 2002).
14. "El barroco y el neobarroco," 174.
15. Ibid., 175.
16. Ibid., 182.
17. Ibid.
18. Ibid., 183.
19. Ibid.
20. Severo Sarduy. *Pájaros de la playa* (Barcelona: Tusquets Editores. 1993). The novel was translated into English in 2007 as *Beach Birds* by Suzanne Jill Levine and Carol Maier.
21. *Pájaros*, 9.
22. *La simulación*, 62.
23. Ibid.
24. Butler points out that "it is important to underscore that drag is an effort to negotiate cross-gender identification, but that cross-gender identification is not the exemplary paradigm for thinking about homosexuality, although it may be one" (*Bodies That Matter*, 235).
25. Eve K. Sedgwick, *Tendencies* (Durham: Duke University Press, 1993), 221–222.
26. Interestingly enough, some gay men who claim the status of "straight acting, straight appearing" want to bring masculinity (or hypermasculinity) as part of their gender and sexual persona, and dispose of drag (transphobia) or effeminacy (sissyphobia) as a gender possibility—this practice often hints at misogyny or self-hatred.
27. *Pájaros*, 20.
28. Ibid., 21–22.
29. It should be noted here that Sarduy's displacement of the body as a way to deal with AIDS/HIV compares dramatically with Lemebel's sickly bodies. Sarduy sees the body as something that must be transcended or disavowed, whereas Lemebel embraces the diseased body, and wants to account for it. These embodiments produce a very distinct politics around how AIDS gets represented.
30. *Pájaros*, 22–23.
31. Ibid., 25.
32. Ibid., 33.
33. Ibid., 43.
34. Ibid., 44.
35. Ibid., 119.
36. Ibid., 124.
37. Ibid., 180.
38. Ibid., 212.

Chapter 9

1. For immigrants to the United States, this question of return, of back home, is a strange one. What does it mean to "go back home"? When and how does the place of national origin cease to be "home"—and the new location becomes home? What these questions point to is that instability of the concept of home. Moreover, either that moment or also that feeling when the home has become another place

signals a transformation of the home to the unhomely, *das Unheimlich*. This loss of certainty and security of the home impacts tremendously the subject's sense of referentiality and situatedness.

2. I would like to be more precise here about this serialization of identity. Of course, some would argue that this serialization is highly affected by generations. For myself, now a middle-aged man who came out in the mid-1980s, that was the sequence of subject formation that I experienced. Nowadays as gay, lesbian, queer, or trans identities circulate more readily in the social imaginary, this serialization may happen otherwise. In this chapter, I wish to hold on to this old system of "first came racial formation, then came sexual awareness," which I experienced, to dramatize and critique the concept of intersectionality.

3. See Kimberlé W. Crenshaw, "Mapping the Margins: Intersectionality, Identity Politics, and Violence Against Women of Color," in *Stanford Law Review* 43, no. 6. (1991), 1241–1299.

4. As I mentioned in the Introduction, I am using the category "Latino American" as first proposed by José Quiroga in his *Tropics of Desire*. This term points to a transnational understanding of how Latino identities in the United States are affected by the gay/lesbian/queer narratives that are imported from the rest of the American continent—but also how Latin American sexualities receive certain influences from the North. This sexy dialectic contains a set of transnational flows and implications that go from the South to the North—and vice-versa—at the same time, though with varying degrees of impact and effect.

5. Reinaldo Arenas, *Before Night Falls: A Memoir*, trans. Dolores M. Koch (New York: Penguin Books, 1993) (noted as *BNF* below). For reasons that will become apparent later on, I will be citing form the English text with some modifications to the translation, then I will be making reference to the Spanish original, *Antes que anochezca (Autobiografía)* (Barcelona: Tusquets Editores, 1992) (noted as *AQA* below).

6. *BNF*, 77.

7. *BNF*: 78; *AQA*: 103–104.

8. *AQA*, 103. My translation: "the common *loca* is the type of homosexual who has a political commitment in Cuba, one who goes to the Cinemateca, who once in a while write a poem, who never takes great risks, and who spends his time drinking tea at his friends' homes. [...] The relationships between these common locas are, generally speaking, with other *locas* and they never come to meet a real man."

It is worthwhile suggesting that what Arenas is describing in his gay taxonomy reveals that there are certain homonormative representations of *locas*—the "common *loca*" being the most exemplary of these homonormative expressions.

9. I thank Larry LaFountain-Stokes for helping me elaborate this insight.

10. On the untranslatability of queer vernaculars and categories, see Martin Manalansan's discussion of a Filipino transnational "queer vernacular/code" in his *Global Divas Filipino Gay Men in the Diaspora* (Durham: Duke University Press, 2003), especially chapters 1 "The Borders Between *Bakla* and Gay (21–44) and 2 "Speaking in Transit: Queer Language and Translated Lives (45–61).

11. Piri Thomas, *Down These Mean Streets* (New York: Vintage Books, 1997).

12. Ibid., 54–55.

13. Ibid., 56.

14. Barbara Johnson, *A World of Difference* (Baltimore: Johns Hopkins University Press, 1988), 16.

15. *Down These Mean Streets*, 56. Italics in original.

16. Ibid., 61.

17. Ibid.

18. I am thinking in particular of two scenes: the sexual fantasy in the subway train and sex with the prostitute. In the train scene, he imagines that the white woman wants to have sex with him as a black man. His masculinity and sexuality get articulated *through* the racial. For an astute reading of the deployment of race between Piri and a white prostitute, see Yolanda Martínez-San Miguel's "Coloniality of Diasporas: Racialization of Negropolitans and Nuyoricans in Paris and New York," *Hispanic Caribbean Literature of Migration* ed. Vanessa Pérez-Rosario (New York: Palgrave, 2010), 191–197.

19. The closest English equivalent for *bugarrón* is "trade."
20. Junot Díaz, *Drown* (New York: Riverhead Book, 1996).
21. *Drown*, 103.
22. Ibid.
23. Ibid., 104.
24. Ibid., 103–104.
25. Ibid., 104.
26. Ibid.
27. In the context of Latin American culture, to be "like a woman" is another way of naming the homosexual. The simile "like a woman" is a slippery slope wherein both homosexual and transgender identities become conflated.
28. *Drown*, 104.
29. I am reminded here of the Latino Fan Club gay porn video company that became popular in the late 1980s and early 1990s. (For a history of the company, see http://www.theoriginallatinofanclub.com/whatsnew/AboutLFC.html [accessed March 15, 2013.]) Spending time in Spanish Harlem at that time, I remember seeing poster on lampposts looking for Latino "models." At that time, I learned that the company was owned by white men, who had a thing or fetish for Latino "thugs." The company hired young Latino men, who would have sex with other Latino men. During the filming of these movies, on the side there would be "straight" porn videos playing to keep the Latino men "hard" throughout the filming. Of course, these "straight" porn movies also gave the Latino men an escape valve to explain that they were heterosexual, and that this experience of having sex with men was only a "one-time deal" and "for pay, and not for 'real.'" The choreography of the white men's desire involves framing the Latino men, who would be looking not at each other for pleasure and satisfaction, but elsewhere. Indeed, to echo Lacan, desire is the desire of the Other.
30. *Drown*, 104.
31. Ibid., 105.
32. Ibid., 106.
33. Manuel Puig, *El beso de la mujer araña* (Barcelona: Seix Barral, 1976), 221.
34. Ibid.
35. Abel Sierra Madero, *Del otro lado del espejo: La sexualidad en la construcción de la nación cubana* (La Habana, Casa de las Américas, 2006), 225–227.

Chapter 10

1. Edward Said, "Traveling Theory," in *The World, the Text, and the Critic*. Cambridge: Harvard University Press, 241–242.
2. Ibid., 226–227.
3. Ibid., 231.
4. One cannot possibly offer a complete list of the important and burgeoning scholarship in queer of color critique. I only mention the following works to

sample the kinds of conversations that queer theory has had: Gloria Anzaldúa and Cherrie Moraga's *This Bridge Called My Back*; Audre Lorde's *Uses of the Erotic*; Roderick A. Ferguson's *Aberrations in Black: Toward a Queer of Color Critique*; Gayatri Gopinath's *Impossible Desires: Queer Diasporas and South Asian Public Cultures*; Daniel H. Justice, Mark Rifkin, and Bethany Schneider's special issue *GLQ: A Journal of Gay and Lesbian Studies*, "Sexuality, Nationality, Indigeneity"; Lawrence LaFountain-Stokes's *Queer Ricans*; Martin Manalansan IV's *Global Divas: Filipino Gay Men in the Diaspora*; Martin Joseph Ponce's *Beyond the Nation: Diasporic Filipino Literature and Queer Reading*; Chandan Reddy's *Freedom with Violence: Race, Sexuality, and the US State*; and Siobhan Somerville's *Queering the Color Line: Race and the Invention of Homosexuality in America*. The list is endless, and it continues to grow. What is important to underline is that each work engages queer theory from a different historical, cultural, and epistemological vantage points. Next, I highlight some tendencies, although many of these works involve more than one disciplinary tradition and epistemology—feminist of color critique as well as poetic practice (Moraga, Anzaldúa, and Lorde), queer of color critique (Ferguson), queer diasporic (Gopinath and Ponce), transnational (LaFountain-Stokes and Manalansan), construction of race (Sommerville), indigenous and two-spirit critiques (Justice), or critiques of the nation-state (Reddy).

It is important to stress that these different interdisciplinary approaches and responses to Queer Theory echo much of Said's critique of universalist theory.

5. José Quiroga, *Tropics of Desire: Interventions from Queer Latino America* (New York: New York University Press, 2000), 7. Among the many strategies of queer intervention that Quiroga details is silence: see chapter 4 on Virgilio Piñera's *La carne de René* appropriately titled "Outing Silence as Code," 101–123.

6. Originally published in Spanish in 1997, *Las historias prohibidas de Marta Veneranda* earned a Premio Extraordinario de Literatura Hispana en los Estados Unidos from Cuba's most prestigious Casa de las Américas. The book appeared in English in 2001. I will quote primarily from the English version of the text—and will make necessary references to the Spanish along the way.

See Emilio Bejel's *Gay Cuban Nation* for a presentation of *Marta Veneranda* as a Latino vis-à-vis Latin American text (218–234). For a perspicacious reading of the text, in particular how the question of polymorphous desires relate to diasporic Cuban identity, refer to Yolanda Martínez-San Miguel's "Más allá de la homonormatividad: Intimidades alternativas en el Caribe hispano," in *Revista Iberoamericana* LXXIV, 225 (2008): 1039–1057.

7. *Marta Veneranda*, 7.
8. Ibid., 7.
9. "Gay Shame, Latina/o Style: A Critique of White Queer Performativity," in *Gay Latino Studies: A Critical Reader*, ed. Michael Hames-García and Ernesto J. Martínez (Durham: Duke University Press, 2011), 55–80.
10. *Marta Veneranda*, 8.
11. Ibid., 8.
12. Ibid.
13. Ibid.
14. Ibid., 9.
15. Ibid.
16. Ibid., 10.
17. Ibid., 12.
18. Ibid.
19. Ibid., 16–17.
20. Ibid., 20.
21. Ibid., 20–21.

22. Ibid., 21.
23. Ibid.
24. Ibid., 23.
25. Readers might consider that Mayté's refusal of a compulsory heterosexuality does not automatically make her to identify her by default as a "lesbian"; in other words, in a queer world, not being heterosexual does not necessarily equal to being "gay" or "lesbian." Indeed, outside of this homo-/heterosexual dichotomy, there are many queer possibilities. I agree in the fluidity of sexual identities that are a central feature of queerness. However, for the sake of argument, I have insisted on Mayté's "lesbian" identity as a result of a particular object choice, conditioned by the specific cultural context and historical moment in the United States, in order to contrast it with Laura's sexual persona. Laura, in fact, seems to have a greater sense of agency; she appears to be more independent, rather than being relationally defined by the sexual object, the other. It is helpful to know that Mayté will reappear in Rivera-Valdés's final story of the collection—"El quinto río" ["The Fifth River"]—still as a lesbian.
26. *Marta Veneranda*, 48.
27. Ibid., 54.
28. Ibid., 54.
29. Richard Rodriguez, *Hunger of Memory: The Education of Richard Rodriguez* (Boston: David R. Godine Publisher, 1981), 126.
30. For a discussion of the relationship between ethnicity and queer sexuality in Richard Rodriguez's work, see Randy A. Rodriguez's "Richard Rodriguez Reconsidered: Queering the Sissy (Ethnic) Subject," in *Texas Studies in Literature and Language* (Winter 1998).
31. Interestingly enough, Rodriguez, a darker man himself, is unable (or unwilling) to literalize the metaphor; instead, his desire is to become "middle class," which throughout the autobiography gets read as "white." Rodriguez must hide his desire to acknowledge the day laborer's dark skin, for it would appear as a narcissistic gesture (like saying "I want to be myself"), and in a certain way as homoerotic and queer.
32. *Marta Veneranda*, 54.
33. Ibid., 55.
34. Ibid., 55–56.
35. Among the extensive bibliography that challenges this notion, see David L. Eng's *Racial Castration: Managing Masculinity in Asian America* (Durham: Duke University Press, 2001); Robert Reid Pharr's *Black Gay Male* (New York: New York University Press, 2001); Phillip Brian Harper's *Are We Not Men? Masculine Anxiety and the Problem of African American Identity* (New York: Oxford University Press, 1996); as well as Dwight A. McBride's *Why I Hate Abercrombie & Fitch: Essays on Race and Sexuality* (New York: New York University Press, 2005). Each critic examines and complicates the vexed position that gay men of color have with masculinity in their racial and cultural communities.
36. *Marta Veneranda*, 56.
37. Ibid., 49–50.
38. *Marta Veneranda* (Spanish original), 57.
39. *Marta Veneranda*, 51.
40. Ibid., 50.
41. Ibid., 50.
42. For an excellent discussion of how hysteria has been construed as a both a biological, physical and psychological disease, as well as a cultural and gendered phenomena, see Mark Micale's *Approaching Hysteria: Disease and Its Interpretations* (Princeton, NJ: Princeton University Press, 1995).

References

Acevedo, David Caleb, Moisés Agosto Rosario, and Luis Negrón. *Los otros cuerpos: Antología de temática gay, lésbica y queer desde Puerto Rico y su diáspora*. San Juan: Editorial Tiempo Nuevo, 2007.
Aching, Gerard. *The Politics of Spanish American* Modernismo: *By Exquisite Design*. Cambridge: Cambridge University Press, 1997.
Alarcón, Norma. "Traddutora, Traditora: A Paradigmatic Figure of Chicana Feminism," in *Cultural Critique* 13, no. 3 (Fall 1989): 57–87
Almaguer, Tomás. 1993. "Chicano Men: A Cartography of Homosexual Identity and Behavior," in *The Lesbian and Gay Studies Reader*, ed. Henry Abelove, Michèle Aina Barale, and David M. Halperin. New York: Routledge, 1993, 255–273.
Altman, Dennis. *The Homosexualization of America: The Americanization of the Homosexual*. New York: St. Martin's Press, 1982.
———.*Homosexual: Liberation and Oppression*. New York: New York University Press, 1993.
———.*Global Sex*. Chicago: University of Chicago Press, 2002.
Anzaldúa, Gloria. *Borderlands/La Frontera: New Mestiza*. San Francisco: Spinsters/Aunt Lute, 1987.
Arenas, Reinaldo. *Antes que anochezca (Autobiografía)*. Barcelona: Tusquets Editores, 1992.
———.*Before Night Falls: A Memoir*, trans. Dolores M. Koch. New York: Penguin Books, 1993.
Arrizón, Alicia. *Queering Mestizaje: Transculturation and Performance*. Ann Arbor: University of Michigan Press, 2006.
Arroyo, Jossianna. *Travestismos culturales: Literatura y etnografía en Cuba y Brasil*. Pittsburgh: Insituto Internacional de Literatura Iberoamericana, 2003.
Austin, J. L. *How to Do Things with Words*. 2nd ed., ed. J. O. Urmson and Marina Sbisà. Cambridge: Harvard University Press, 1975.
Barbachano Ponce, Miguel. *El diario de José Toledo*. Mexico, DF: Premiá, 1988.
———.*The Diary of José Toledo: A Translation Critical Edition*, trans. Clary Loisel. New Orleans: University Press of the South, 2001.
Barthes, Roland. *Incidents*, trans. Richard Howard. Berkeley: University of California Press, 1992.
Bejel, Emilio. *Gay Cuban Nation*. Chicago: University of Chicago Press, 2001.
Bellatín, Mario. *Salon de belleza*. Mexico, DF: Ediciones del equilibrista, 1996.
Bennett, Paula, and Vernon Rosario, eds. *Solitary Pleasures: The Historical, Literary, and Artistic Discourses of Autoeroticism*. New York: Routledge, 1995.

Bersani, Leo. "Is the Rectum a Grave?" in *AIDS: Cultural Analysis, Cultural Activism*, ed. Douglas Crimp. Cambridge, Mass.: The MIT Press, 1988, 197–222.
Beverley, John. *Testimonio: On the Politics of Truth*. Minneapolis: University of Minnesota Press, 2004.
Biron, Rebecca. *Murder and Masculinity: Violent Fictions of 20th-Century Latin America*. Nashville: Vanderbilt University Press, 2000.
Bhabha, Homi. *The Location of Culture*. New York: Routledge, 1994.
Blanco, José Joaquin. *Funciones de medianoche: ensayos de literatura cotidiana*. Mexico, DF: Ediciones Era, 1981.
———.*Las púberes canéforas*. Mexico, DF: Ediciones Océano, 1983.
Bloom, Harold. "The Breaking of Form," in *Deconstruction and Criticism*. London and New York: Continuum, 1979, 1–31.
Brooks, Peter. *Reading for the Plot*. New York: Vintage Books, 1984.
Browning, Frank. *The Culture of Desire: Paradox and Perversity in Gay Lives Today*. New York: Crown, 1993.
Butler, Judith. *Gender Trouble: Feminism and the Subversion of Identity*. New York and London: Routledge, 1990.
———.*Bodies That Matter: On the Discursive Limits of "Sex."* New York: Routledge, 1993.
———.*The Psychic Life of Power: Theories in Subjection*. Stanford, Calif.: Stanford University Press, 1997.
Caminha, Adolfo. *Bom Crioulo: texto integral*. São Paulo: Editora Atica, 2002.
Camus, Albert. *La chute*. Paris: Éditions Gallimard. 1956.
Carrier, Joseph. *De los otros: Intimacy and Homosexuality Among Mexican Men*. New York: Columbia University Press, 1995.
Caruth, Cathy. *Unclaimed Experience: Trauma, Narrative and History*. Baltimore: Johns Hopkins University Press, 1996.
Castro-Klaren, Sara. *Understanding Mario Vargas Llosa*. Columbia: University of South Carolina Press, 1990.
Chauncey, George. *Gay New York: Gender, Urban Culture, and the Making of the Gay World, 1890–1940*. New York: Basic Books, 1994.
Chávez-Silverman, Susana, and Librada Hernández, eds. *Reading and Writing the Ambiente: Queer Sexualities in Latino, Latin American, and Spanish Culture*. Madison: University of Wisconsin Press, 2000.
Chiampi, Irlemar. "La proliferación barroca en *Paradiso*," in *José Lezama Lima: Textos críticos*, ed. Justo C. Ulloa. Miami: Ediciones Universales, 1979, 82–90.
———."Sobre la lectura interrupta de *Paradiso*," in *Revista Iberoamericana* LVII, no. 154 (1991): 63–76.
Christ, Ronald. "An Interview with Manuel Puig," in *Partisan Review* 44 (1977): 52–61.
———."A Last Interview with Manuel Puig," in *World Literature Today* 65.4 (1991): 571–580.
Conrad, Joseph. *Heart of Darkness* (A Norton Critical Edition), ed. Robert Kimbrough New York: Norton, 1988.
Cortázar, Julio. "Para llegar a Lezama Lima," in *La vuelta al día en ochenta mundos*, vol. II, 6th ed. Mexico, DF: Siglo XXI Editores, S.A. (1967)19721967, 41–81.
Covarrubias, Alicia. "*El vampiro de la colonia Roma, de Luis Zapata*: La nueva picaresca y el reportaje ficticio," in *Revista de Crítica Literaria Latinoamericana* XX, no. 39 (1994): 183–197.
Crenshaw, Kimberlé W. "Mapping the Margins: Intersectionality, Identity Politics, and Violence Against Women of Color," in *Stanford Law Review* 43, no. 6. (1991), 1241–1299.
de la Cruz, Sor Juana Inés. *Obras completas*, vol. I, ed. Alfonso Méndez Plancarte. Mexico, DF: Fondo de Cultura Económica, 1951.

Cruz Malavé, Arnaldo. "El destino del padre: *Künstlerroman* y falocentrismo en *Paradiso*," in *Revista Iberoamericana* LVII, no. 154 (1991): 51–64.
———."'What a Tangled Web ... !' Masculinidad, abyección y la fundación de la literatura puertorriqueña en los Estados Unidos," in *Revista de crítica literaria latinoamericana* 23, no. 45 (1997): 327–340.
Cruz Malavé, Arnaldo, and Martin Manalansan, eds. *Queer Globalization: Citizenship and the Afterlife of Colonialism*. New York: New York University Press, 2002.
Darío, Rubén. *Prosas profanas* in *Poesías completas*, vol. 1. Madrid: Aguilar, 1967, 543–622.
Dean, Tim. *Unlimited Intimacy: Reflections on the Subculture of Barebacking*. Chicago: University of Chicago Press. 2009.
"Raras rarezas." *Debate feminista* 16 (1997).
"Las raras." *Debate feminista* 29 (2004).
"Cuerpos transexuales y trangéneros." *Debate feminista* 39 (2009).
Decena, Carlos U. *Tacit Subjects: Belonging and Same-Sex Desire Among Dominican Immigrant Men*. Durham: Duke University Press, 2011.
Deleuze, Gilles. "Coldness and Cruelty," in *Masochism*. New York: Zone Books. 1989.
D'Emilio, John. "Capitalism and Gay Identity," in *The Gay and Lesbian Studies Reader*, ed. Henry Abelove, Michele Aina Barale, and David Halperin. New York: Routledge, 1993, 467–476.
Derrida, Jacques. "Living on: Border Lines," in *A Derrida Reader: Between the Blinds*, ed. Peggy Kamuf. New York: Columbia University Press, 1991, 254–268.
de Villiers, Nicholas. *Opacity and the Closet: Queer Tactics in Foucault, Barthes, and Warhol*. Minneapolis: University of Minnesota Press, 2012.
Díaz, Junot. *Drown*. New York: Riverhead Book, 1996.
———.*The Brief Wondrous Life of Oscar Wao*. New York: Riverhead Book, 2007.
———.*This Is How You Lose Her*. New York: Riverhead Book, 2012.
Donoso, José. *El lugar sin límites*. Barcelona: Seix Barral (1966)1987.
———.*Hell Has No Limits* in *Triple Cross*, trans. Hallie D. Taylor and Suzanne Jill Levine. New York: E. P. Dutton & Co., 1972.
Duany, Jorge. "Race and Racialization," in *The Oxford Encyclopedia of Latinos and Latinas in the United States*, ed. Suzanne Oboler and Deena J. González. New York: Oxford University Press, 2005, 535–544.
Duggan, Lisa. "The New Homonormativity: The Sexual Politics of Neoliberalism," in *Materializing Democracy: Toward a Revitalized Cultural Politics*, ed. Russ Castronovo and Dana D. Nelson. Durham, NC and London: Duke University Press, 2002, 175–194.
Edelman, Lee. *Homographesis: Essays in Gay Literary and Cultural Theory*. New York: Routledge. 1994.
Eng, David L. *Racial Castration: Managing Masculinity in Asian America*. Durham: Duke University Press, 2001.
Felman, Shoshana. "To Open the Question," in *Yale French Studies* 55/56 (1977): 5–10.
———.*Jacques Lacan and the Adventure of Insight: Psychoanalysis and Contemporary Culture*. Cambridge: Harvard University Press, 1987.
Felman, Shoshana, and Dori Laub, *Testimony: Crises of Witnessing in Literature, Psychoanalysis and History*. New York: Routledge, 1992.
Ferguson, Roderick A. *Aberrations in Black: Toward a Queer of Color Critique*. Minneapolis: University of Minnesota Press, 2003.
Foster, David William. *Gay and Lesbian Themes in Latin American Writing*. Austin: University of Texas Press, 1991.
———.*Sexual Textualities: Essays in Queer/ing Latin American Writing*. Austin: University of Texas Press, 1997.

Foucault, Michel. "Preface to Transgression," in *Language, Counter-Memory, Practice*. Ithaca, NY: Cornell University Press, 1977, 29–52.
———.*Surveiller et punir. Naissance de la prison*. Paris: Éditions Gallimard, 1975.
———.*Histoire de la sexualité 1: La volonté de savoir*. Paris: Gallimard, 1978.
———.*Discipline and Punish*, trans. Alan Sheridan. New York: Vintage, 1979.
Franco, Jean. *Plotting Women: Gender and Representation in Mexico*. New York: Columbia University Press, 1989.
Freud, Sigmund. *The Standard Edition of the Complete Psychological Works of Sigmund Freud*, ed. James Strachey. London: Hogarth Press and The Institute of Psycho-Analysis, 1957–1973.
———.*Three Essays on the Theory of Sexuality. SE* VII, 1905, 123–246.
———."Character and Anal Erotism." *SE* IX, 1908, 167–176.
———.*From the History of an Infantile Neurosis. SE* XVII (1914)1918, 1–124.
———."Instincts and Their Vicissitudes." *SE* XIV, 1915, 117–140.
———."On Transformations of Instinct as Exemplified in Anal Erotism." *SE* XVII, 1917, 125–134.
———."'A Child Is Being Beaten': A Contribution to the Study of the Origin of Sexual Perversions" *SE* XVII, 1919, 175–204.
———.*Beyond the Pleasure Principle SE* XVIII, 1920, 7–64.
———."Group Psychology and the Analysis of the Ego" *SE* XVIII, 1921, 67–143.
———."The Economic Problem of Masochism," *SE* XIX, 1924, 157–170.
Fuss, Diana. *Identification Papers*. New York: Routledge. 1995.
Gallo, Rubén. "Severo Sarduy, Jacques Lacan y el psicoanálisis. Entrevista con François Wahl, in *Revista hispánica moderna* 59, no. 1/2 (2006): 51–59.
———."Sarduy avec Lacan: The Portrayal of French Psychoanalysis in Cobra and La simulación," in *Revista hispánica moderna* 60, no. 1 (2007): 34–60.
Garber, Marjorie B. *Vested Interests: Transvestism and Cultural Anxiety*. New York: Routledge, 1991.
Gide, André. *L'immoraliste* in *Romans*. Paris: Gallimard (Bibliothéque de la Pléiade), 1958.
Giorgi, Gabriel. *Sueños de exterminio. Homosexualidad y representación en la literatura argentina contemporánea*. Rosario: Beatriz Viterbo Editora, 2004.
Girard, René. *Deceit, Desire, and the Novel: Self and Other in Literary Structure*, trans. Yvonne Freccero. Baltimore: Johns Hopkins University Press, 1972.
González Echevarría, Roberto. *Relecturas: Estudios de literatura cubana*. Caracas: Monte Avila, 1976.
———."Lo cubano en *Paradiso*," in *Coloquio Internacional sobre la obra de José Lezama Lima. Vol. II: Prosa*, ed. y Cristina Vizcaino and Eugenio Suárez Galbán. Poitiers: Centro de Investigaciones Latinoamericanas, Universidad de Poiters, 1984, 31–51.
Gopinath, Gayatri. *Impossible Desires: Queer Diasporas and South Asian Public Cultures*. Durham: Duke University Press, 2005.
Grosz, Elizabeth. "Lesbian Fetishism?" in *differences* 3, no. 2 (1991): 39–54.
———.*Volatile Bodies: Towards a Corporeal Feminism*. Bloomington: Indiana University Press, 1994.
Guerrero, Gustavo. *La estrategia neobarroca: estudio sobre el resurgimiento de la poética barroca en la obra narrativa de Severo Sarduy*. Barcelona: Ediciones del Mall, 1987.
Gutiérrez, Laura G. *Performing Mexicanidad: Vendidas y Cabareteras on the Transnational Stage*. Austin: University of Texas Press. 2010.
Gutiérrez Alea, Tomás, Juan Carlos Tabío, Jorge Perugorría, and Vladmir Cruz. *Fresa y chocolate* [*Strawberry and Chocolate*]. DVD. Dir. Tomás Gutiérrez Alea and Juan Carlos Tabío. New York: Miramax Films, 2004.

Guzmán, Manolo. *Gay Hegemony/Latino Homosexualities*. New York: Routledge, 2006.
Halperin, David M. *Saint Foucault: Towards a Gay Hagiography*. New York: Oxford University Press. 1995.
Harper, Phillip Brian. *Are We Not Men? Masculine Anxiety and the Problem of African American Identity*. New York: Oxford University Press, 1996.
Henríquez Ureña, Max. *Breve historia del modernismo*. Mexico, DF: Fondo de Cultura Económica, 1954.
Herrero Olaizola, Alejandro. "Homosexuales en escena: Identidad y performance en la narrativa de Luis Zapata," in *Antipodas* 11–12 (1999–2000): 249–262.
Hinojosa, Claudia. "Una perspectiva lesbiana del lesbianismo," in *fem.: 10 años de periodismo feminista*. Mexico, DF: Fascículos Planeta, S.A. de C.V., 1988, 149–153.
———."Confessiones de una mujer de costumbres raras," in *fem.: 10 años de periodismo feminista*. Mexico, DF: Fascículos Planeta, S.A. de C.V., 1988, 215–217.
Ingenschay, Dieter. "Mario Vargas Llosa y el 'pecado nefando,'" in *Revista chilena de literatura* 80 (2011): 51–63.
Irigaray, Luce. *Ce sexe qui n'en est pas un*. Paris: Éditions de minuit, 1977.
———.*Speculum of the Other Woman*, trans. Gillian C. Gill. Ithaca, NY: Cornell University Press, 1985.
Irwin, Robert McKee. *Mexican Masculinities*. Minneapolis: University of Minnesota Press, 2003.
Jaén, Didier T. "La neopicaresca en México: Elena Poniatowska y Luis Zapata," in *Tinta* 1 no. 5 (1987): 23–29.
Jagose, Annamarie. *Queer Theory, An Introduction*. New York: New York University Press, 1996.
Jameson, Frederic. "Third-World Literature in the Era of Multinational Capitalism," *Social Text* 15 (1986): 65–88.
Johnson, Barbara. *A World of Difference*. Baltimore: Johns Hopkins University Press, 1989.
Johnson, E. Patrick. *Appropriating Blackness: Performance and the Politics of Authenticity*. Durham, NC: Duke University Press, 2003.
Jrade, Cathy. *Modernismo, Modernity, and the Development of Spanish American Literature*. Austin: University of Texas Press, 1998.
Justice, Daniel Heath, Mark Rifkin, and Bethany Schneider, eds. "Sexuality, Nationality, Indigeneity," in *GLQ: A Journal of Gay and Lesbian Studies* 16 (2010): 1–2.
Kaminsky, Amy K. *Reading the Body Politic: Feminist Criticism and Latin American Women Writers*. Minneapolis: University of Minnesota Press, 1993.
Kerr, Lucille. *Suspended Fictions: Reading Novels by Manuel Puig*. Urbana: University of Illinois Press, 1987.
Kirkpatrick, Gwen. *The Dissonant Legacy of Modernismo: Lugones, Herrera y Reissig, and the Voices of Modern Spanish American Poetry*. Berkeley: University of California Press, 1989.
Kristal, Efraín. *Temptation of the Word: The Novels of Mario Vargas Llosa*. Nashville: Vanderbilt University Press, 1998.
Lacan, Jacques. *Écrits* I. Paris: Éditions du Seuil, 1966.
———.*Écrits. The First Complete Edition in English*, trans. Bruce Fink. New York: W. W. Norton & Co., 2006.
———.*The Four Fundamental Concepts of Psycho-analysis*, trans. Alan Sheridan. London: Hogarth, 1977.
———.*The Seminar of Jacques Lacan, Book XX: Encore. On Feminine Sexuality, the*

Limits of Love and Knowledge, ed. Jacques-Alain Miller. New York: Norton, 1998.
LaFountain-Stokes, Lawrence. Queer Ricans: Cultures and Sexualities in the Diaspora. Minneapolis: University of Minnesota Press, 2009.
———."Gay Shame, Latina/o Style: A Critique of White Queer Performativity," in Gay Latino Studies: A Critical Reader, ed. Michael Hames-García and Ernesto J. Martínez. Durham: Duke University Press, 2011, 55–80.
Laguarda, Rodrigo. Ser gay en la ciudad de México: Lucha de representaciones y apropiación de una identidad, 1968–1982. Mexico, DF: Instituto Mora: CIESAS, 2009.
Laplanche, Jean, and Jean-Bertrand Pontalis, "Fantasy and the Origins of Sexuality," in International Journal of Psychoanalysis 49, no. 1 (1968): 1–18.
Laqueur, Thomas W. Solitary Sex: A Cultural History of Masturbation. New York: Zone Books, 2003.
Laqueur, Thomas, and Catherine Gallagher, eds. The Making of the Modern Body: Sexuality and Society in the 19th Century. Berkeley: University of California Press, 1987.
Lazarillo de Tormes, ed. Francisco Rico. Madrid: Ediciones Cátedra, 1987.
Lee, Spike, Danny Aiello, Ossie Davis, Ruby Dee, and Giancarlo Esposito. Do the Right Thing, 20th Anniversary Edition. Blu-ray. Dir. Spike Lee. Los Angeles: Universal Studios Home Entertainment, 1989.
Lemebel, Pedro. Loco afán: Crónicas de sidario. Santiago de Chile: LOM Ediciones, 1996.
Levine, Suzanne Jill. "Discourse as Bricolage" Review 74 (1974): 32–37.
Lewis, Paul Vek. "La noche delincuente: La representatión del prostituto en El vampiro de la colonia Roma, Las púberes canéforas y La Virgen de los Sicarios," in Journal of Iberian and Latin American Research 9, no. 1 (2003): 73–94.
———.Crossing Gender and Sex in Latin America. New York: Palgrave Macmillan, 2010.
Lezama Lima, José. La expresión americana. La Habana: Instituto Nacional de Cultura, 1957.
———.Paradiso (Critical Edition by Cintio Vitier). Argentina: Colección Archivos (1966)1988.
———.Paradiso, trans. Gregory Rabassa. New York: Farrar, Straus and Giroux, 1974.
Limentani, Adam. Between Freud and Klein: The Psychoanalytic Quest for Knowledge and Truth. London: Free Association, 1989.
Livingston, Jennie, Dorian Corey, Pepper LaBeija, and Willi Ninja. Paris Is Burning. DVD. Dir. Jennie Livingston. New York: Miramax Home Entertainment, 2005.
Loisel, Clary. "Interview with Miguel Barbachano Ponce," in Harrington Gay Men's Fiction Quarterly 3, no. 2 (2001): 17–25.
Ludmer, Josefina. "Tretas del débil," in La sartén por el mango, ed. Patricia Elena González and Eliana Ortega. Río Piedra, PR: Ediciones Huracán, 1985, 47–54.
Manalansan IV, Martin. Global Divas Filipino Gay Men in the Diaspora. Durham, NC: Duke University Press, 2003.
Mann, Thomas. Death in Venice (A Norton Critical Edition), ed. and trans. Clayton Koelb. New York: W. W. Norton & Co., 1994.
Maravall, José Antonio. Culture of the Baroque: Analysis of a Historical Structure, trans. Terry Cochran. Minneapolis: University of Minnesota Press, 1986.
Martí, José. "Nuestra América," in Ensayos y crónicas, ed. José Olivio Jiménez. Madrid: Cátedra, 2004.
Martinetto, Vittoria. "The Buenos Aires Affair: anatomía de una censura," in Encuentro Internacional Manuel Puig, ed. José Amícola and Graciela Speranza. Rosario: Beatriz Viterbo Editora, 1998, 212–223.
Martínez-San Miguel, Yolanda. Saberes americanos: Subalternidad y epistemología

en los escritos de Sor Juana. Pittsburgh: Instituto Internacional de Literatura Iberoamericana, 1999.
———."(Neo) Barrocos de Indias: Sor Juana y los imaginarios coloniales de la crítica latinoamericana," in *Revista de Estudios Hispánicos* 44 no.2 (2010): 433–463.
———."Coloniality of Diasporas: Racialization of Negropolitans and Nuyoricans in Paris and New York." *Hispanic Caribbean Literature of Migration,* ed. Vanessa Pérez-Rosario. New York: Palgrave, 2010, 189–206.
———."Female Sexiles? Towards an Archeology of Displacement of Sexual Minorities in the Caribbean," in *Signs* 36 no. 4 (Summer 2011), 813–836.
McBride, Dwight A. *Why I Hate Abercrombie & Fitch: Essays on Race and Sexuality.* New York: New York University Press, 2005.
Micale, Mark. *Approaching Hysteria: Disease and Its Interpretations.* Princeton, NJ: Princeton University Press, 1995.
Miles, Robert, and Malcolm Brown. *Racism (Key Ideas),* 2nd ed. New York: Routledge, 2003.
Miller, D. A. *Bringing Out Roland Barthes.* Berkeley: University of California Press, 1992.
Mitchell, David T., and Sharon L. Snyder. *Narrative Prosthesis: Disability and the Dependencies of Discourse.* Ann Arbor: University of Michigan Press, 2000.
Mitchell, Juliet. *Mad Men and Medusas: Reclaiming Hysteria.* New York: Basic Books, 2000.
Molloy, Sylvia. *En breve cárcel.* Barcelona: Seix Barral, 1981.
———.*At Face Value: Autobiographical Writing in Spanish America.* Cambridge: Cambridge University Press, 1991.
———."Too Wilde for Comfort: Desire and Ideology in Fin-de-Siècle Spanish America." *Social Text* 31/32 (1992): 187–201.
———."The Politics of Posing," *Hispanisms and Homosexualities,* ed. Sylvia Molloy and Robert Irwin. Durham, NC: Duke University Press, 1998, 141–160.
———."Voice Snatching: *De sobremesa,* Hysteria, and the Impersonation of Marie Bashkirtseff." *Latin American Literary Review* XXV, no. 50 (1997): 11–29.
———.*Poses de fin de siglo: Desbordes del género en la modernidad.* Buenos Aires: Eterna Cadencia Editora, 2012.
Molloy, Sylvia, and Robert Irwin, eds. *Hispanisms and Homosexualities.* Durham, NC: Duke University Press, 1998.
Monsiváis, Carlos. "El mundo soslayado." Prologue to *La estatua de sal* by Salvador Novo. Mexico, DF: Consejo Nacional para la Cultura y las Artes, 1998, 11–41.
———."De la marginidad sexual en America Latina," in *Debate feminista* 40 (2009): 127–145.
Montaldo, Graciela. *La sensibilidad amenazada. Fin de siglo y modernismo.* Rosario: Beatriz Viterbo Editora, 1994.
Moraga, Cherríe, and Gloria Anzaldúa, eds. *This Bridge Called My Back: Writings by Radical Women of Color,* 2nd ed. Boston: Kitchen Table, Women of Color Press, 1983.
Mulvey, Laura. *Visual Pleasure and Narrative Cinema,* 2nd ed. New York: Palgrave Macmillan, 2009.
Muñoz, José E. *Disidentifications: Queers of Color and the Performance of Politics.* Minneapolis: University of Minnesota Press, 1999.
Murray, Stephen O. *Latin American Male Homosexualities.* Albuquerque: University of New Mexico Press, 1995.
Nervo, Amado. *El bachiller* in *Obras completas, Volumen 1, Prosas,* ed. Francisco González Guerrero and Alfonso Méndez Plancarte. Madrid: Aguilar, 1954.
Noyes, John K. *The Mastery of Submission: Inventions of Masochism.* Ithaca, NY: Cornell University Press, 1997.

Nuñez Noriega, Guillermo. *Sexo entre varones: Poder y resistencia en el campo sexual.* Mexico, DF: UNAM/PUEG, 2000.
Oropesa, Salvador A. *The Contemporáneos Group: Rewriting Mexico in the Thirties and Forties.* Austin: University of Texas Press, 2003.
Ortíz, Fernando. *Cuban Counterpoint: Tobacco and Sugar,* trans. Harriet de Onís. Durham, NC: Duke University Press, 1995.
Ortíz, Ricardo L. *Cultural Erotics in Cuban America.* Minneapolis: University of Minnesota Press, 2007.
Osorio, Manuel. "Entrevista con Manuel Puig: 'Soy tan macho que las mujeres me parecen maricas.'" *Cuadernos para el diálogo* 231 (1977): 51–53.
Ovid. *The Metamorphoses of Ovid,* trans. Allen Mandelbaum. San Diego: Harcourt Brace and Co., 1995.
Palaversich, Diana. "The Wounded Body of Proletarian Homosexuality in Pedro Lemebel's *Loco afán,*" trans. Paul Allaston, in *Latin American Perspectives,* "Gender, Sexuality, and Same Sex Desire in Latin American" 29, no. 2 (March 2002): 99–118.
Parkinson Zamora, Lois, and Monika Kaup, eds. *Baroque New Worlds: Representation, Transculturation, Counterconquest.* Durham, NC: Duke University Press, 2009.
Paz, Octavio. *El laberinto de la soledad,* ed. Enrico Mario Santí. Madrid: Cátedra, (1950) 1993.
———. "El espejo indiscreto," in *Obras completas,* vol. 8, *El peregrino en su patria: Historia y política de México.* Mexico: Fondo de Cultura Económica, 1993.
Pellón, Gustavo. *José Lezama Lima's Joyful Vision.* Austin: University of Texas Press, 1989.
Pérez de Mendiola, Marina. *Gender and Identity Formation in Contemporary Mexican Literature.* New York: Garland Publishing, 1998.
Perlongher, Nestor. *La prostitución masculina.* Buenos Aires: Ediciones de la Urraca, 1993.
Pino-Ojeda, Walescka. "Gay Proletarian Memory: The Chronicles of Pedro Lemebel," in *Continuum: Journal of Media & Cultural Studies* 20, no. 3 (September 2006): 395–406.
Ponce, Martin Joseph. *Beyond the Nation: Diasporic Filipino Literature and Queer Reading.* New York: New York University Press, 2012.
Pratt, Mary Louise. "Arts of the Contact Zone," in *Profession* (1991): 33–40.
Puig, Manuel. "Growing up at the Movies: A Chronology" *Review* 72 (Winter 1971–Spring 1972): 49–51.
———. *El beso de la mujer araña.* Barcelona: Seix Barral, 1976.
———. *The Buenos Aires Affair.* Barcelona: Seix Barral, 1986.
———. "Puig por Puig." *Zona Franca* 51–54 (1977): 49–54.
———. *The Buenos Aires Affair,* trans. Suzanne Jill Levine. Champaign, Ill.: Dalkey Archive Press, 2010.
Quiroga, José. *Tropics of Desire: Interventions for Queer Latino America.* New York: New York University Press, 2000.
———. *Cuban palimpsests.* Minneapolis: University of Minnesota Press, 2005.
———. *Law of Desire.* Vancouver, BC: Arsenal Pulp Press, 2009.
Ramírez, Rafael L. *What It Means to Be a Man: Reflections on Puerto Rican Masculinity.* New Brunswick, NJ: Rutgers University Press. 1999.
Ramos, Julio. *Divergent Modernities: Culture and Politics in 19th Century Latin America.* Durham, NC: Duke University Press, 2001.
Reddy, Chandan. *Freedom with Violence: Race, Sexuality, and the US State.* Durham, NC: Duke University Press, 2011.
Reid Pharr, Robert. *Black Gay Male.* New York: New York University Press, 2001.

Rich, Adrienne. "Compulsory Heterosexuality and Lesbian Existence," in *Signs* 5, no. 4 (1980): 631–660.
Ríos Avila, Rubén. *La raza cómica de sujeto en Puerto Rico*. San Juan: Ediciones Callejón, 2002.
Rivera-Valdés, Sonia. *Las historias prohibidas de Marta Veneranda*. New York: Seven Stories Press, 2001.
———. *The Forbidden Stories of Marta Veneranda*, trans. Dick Cluster, Marina Harss, Mark Schafer, and Alan West-Dúran. New York: Seven Stories Press, 2001.
Rivière, Joan. "Womanliness as a Masquerade," in *International Journal of Psychoanalysis* 10 (1929): 303–313.
Rodríguez, Juana María. *Queer Latinidad: Identity Practices, Discursive Spaces*. New York: New York University Press, 2003.
Rodriguez, Randy A. "Richard Rodriguez Reconsidered: Queering the Sissy (Ethnic) Subject," in *Texas Studies in Literature and Language* 40, no. 4 (1998): 396–423.
Rodriguez, Richard. *Hunger of Memory: The Education of Richard Rodriguez*. Boston: David R. Godine Publisher, 1981.
Rodríguez Monegal, Emir. "Sobre el *Paradiso* de Lezama," in *Mundo Nuevo* 16 (1967): 90–95.
———. "*Paradiso* en su contexto," in *Mundo Nuevo* 24 (1968): 40–44.
———. "Conversación con Severo Sarduy." *Revista de Occidente* 93 (1970): 315–343.
Roof, Judith. *Come as You Are: Sexuality and Narrative*. New York: Columbia University Press, 1996.
Rubin, Gayle. "The Traffic in Women: Notes on the 'Political Economy' of Sex," in *Toward and Anthropology of Women*, ed. Rayna R. Reiter. New York: Monthly Review Press, 1975, 157–210.
———. "Thinking Sex: Notes for a Radical Theory of the Politics of Sexuality," in *Pleasure and Danger: Exploring Female Sexuality*, ed. Carole S. Vance. Boston: Routledge & Kegan Paul, 1984, 267–319.
Ruiz, Bladimir. "Prostitución y homosexualidad: interpelaciones desde el margen en *El vampiro de la colonia Roma* de Luis Zapata," in *Revista iberoamericana* 65, no. 187 (1999): 327–339.
Said, Edward. *The World, the Text and the Critic*. Cambridge: Harvard University Press, 1983.
Salessi, Jorge. *Médicos, maleantes y maricas: higiene, criminología y homosexualidad en la construcción de la nación argentina (Buenos Aires, 1871–1914)*. Rosario: Beatriz Viterbo Editora, 1995.
Santí, Enrico Mario. "Parridiso," in *José Lezama Lima: Textos críticos*, ed. Justo C. Ulloa. Miami: Ediciones Universales, 1979, 91–114.
Sarduy, Severo. *De donde son los cantantes*. Mexico, DF: Joaquin Mortiz, 1967.
———. "El barroco y el neo-barroco," in *América en su literatura*, ed. César Fernández Moreno. Mexico and Paris: Siglo XXI-UNESCO, 1972, 167–184.
———. *Cobra*. Buenos Aires: Editorial Sudamericana, 1972.
———. "The Baroque and the Neobaroque," in *America in Its Literature*, ed. César Fernández Moreno. English text ed. Iván Schulman, trans. Mary Berg. New York: Holmes & Meier, 1980, 115–132.
———. *La doublure*. Paris: Flammarion, 1981.
———. *La simulación*. Caracas: Monte Ávila Editores, 1982.
———. *Ensayos generales sobre el barroco*. Mexico, DF: Fondo de Cultura Económica, 1987.
———. *Written on a Body*, trans. Carol Maier. New York: Lumen Books, 1991.
———. *Pájaros de la playa*. Barcelona: Tusquets Editores. 1993.
———. "Diario de la peste," in *Vuelta* 18, no. 206 (1994): 33–35.
———. "El estampido de la vacuidad," in *Vuelta* 18, no. 206 (1994): 36–38.

---. *Beach Birds*, trans. Suzanne Jill Levine and Carol Maier. Los Angeles: Otis Books/Seismicity Editions, 2007.
Schaefer, Claudia. *Danger Zones: Homosexuality, National Identity, and Mexican Culture*. Tuscon: University of Arizona, 1996.
Schneider, Luis Mario. *La novela mexicana entre el petróleo, la homosexualidad y la política*. Mexico. DF: Nueva Imagen, 1997.
Sedgwick, Eve Kosofsky. *Between Men: English Literature and Male Homosocial Desire*. New York: Columbia University Press, 1985.
---. *The Epistemology of the Closet*. Los Angeles: University of California Press, 1991.
---. "Queer Performativity: Henry James's *The Art of the Novel*," in *GLQ: A Journal of Lesbian and Gay Studies* 1, no. 1 (1993): 1–16.
---. *Tendencies*. Durham: Duke University Press, 1993.
Sierra Madero, Abel. *Del otro lado del espejo: La sexualidad en la construcción de la nación cubana*. La Habana, Casa de las Américas, 2006.
Sifuentes-Jáuregui, Ben. "National Fantasies: Peeking into the Latin American Closet," in *Queer Representations: Reading Lives, Reading Cultures*, ed. Martin B. Duberman. New York: New York University Press, 1997, 290–301.
---. "The Swishing of Gender: Homographetic Marks in *Lazarillo de Tormes*," in *Hispanisms and Homosexualities*, ed. Sylvia Molloy and Robert M. Irwin. Durham, NC: Duke University Press, 1998, 123–140.
---. *Transvestism, Masculinity and Latin American Literature: Genders Share Flesh*. Nueva York: Palgrave, 2002.
---. "Cuerpos, intelectuales y homosocialidad en *Los de abajo*," in *Revista de Crítica Literaria Latinoamericana* 33, no. 66 (2007): 95–111.
Silverman, Kaja. *Male Subjectivity at the Margins*. New York: Routledge, 1992.
Sommer, Doris. *Foundational Fictions: The National Romances of Latin America*. Berkeley: University of California Press, 1993.
Sommerville, Siobhan B. *Queering the Color Line: Race and the Invention of Homosexuality in American Culture*. Durham, NC: Duke University Press, 2000.
Spivak, Gayatri C. "The Politics of Translation," in *Outside the Teaching Machine*. New York: Routledge, 1993, 179–200.
Taylor, Clark L. "Mexican Male Homosexual Interaction in Public Contexts." *The Many Faces of Homosexuality*, ed. Evelyn Blackwood. New York and London: Harrington Park Press, 1986, 117–136.
Thoma, Benno. *Somos Cubanos*. Berlin: Gmünder, 1998.
Thomas, Piri. *Down These Mean Streets*. New York: Vintage Books, 1997.
"Those Hot Chile Nights," in *Time Magazine*, May 29, 1972. http://www.time.com/time/magazine/article/0,9171,903554,00.html (accessed August 1, 2009).
Torres Bodet, Jaime. *Tiempo de arena* in *Obras escogidas*. Mexico, DF: Fondo de Cultura Económica, 1961, 189–384.
Vargas Llosa, Mario. *La ciudad y los perros*, 3rd ed. Barcelona: Seix Barral, (1963)1985.
---. *Los cachorros*, ed. Guadalupe Fernández Ariza. Madrid: Cátedra, (1967)2010.
---. "Sobre el *Paradiso* de Lezama," in *Mundo Nuevo* 16 (1967): 89–90.
---. *Conversación en La Catedral*. Barcelona: Seix Barral, 1969.
---. *The Cubs and Other Stories*, trans. Gregory Kolovakos and Ronald Christ. New York: Harper & Row, 1979.
---. "Breve discurso sobre la cultura," in *Letras libres* 139 (June 2010): 48–55
Warner, Michael. "Introduction: Fear of a Queer Planet" *Social Text* 29 (1991): 3–17.
Weston, Kath. "Get Thee to a Big City: Sexual Imaginary and the Great Gay Migration," in *GLQ* 2 (1995): 253–277.
Whitam, Frederick L., and Robin M. Mathy. *Male Homosexuality in Four Societies:*

Brazil, Guatemala, the Philippines, and the United States. New York: Praeger, 1986.
Wigozki, Karina. "El discurso travesti o el travestismo discursivo en *La esquina es mi corazón: crónica urbana* de Pedro Lemebel," in *La Casa* 2 (2006). http://www.class.uh.edu/MCL/faculty/zimmerman/lacasa/Estudios%20Culturales%20Articles/Karina%20Wigozki.pdf (accessed August 1, 2009).
Wölfflin, Heinrich. *Principles of Art History: The Problem of the Development of Style in Later Art*. New York: Dover Publications, 1950.
Zapata, Luis. *Las aventuras, desventuras y sueños de Adonis García. El vampiro de la colonia Roma*. Mexico, DF: Grijalbo, 1979.
———.*Adonis García: A Picaresque Novel*, trans. E. A. Lacey. San Francisco: Gay Sunshine Press, 1981.

Index

Aching, Gerard, 26, 234–35n6
affiliative versus filiative spaces, 64–65
AIDS, 19, 117, 124, 127, 129–30, 184, 188, 250n29, 258n29
Alarcón, Norma, 232n14
albur, 71, 147, 184, 241n12, 251n38
Allegri, Gregorio, 235–36n26
Almaguer, Tomás, 233–34n45
Alter, Robert, 88
Altman, Dennis, 3, 249–50n24
Americanization of the homosexual, 3
Anzaldúa, Gloria, 232n16
Arenales, Ricardo, 141–42, 252n9
Arenas, Reinaldo: *Before Night Falls*, 198–201, 210, 259n8
Arévalo Martínez, Rafael, 191
Arroyo, Jossianna, 171
assujetissement, 70, 90, 111
autoeroticism, 89, 96, 104, 106, 114. See also masturbation

Bakhtin, Mikhail, 179
Barba Jacob, Porfirio. See Arenales, Ricardo
Barbachano Ponce, Miguel: *El diario de José Toledo*, 17–18, 51–64, 237–38n2
Baroque allegory, 122–23
Baroque, 173–84; condensation, 174, 177–78; proliferation, 175–78, 182–83, 185, 255n39; substitution, 174–75, 178, 182. See also Homo-Baroque; Neo-Baroque
Barthes, Roland, 73, 183
Bayly, Jaime, 124–25, 127, 250n26

Bejel, Emilio, 261n6
Bhabha, Homi, 100
blank spaces, 74–75, 79, 81
Bloom, Harold, 122
Boom (literary movement), 16, 137, 158
Brooks, Peter, 97
Browning, Frank, 32
Butler, Judith, 2, 10–11, 70–72, 120, 123, 184, 186, 258n24

Caminha, Adolfo: *Bom crioulo*, 251n2
Camus, Albert: *La chute*, 69, 75–76
capitalism, 65–67
Carrier, Joseph, 233–34n45
castration, 102, 104, 112–13, 118, 141, 143, 150, 163, 203, 237n60; disavowal of, 7, 148–49, 252n25; as a Lacanian fault, 46–47; and Origènes, 46
Chiampi, Irlemar, 255n39
chingada/chingado, 9, 15
closetedness, 1–3, 5, 12, 21. See also "coming out" narrative
colonialism, 9, 79, 83, 99–102, 104, 127, 179, 183, 240n4, 240–41n10
"coming out" narrative, 2–3, 5, 21, 61, 199, 214, 222, 225
confessions, 80–81
Conrad, Joseph: *Heart of Darkness*, 97, 100–104
contact zones, 97, 99, 103
conversion of the object, 41–42
Cortázar, Julio, 158, 168, 170
cross-dressing, 122–23, 186–87. See also transvestism

Cruz, Sor Juana Inés de la, 7, 182, 242n26
cultural transvestism, 171. *See also* transvestism

D'Emilio, John, 65–68
Darío, Rubén, 25–26, 234n1, 235n12
de Villiers, Nicholas, 231–32n8
Death in Venice (film), 193–94. *See also* Mann, Thomas: *Death in Venice*
Decena, Carlos U., 231–32n8, 232n9
Deleuze, Gilles, 236n32, 255n34
Derrida, Jacques, 69, 98, 235n23
Díaz, Junot: *Drown*, 21, 198, 202, 204–208
disavowal, 7, 9, 11, 16, 20, 133, 138, 144, 148–49, 153, 187, 252n25, 258n29
disidentification, 2, 49, 102, 231n3
domesticity, 18, 54, 64–67, 126, 166, 224, 229
Donoso, José: *El lugar sin límites*, 115–21, 123, 192
drag, 122, 124, 131–33, 185–87, 258n24, 258n26
Duggan, Lisa, 126

ecstasy, 34, 38–42, 47
Edelman, Lee, 240n7
effeminacy, 105, 186, 201–202, 246n40, 248–49n6, 249n23, 258n26
ellipses (trope), 132–34, 210
epistemerotics, 18, 104–106, 208–10, 246–47n53
eroticism, 10, 133, 161, 163–67, 171–75, 180–82, 208–12, 227–28. *See also* autoeroticism; epistemerotics; homoerotics
erotogenic masochism, 35–37, 42, 164–65, 232n21
espacios en blanco (blank spaces), 74–75, 79, 81

Felman, Shoshana, 75
fetishism, 9, 21, 114, 226, 252n25
filiative relations, 64–68, 239n42
Form (*la forma*), 14–15
Foster, David William, 237–38n2
Foucault, Michel, 89, 100, 235n20, 245n36; and *assujettissement*, 70, 157–58, 165, 168; Vargas Llosa on, 155–56
Franco, Jean, 232n14

Freud, Sigmund, 48; on disavowal of castration, 252n25; "The Economic Problem of Masochism," 35–37; on identification, 15, 119–20, 123, 182, 231n3; on loving, 50–51; on masochism, 35–37, 164–65, 236n38, 254n26, 255n34; on melancholia, 56–57; on pleasure as absence of pain, 190; on the primal scene, 97–98, 120; on sadism, 35–37, 164–66, 254n26; and retelling of the Wolf Man, 87–88, 96–99, 106–107, 118–20; *Three Essays on the Theory of Sexuality*, 197, 211, 241n16, 254n26
Fuentes, Carlos, 138

gay identity, 1, 18–19, 65–66, 70, 73–75, 78, 80, 127, 131, 240n7. *See also* identification
gaze, 9, 26, 33–34, 42, 58–62, 99–102, 190, 245n31
ghetto, 13
Gide, André, 252n15; *L'immoraliste*, 19, 140–42, 144
Giordano, Alberto, 247n59
Girard, René, 10
Góngora, Luis de, 174
González Echevarría, Roberto, 80, 239–40n2
González Martínez, Enrique, 141
Gutiérrez Alea, Tomás, 242n20
Guzmán, Manolo, 245n31

Halperin, David, 165
Henríquez Ureña, Max, 245n5
Hesse, Hermann: *Demain*, 244n10
HIV/AIDS, 19, 117, 124, 127, 129–30, 184, 188, 250n29, 258n29
Homo-Baroque, 19–20, 183–84
homoerotics, 10, 96, 133, 164, 199, 211–12, 241n12, 245n31, 251n2. *See also* erotics
homographesis, 177
homonormativity, 18–19, 126–27, 131, 199, 214, 225, 230, 259n8
homophobia, 11, 13–14, 26, 51, 72, 90, 115–16, 119, 147, 187, 204, 247–8n70
homosexual panic, 10, 108, 147, 187, 204
homosocial bonding, 146–47
hysteria, 230, 262n42

identification, 3, 5–6, 119–33, 182–83, 198, 206; and ambivalence, 120–21; crisis of, 89; gay, 1, 18–19, 65–66, 70, 73–75, 78, 80, 127, 131, 240n7; filiative relations and, 64–68; queer, 3, 61, 88, 198, 214–16; and serialization, 259n2; *See also* disidentification
illegitimacy, 121, 124–26
Irwin, Robert McKee, 233–34n45, 241n15

Jagose, Annamarie, 2
Jiménez, José Alfredo, 137
Johnson, Barbara, 202
Johnson, E. Patrick, 242n23
Jrade, Cathy L., 42, 234n4

Kerr, Lucille, 243–44n4, 247n59
Kirkpatrick, Gwen, 28

Lacan, Jacques, 25, 39, 46–47; and desire, 180, 260n29; and the Real, 43, 167, 255n39; and Sarduy, 174, 180, 183, 192, 257n4, 257n9; and the Saussurean sign, 257n9; and the Symbolic order, 54
LaFountain-Stokes, Lawrence, 216
Laplanche, Jean, 87, 104, 106
Latino American, use of the term, 232–3n27, 259n4
Lazarillo de Tormes, 77–79, 240n3
Lee, Spike, 244n17
Lemebel, Pedro, 18–19; *Loco afán*, 115–16, 121–27; on *El lugar sin límites*, 116; "La noche de los visones," 127–32; "La Regine de Aluminios El Mono," 132–34
Lévi-Strauss, Claude: *The Elementary Structures of Kinship*, 8
Lima, José Lezama, 174; and Llosa on *Paradiso*, 158–59, 167–68; and Rodríguez Monegal on *Paradiso*, 158–59, 168; *Paradiso*, 19, 137, 157–73, 253n2, 255n39, 256n51
Llosa, Vargas: "Breve discurso sobre la cultura," 153–56; *Los cachorros*, 19, 137–56, 251n2, 251–52n3, 252n25; *La ciudad y los perros*, 137, 139, 251–52n3; on culture, 153–56; on Foucault, 155–56; on *Paradiso*, 158–59, 167–68

Luna, Juan de, 243n34
lurk, the, 100–101

machismo, 7, 80, 113
Mann, Thomas: *Death in Venice*, 4–5, 194, 232n10
maps, 97, 100–104
Martí, José, 11, 141–42
Martinetto, Vittoria, 248n73
Martínez-San Miguel, Yolanda, 260n18, 261n6
Mary Magdalene, 35
masculinity, 9, 113–14, 119, 145–53, 203–205, 232n21, 236n38, 236–37n48, 238n28, 244n18, 246n40
masks and masking, 6, 9, 12–14, 32, 71, 73, 78, 117, 166–67, 169–72, 255n37, 256n49
masochism, 30, 38, 42–47, 70, 144, 157–58, 163–69, 232n21; Christian, 38; erotogenic, 35–37, 42, 164–65, 232n21; Freud on, 35–37, 164–65, 236n38, 254n26, 255n34
masturbation, 46, 50, 90, 96–104, 106–107, 114, 205, 245n35–36. *See also* autoeroticism
melancholia, 7–8, 47, 56–57, 61–62
memory, 9, 87–91, 95, 97, 104, 113, 129, 178, 190, 227–30
metaphor, 28–29, 122–24, 131, 145
Mexican identity, 6, 71, 241n14
mirrors and mirroring, 13–14, 49, 80, 83, 99, 129, 125, 181, 193, 220, 247–48n70
Mitchell, David T., 244n14
modernismo (literary movement), 16–17, 20, 25–29, 42, 64, 178, 234n1, 236–7n48, 247n61; central features, 28; and language, 234n4, 235n24
Molloy, Sylvia, 12, 141–42, 251n1
Monsiváis, Carlos, 12–14, 243n29
Montaldo, Graciela, 29
Movimiento Magisterial de 1958 (Teachers' Movement of 1958), 59–60
Muñoz, José, 231n3

narcissism, 9, 30, 40–41, 43–44, 125–26, 192, 221, 262n31
narcissistic injury, 58, 62–64, 141, 148
Narcissus, 33, 40
Neo-Baroque, 16, 19, 158, 173–74, 178–81, 255n39. *See also* Baroque

278 Index

neoliberalism, 18, 124–26, 131, 134, 250n26, 252n5
Nervo, Amado, 235n7; *El bachiller*, 17, 27–50, 64, 235n19, 235n24, 235–6n26, 236n47, 236–37n48, 237n60–61, 247n61
Novo, Salvador, 12–14, 233n41

Oedipus and Oedipal narrative, 30, 40, 47, 79, 91, 102, 104, 118, 206
Orígènes, 44–46
Oropesa, Salvador A., 252n15
Ortíz, Fernando, 99, 170–71
Osorio Benítez, Miguel Ángel. *See* Arenales, Ricardo

Paz, Octavio, 1, 72, 232n21, 242n26; on homosexual identity, 14–15, 71–72, 241n16; "Máscaras mexicanas," 1, 5–13, 71, 255n37
pedagogy, 138, 151–53, 156
Pellón, Gustavo, 254n24
penetration paradigm, 72
Pérez de Mendiola, Marina, 237–38n2
performativity, 2, 3, 10–11, 80–81, 167, 184–85, 201, 214
picaresque, 77–78, 243n33
Pino-Ojeda, Walescka, 248n5
Platonic dialogue, 140
Pontalis, Jean-Bertrand, 87, 104, 106
postcolonial, use of the term, 240n4
Pratt, Mary Louise, 97, 99
prayer, 34, 38, 41
primal scene, 97–102, 104, 115–24, 188, 191, 231n3, 249n11
prostitution, 35, 58, 75, 82, 108–109, 151, 259–60n18
Proust, Marcel, 142
Puig, Manuel, 246n40; *Boquitas pintadas*, 105, 246n40; *The Buenos Aires Affair*, 18, 89–97, 102–104, 114; *Kiss of the Spider Woman*, 96, 125, 208–11; *La traición de Rita Hayworth*, 105

queer identification, 3, 61, 88, 198, 214–16. *See also* identification
queer realization, 47–48
queer theory, 2
queer, use of the term, 2
queerness, definition of, 5
Quiroga, José, 3, 11–12, 261n5; *Tropics of Desire*, 12, 215, 232–33n27, 259n4

radial reading, 176–77, 182
rajada/rajado, 6–7, 9. *See also* castration
Reik, Theodor, 38, 236n38
reino interior (interior kingdom), 17, 27–35, 42–43, 47–48, 64, 234–35n6
Rivera-Valdés, Sonia: "Five Windows on the Same Side," 217–24; *Forbidden Stories of Martha Veneranda*, 21, 215–30; "Lunacy," 224–30
Rodríguez Monegal, Emir, 158–59, 168, 253n2, 255n40
Rodríguez, Richard: *Hunger of Memory*, 225–26, 262n31
Rubin, Gayle, 8–10, 19

sadism, 35–37, 42, 164–65, 236n32, 247n59, 254n26, 255n34
sadomasochism, 157–58, 163–69, 171–72. *See also* masochism
Said, Edward, 64, 213–15, 217, 223, 261n4
Sarduy, Severo, 123; "El barroco y el neobarroco," 173–84; on the body, 258n29; *Cobra*, 185, 187; *Escrito sobre un cuerpo*, 185; *De donde son los cantantes*, 185, 187; Lacan's influence on, 183, 257n4; and *leer en filigrana*, 179, 183; *Pájaros de la playa*, 173, 184–94; on signifier/signified, 257n9; *La simulación*, 185; and simulation, 185–93, 257n1; and theory of the Neo-Baroque, 173–84
Schaefer, Claudia, 237–38n2, 239–40n2
Sedgwick, Eve K., 2, 10, 19, 146–47, 186–87, 245n36, 247–8n70
sensibility, 26–28, 34
She's Gotta Have It (film), 244n17
Sierra Madero, Abel, 211–12
silence, 3–5, 18–22, 47–48, 55, 75–76, 79, 132–34, 184, 204–10, 231–32n8, 232n10, 242n24, 242n26
Silverman, Kaja, 37–38, 236n38
Simmel, Georg, 14
simulation, 185–93, 257n1
Snyder, Sharon L., 244n14
Socrates, 138
Sollers, Philippe, 183
Sommers, Doris, 251n2
Spivak, Gayatri, 242n24
Stoler, Ann Laura, 246–47n53
Stonewall riots, 214

Tabío, Juan Carlos, 242n20
terrain vague of sexuality, 109–12, 134
testimonio, 75, 78, 242n23
theatricality, 116–17
Thomas, Piri: *Down These Mean Streets*, 21, 198, 202–204, 208, 210, 212
Torres Bodet, Jaime, 252n15; *Tiempo de arena*, 140–42
total sexuality, 87, 114
transculturation, 99, 170–71
transphobia, 119, 258n26
transvestism: cultural, 171; in *El lugar sin límites* (Donoso), 115–19; and homosexual identity, 238n28; Lemebel on, 115, 121–27, 249n6, 249n23; and masculinity, 249n11; Sarduy on, 185–87, 190; as a trope, 249n8
trope, defined, 249n8

Visconti, Luchino, 193–94

Wahl, François, 183
Wilde, Oscar, 32, 141–42, 233n41

Zapata, Luis: *El vampiro de la colonia Roma*, 18, 69, 73–83, 239n1, 241n18, 243n33

www.ingramcontent.com/pod-product-compliance
Lightning Source LLC
Chambersburg PA
CBHW020641230426
43665CB00008B/261